HIS BURDEN IS LIGHT

CULTIVATING PERSONAL HOLINESS

David R. Downey

ACKNOWLEDGMENTS

This book is dedicated first to my wife, Kim, who is always the first to believe and love (and to read!), and to my son Davey, who is unflagging in his zeal for his father and his work. Also, to my parents, Charles and Joan, whose diligent teaching of "The Lord is Our God, the Lord is One" started this lifelong process, and to Vernon White, a constant encourager and joyful supporter.

Thanks also to my readers Dr. Chad Bennett, Dr. Tige Bennett, Dr. Michael Dean, Kim Downey, Davey Downey, Dr. F.B. Huey, Dr. Mike Morris, Randy Reeder, and Vernon White for their diligent efforts in reading every word of this manuscript.

Contents

Introduction

I was recently driving in a rough area of the large city in which I live. Surrounded by urban squalor, I was aware I was in an area that had never been great and had only declined in recent years.

I passed the type of house that most of us have seen at one time or another. It was small, there was a chain link fence surrounding the tiny front yard facing a very busy street. The residents had filled the yard with brightly colored yard decorations—gnomes, flags, plastic flowers, gazing balls, Asian incense pots—even where to my taste, it was too bright and overdone. Yet, it was obvious the people who lived there had joy in their existence and wanted to share it with others.

As I thought about this, I remembered the phrase I had heard once, "I believe most in humankind when I see flowers in a ghetto window box."

This can be an allegory for what I will share in this book. Holiness radiates hope in all circumstances. Holiness is like the creative beauty behind plastic flowers on an ugly street. It is life itself springing up amid our weakness and surrounding bleakness, showing the incomparable power of God.

Motivation

Some years ago, I began reading great teachers like John Bunyan, Watchman Nee, Andrew Murray, Charles Spurgeon, and Dietrich Bonheoffer, and was captivated by their consistently holy lives. This piqued my interest and I have since pursued this subject of walking with God throughout my spiritual life. I have tested theories and outcomes all on what I would call the "guinea pig of self." What I bring in this book is my testimony of a growing experiment.

When I was a child, one of the sayings we used on each other was "Prove it!" One person would say, "I am stronger than you;" and the response would be, "*Prove* it!" "I could climb that tree to the top." "*Prove* it!" I do not know if this saying is still used but it would apply to teaching about holiness. "Holiness is possible." "*Prove it!*" I have proven the principles of this book by testing them in my life. Now all that remains is for the reader to prove them as well.

However, we must go beyond experience. Experience is secondary to authority, and we live according to the authority of God's Word. I have expended every effort to make this book thoroughly biblical, and we should test it according to that. If it is biblical, then we have no other choice than to apply it.

Accessible Holiness

Six times in Leviticus, God tells His children, "Be holy for I am holy." Later, when the apostle Peter reminds his audience of these words, he says, "Like the Holy One who called you, be holy yourselves also in all your behavior" (1 Peter 1:15). These words, and others like them in the Bible, are very clear...but we seem to be less so.

It has been my observation that some people think "holiness" is for the unusually devoted, or the spiritually elite. Others seem to think that holiness is difficult, if not impossible, and they shy away from these "pinnacles of righteousness." Some teachers of holiness have possibly contributed to this by making the subject a contemplative, mystic, and arduous task for the special few.

That is erroneous, for holiness is accessible, it is for all of us, and it is not arduous.

Since God created us in His image, it is natural that we have a desire to be more like the Creator. Even though we may try to ignore this basic need, it will remain insistent. God created man to be in close relation to Him, and He will accept no substitute. He actually expects all people—of all stripes— to remain in this state. Since this is so, we know it is not an impossible task.

Our Father in Heaven knows our personal weaknesses better than anyone could know them. This can be a staggering thought when we are acquainted with our own frailty (though we may be more acquainted with the frailties of others!). However, having an intimate knowledge of our failures God *still* accepts nothing from us but total holiness.

It is also possible that our desire to live holy lives will be frustrated because we fear such a state as it is unknown. We might wonder if we will be weird, unloving, or become isolated. Why should we worry, as holiness is simply the natural state of the creature in right relation to the Creator.

It is interesting that when people asked me about the subject of this book, and I told them "holiness," most seemed excited. However, some were neutral, and their responses often fell into two categories: "Oh, that *is* needed (with a faraway look)," or "That's nice (with a look that said "*Huh?*")."

I think we have might have mistaught holiness, when we have taught it at all. Because we have concentrated on discussions about holiness, we might have made it appear unattainable—an elusive Holy Grail.

Therefore, holiness itself is not the subject of this book, as much as what we can do to experience it. I have reserved definitions of holiness for this chapter of introduction, because the rest of the book is more concerned with mental steps, spiritual attitudes, and the actions that we take that cultivate personal holiness. The motivation is that more of us will walk daily in holiness, and humbly lead others there.

Systematically, we can liberate the Holy Spirit in our lives. Herein are certain standards to apply to allow the Lord to use His remarkable power to generate change in us. The solution will not be in difficult efforts to comply with the will of the Lord with our strength. Rather, we will give up our self-enthroned, and surrender to daily communion that will result in holiness through holy influence.

What holiness we obtain is God's gift because we are not able to create or work up one iota of true holiness. Growth in grace is only possible through the work of the Holy Spirit in us. When we try it any other way, we learn quickly that holiness belongs to God and we have it only when He shares it with us.

I was waiting for those who asked about this book to say, "And why are *you* writing about holiness?" Thankfully, they did not. However, I would have said, "*Only Jesus is holy; however, when I walk with Him unhindered, I am holy, for it is a work of grace.*" Holiness rests on the shoulders of the One that can bear it, that is Jesus; and the recipients of the grace of holiness are those who walk with Him.

Some Definitions

It will help to look at a few key points to biblical holiness.

First, *God is the only author of holiness*. When the four living creatures of Revelation refer to God unceasingly as being *Holy, Holy, Holy* (Revelation 4:8), in part they are saying that God is of a nature which nothing in heaven or earth can participate, unless He gifts it. He has an essence of purity, rightness, and exalted perfection (morally and otherwise) that cannot be imitated, only reflected. The creatures say God who is holy "was, is, and is to come." He shows His holiness in that which He has done, in that which He is doing, and that which He will do throughout eternity. He is everlastingly consistent in His perfection.

Second, *God wishes to share holiness*. When the Bible speaks of holiness in reference to anything other than God, it is referring to what is set apart *by* God. Kenneth Wuest further clarifies that it does not mean to be merely "set apart," but to be "set apart *to* God."[1] Therefore, what is holy is set apart *by* and *to* God.

In the Old Testament the tabernacle and temple, the objects of the temple, the sacrifices of the Old Testament, even the articles of clothing worn by those participating in the rites were *holy*. The people of God were *holy*: the children of Israel as a nation were *holy*, as were the individual priests that performed the services and those that were obedient to the commands of God.

In the New Testament, all those God called and who accepted the rule of the Messiah were the "holy ones" or "saints" (From the Greek, *Hagios*). There are no exceptions. God has set every Christian apart to Himself.

Third, stated in the negative, *the recipient of holiness does not have a "holier than thou" attitude.* This attitude is foreign to true holiness and is in fact, anti-holy. Since true holiness is a gift, the one who receives it and wishes to keep it is not self-absorbed. Ultimately, we do not *have* holiness; we *borrow* it, as it emanates from God. The holiness imparted to us at our salvation is unassailable, but that which we walk in can wane when we are careless.

The apostle Paul said that he wished to be found *in* Christ: "Not having a righteousness of my own derived from the Law, but that which is through faith in Christ, the righteousness which comes from God on the basis of faith" (Philippians 3:9). Since holiness is accessible to everyone who is willing to walk in it by faith, and since it is not "owned" by any of us, this would preclude any sense of superiority.

You might ask "Why?"

If you are a Christian, you probably do not have to be convinced that personal holiness is important, but you might honestly wonder why you should bother. (You might be fingering this book in the bookstore, trying to determine whether you will buy it or one titled *Enjoying Your Recreation,* or one called *Watching Your Finances Grow...Spiritually.*) Why should you bother? *Do you know that holiness will make your life both effective and enjoyable.* I skipped over the obvious answer, that *God commands holiness.* I am not minimizing that, He does command it, but did you also know that you would not be satisfied without it.

There is no guarantee that holiness will cause everything to go well. In fact, I can guarantee sometimes it will not. However, God promised that when we walk in holiness everything would go according to His will (at least in respect to us). That is deeply satisfying, because God's rewards are simply unsurpassed, and He promised His full benefits—now and later—to those who walk in holiness.

Paul said, "I am speaking in human terms because of the weakness of your flesh. For just as you presented your members as slaves to impurity and to lawlessness, resulting in further lawlessness, so now present your members as slaves to righteousness, resulting in sanctification...but now having been freed from sin and enslaved to God, you derive your benefit, resulting in sanctification, and the outcome, eternal life" (Romans 6:19, 22). The apostle is suggesting that we are giving up what we thought we wanted to get what we truly need. Before, we gave ourselves to wickedness, sometimes ignorantly, but now we give ourselves purposely as slaves to a new master, which is righteousness or holiness, a by-product of a fruitful relationship with God. When we give ourselves entirely and energetically to these spiritual principles, we are "sanctified," or made holy.

Years ago, my son was watching me organize my fishing tackle box. I was cleaning items, sharpening hooks, and throwing old pieces away. I was about to dispose of a tiny brass swivel (which is used to allow freedom of movement to two lines, tied to both ends), when he asked if he could have it. Knowing he found joy from many things—sometimes, *unusual* things—I gave it to him.

He made the swivel a pet. He named it "Tim."

The swivel was green with corrosion, so that it would no longer move on both sides. He explained to his mother that Tim had a handicap: he could not swivel, as he should...he could only *swiv*.

It seems to me that many Christians are only *swiving* when they could *swivel*. God desires for us to have freedom of movement as we achieve His purposes. This is possible in holiness, and it is for this reason that we approach this subject with joy.

---

1. Kenneth S. Wuest, "Studies in the Vocabulary of the Greek New Testament," in *Wuest's Word Studies from the Greek New Testament,* rev. ed. (1945; repr., Grand Rapids: Wm. B. Eerdmans, 1973), 3:4:30.

Section 1: Reassessing Our Call

"Would You be Free From the Burden of Sin?"

CHAPTER 1

His Burden is Light and His Yoke Is Easy

Jesus said, "Come unto me all who are weary and heavy-laden, and I will give you rest" (Matthew 11:28), and our minds fly to His offer of salvation. This is not surprising since salvation is foremost of the gifts He has given us. He said, "My Burden is light," (v. 30) and we rejoice that the burden of our salvation on the Lord's shoulders is light enough to be completely free for us.

However, Warren Wiersbe points out the double use of the word "rest" in the words of Jesus. "'I will give you rest'—this is the peace with God that comes with salvation. 'You will find rest'—this is the peace of God that comes with surrender (see Phil. 4:6–9). To be yoked to Christ is the greatest blessing possible."[1]

For the purpose of this book, we are focusing on the continuing properties of this verse, or that rest that "comes with surrender." Jesus wants to provide "lightness" for those who walk in Him. Our salvation is certain and once for all, but we also need to progress daily in an enjoyment of this salvation. How can we walk worthy of our great salvation? The answer is the focus of this book, which is that the holiness of Jesus is effortless and will assure our success, where we tend to fill our attempts with impractical labor.

Richard Foster points out that the Jerusalem Bible translates Ecclesiastes 7:29 this way: "God made man simple; man's complex problems are of his own devising."[2] Our leaning toward complexity is such that we began to believe anything worthwhile has to be difficult!

Jesus did not call us in this way. He offers us "rest." How wonderful that sounds to weary people! We often feel that our burdens will never ease, and then we come to this passage and it offers harmony for our discordant lives: "I will give you rest," and then, "You will find rest for your souls." The word Jesus uses in both cases is from the root word *Anapouo*, which means refreshment or release from weariness. This is far from complex.

Jesus also said that His yoke is "easy," which in the Greek is the word *Chrestos*. Many people in the first century had the name *Chrestos* because of its pleasant meaning, which is "kind" or "benevolent." By using this word, Jesus assured us that His yoke is friendly.

Nevertheless, we should remember that the yoke of that day was a term for service. To "take a yoke" meant to become a disciple. The literal yoke of that day was a wooden device that fitted over the shoulders of two animals that connected them to each other and jointly attached them to the load. They pulled together and they helped each other in moving the burden. Our easy yoke is our service under Jesus' authority, but it seems that He will share the yoke with us as we pull together.

The word "yoke" normally may bring to mind containment or even entrapment, but not in this passage. A.T. Robertson said, "In portions of Europe today people place yokes on the shoulders to make the burden easier to carry."[3] Not only is the load that is carried easier, but because of the yoke, more can be carried. Jesus makes the labor lighter and more efficient.

Rest is Found in the Ancient Path

If we return to the idea of "rest" in Jesus' words, for instruction we can turn to the words of Jeremiah from which Jesus was probably quoting. "Thus says the Lord, 'Stand by the ways and see and ask for the ancient paths, Where the good way is, and walk in it; And you will find rest for your souls.' But *they* said, 'We will not walk in it'" (Jeremiah 6:16).

The way that Jesus offers is the "Ancient Path," and it has been tested. Abraham walked in this way and found it "good." Moses walked in this tested way and found rest. King David, with his catastrophic failures, walked in the old path and was beloved and a man like God's "own heart." Jesus understood the "old paths" better than anyone did—He knew their importance and He walked in them.

In contrast to many good examples in the Bible, Israel failed her test. Jeremiah said that Israel had the choice concerning the way but she said, "We will not walk in it."

We also have to make a choice. We can walk in the ancient way with Jesus and find our burdens lifted, or continue to carry them in our own strength and be weary. The right choice seems obvious, but too often, we have chosen the wrong way. Jesus said we must "learn" of Him. Surrendering to Jesus always yields the same positive results but we are often stubborn! We can learn to trust Him more and rely on our strength less.

The burden Jesus offers is "light." It is light is because He is "gentle and humble in heart." Robertson said, "Humility was not a virtue among the ancients. It was ranked with servility. Jesus has made a virtue of this vice. He has glorified this attitude so that Paul urges it (Phil. 2:3), 'in lowliness of mind each counting other better than himself.'"[4]

How much the teachings of Jesus have changed us! Where humility used to be a lowly state, Jesus has elevated it to be a trait that marks a great person. Today, humility rarely has any negative connotation. How wonderful are these words, "Learn from Me, for I am gentle and humble of heart" (Matthew 28:29).

A Garden Analogy

Another famous passage that can help us as we consider holiness and how to attain it is John 15:1-11:

> I am the true vine, and My Father is the vinedresser. Every branch in Me that does not bear fruit, He takes away; and every branch that bears fruit, He prunes it so that it may bear more fruit. You are already clean because of the word which I have spoken to you. Abide in Me, and I in you. As the branch cannot bear fruit of itself unless it abides in the vine, so neither can you unless you abide in Me. I am the vine, you are the branches; he who abides in Me and I in him, he bears much fruit, for apart from Me you can do nothing. If anyone does not abide in Me, he is thrown away as a branch and dries up; and they gather them, and cast them into the fire and they are burned. If you abide in Me, and My words abide in you, ask whatever you wish, and it will be done for you. My Father is glorified by this, that you bear much fruit, and so prove to be My disciples. Just as the Father has loved Me, I have also loved you; abide in My love. If you keep My commandments, you will abide in My love; just as I have kept My Father's commandments and abide in His love. These things I have spoken to you so that My joy may be in you, and that your joy may be made full.

It is a matter of abiding! When we abide in something we live in it, and so the word *abode* is a dwelling or is where we live. The abode that Jesus refers to is spiritual and the "vine" is where it is located. Several things to notice in the above passage:

1. *The Father is the vinedresser.*
   God manages everything. He wants to be sure His vineyard grows well, but by His design, the plant that gives us direct sustenance is Jesus.
2. *Jesus is the vine, from which the sap and nutrients all flow.*
   Much of this is hidden from our eyes but is true nonetheless. As we shall see in this book, it is in the finished work of Jesus that our holiness resides. Jesus is a towering success and our success follows. (Do you see how much power He wields to make us strong? The Father and the Son work so that we might have rest!)

3. *We are the branches.*
   We attach to the vine, which means once we have chosen Jesus as our Savior, we have chosen His way as our way. It is impossible for branches to live independent of the vine.

4. *How we attach to the vine is in view.*
   If we disconnect from the vine to some extent, we will produce weakly. If we separate ourselves entirely we will die. Trace the branch from the outside in and a branch healthy and loaded with fruit is always well attached to the vine.

5. *We fully attach to the vine when we abide.*
   "If you abide in Me and My words abide in you, ask and it will be done." Our power in prayer is the result of abiding in the vine. Abiding in the vine is only possible if we continue to allow His words to grow in us.

6. *The result is the production of fruit.*
   What is this fruit? Jesus did not define it. However, we see that when we are abiding we will produce what Jesus is producing. That would be enough.

7. *Jesus wishes our joy to be full.*
   Our joy is "made full," which means it is produced by the vine and not by us. Our responsibility is to stay attached; Jesus provides the power for effective and joyful living.

There is nothing difficult about receiving power from another. These verses tell us that Jesus wants our "joy to be full," and this will happen when we are working in His power. The oft-quoted phrase is true, "God's work done in God's way will never lack for God's supply."

It is equivalent to theological nonsense to say we are Christians but reject the clear teachings of the Bible. Matthew Henry said, "From a vine we look for grapes (Isaiah 5:2), and from a Christian we look for Christianity."[5] Our world is filled with people who say they love Christ, but ignore or attack His teachings. This cannot be! Every Christian has for their marching orders the words of the infallible Word of God.

Some say, "I believe in an inerrant Scripture but I do not believe in inerrant interpretations." That is reasonable, but we cannot let it detract from the fact that the Bible is very clear in its teaching. There are obscure passages, to be sure, and we should approach all interpretation with open minds and humility. However, the truth of the Bible is knowable and every one of us who names Christ as Lord is responsible to its commands. This is abiding!

The words of Christ in John 15 are overwhelmingly positive. The compelling reason to abide in Christ is the effectiveness and joy that He brings. Certainly, these verses point to the decay that will be inevitable if we do not follow Christ's teachings; however, our primary reason for following Him is that it gives us joy to serve Him! It is always best when our relationship of love generates what we do in the name of Jesus.

As we seek to follow Jesus and share His holiness we should recall these two passages, that of the light burden and the vine and the branches. Our complexity is of our own devising. The way of God is intelligible and our lives will be simpler in His light.

1. W. W. Wiersbe, *Wiersbe's Expository Outlines on the New Testament* (Wheaton, Illinois: Victor Books, 1992), 47.

2. Richard Foster, *The Celebration of Discipline* (San Francisco: Harper & Row, 1978), 69.

3. A. T. Robertson, *Word Pictures in the New Testament* (Nashville: Sunday School Board of the Southern Baptist Convention, 1930), 1:92.

4. Ibid.

5. Matthew Henry, *Matthew Henry's Commentary on the Whole Bible* (Old Tappan, New Jersey: Fleming H. Revell Company, 1721), 2:1123.

CHAPTER 2

Simple Devotion

A life of holiness is not only possible, but God gives us the tools so that it will also not be burdensome. God does not want us to "rust out" but neither does He want us to "burn out." When we are living spiritually as God intended, we can be efficient and powerful, because He is.

Think for a minute what a day spent with an incarnate Jesus would be like. If He were to physically appear and stay with you throughout the day, what would be the result? I do not think that you would be nervous, eager to please, or carefully watching every word and deed. I think that you would be entirely free, with a sense of well-being unlike you have ever had. The people in the Bible flocked to Jesus because He was a *wonder*! He was direct and unflinching in what He said—which only kept the "Pharisees" away—because His authority and His love were surely evident to all.

Likely, if someone were to ask us after a day spent with Jesus, "What was the overwhelming result of Jesus' presence?" I think we would say, "Change!" Just being with Jesus means change or revival if you will.

One purpose for this book is to experience a *Jesus revival* and it only takes His presence. "Simple devotion" is a title carefully chosen for this chapter, for our devotion should be simple or it may become something other than devotion, like artifice. When we find the simple path to full devotion to Christ then His presence is made manifest in our lives and results in holiness.

Like a Child

Jesus told us to come to Him like a child (Matthew 18:3, Mark 10:14-15). Further, He said that we should all become like children to enter the kingdom at all, which begs the question: what *is* a child like?

A child is *humble*. This is specifically what Jesus addressed in Matthew 18. He said we should "humble ourselves" as children. A child is unassuming and candid (most of the time). This is one of the reasons society should carefully guard them, because they are trusting and easily led. We should trust Jesus.

A child is *dependent*. Children are dependent on others and they know it. When we come to Jesus, we should realize we are dependent on Him. We might never surrender completely to other people, but with Jesus there is nothing to hold back. He is always trustworthy.

A child is *buoyant*. At this writing, my son is ten years old. He is his parents' joy and health. He is sprightly and fresh and His newest antics constantly entertain us. When we approach Jesus, buoyancy and joy should be natural. In my mind's eye, I can hear the children laughing as they sat on Jesus' lap where they probably played with His beard.

A child is *curious*. I worked once as a maintenance man in a church school. I was painting a picnic bench and the preschoolers gathered around me as if I were a rock star, enthralled with my every move. They began asking questions:

"Whacha' doin'?" One asked.
"I'm painting," I responded. Knowingly, one turned to the other and
    said, "He's paintin'."
"Why're ya' paintin'?"
"Because you guys tore the paint off."
(Pause...)
"What color is that?"
"This is yellow."
"Why're ya' paintin' it yellow?"

On and on it went. A teacher had to shoo them off to class.

When we approach our Maker, there is so much to learn and so much to understand that we should come to Him with curiosity and the joy of discovery.

A child is *unbent*. The child has not been hurt enough to be cynical. They are still innocent of the world's meanness. Not only can we come to Jesus unbent (Jesus does not deserve cynicism), but being close to Him will straighten us out.

A person becomes like Jesus when they habitually walk with Him. However, as the false religionists of Jesus' day soon discovered, there will be no benefit unless we approach Jesus honestly. I believe that if our true purpose is to glorify Jesus when we approach Him, He will see to it that we do not fail.

A simple approach to Jesus sets powerful changes in motion. What happens to us when we open ourselves up to His influence?

The Mind as a Pilothouse

When we approach Jesus honestly and effectively, we will see the power of the mind to affect change. We must get this to understand God's method of change.

There are spiritual groups today that distrust the mind, and some go so far as to view the mind as an enemy to the Spirit. It is true that our minds *could* be used to the detriment of the Holy Spirit's work. It is enough of a danger that Charles Spurgeon once said, "Oh, what a burden reason is to faith." More disdainfully, Martin Luther said, "Reason is a whore, the greatest enemy that faith has." However, God did not design our reason to be contrary to the work of the Holy Spirit, rather in its proper place it can unlock the things of the Spirit.

The mind can be compared to the pilothouse (or deckhouse) of a ship. This room, usually facing forward with panoramic windows is where the pilot oversees the operation of the entire ship. The captain is often in this room, and if he is not, he appoints a trusted subordinate to "man the ship." The steering wheel is located in the pilothouse, as is the compass and the navigating equipment. This room also has the public address where the steersman can address any room in the ship or the entire ship at once. The engine, rudder, weaponry, radio room, and all other parts of the ship have their individual purpose; however, they are ultimately under the control of the pilot. Our mind is something like this and as it goes, so goes the "ship." God wishes to change our mind, which will lead to change everywhere else.

Paul said to the Ephesians, " This I say... that you walk no longer just as the Gentiles also walk, in the futility of their *mind*, being darkened in their *understanding*, excluded from the life of God because of the *ignorance* that is in them...But you did not *learn* Christ in this way, if indeed you have heard Him and *have been taught* in Him, just as truth is in Jesus, that, in reference to your former manner of life, you lay aside the old self, which is being corrupted in accordance with the lusts of deceit, and that you be *renewed in the spirit of your mind*, and put on the new self, which in the likeness of God has been created in righteousness and holiness of the truth" (Ephesians 4:17-24, emphasis added).

Paul said that unlike those who walk in the futility of the mind, "You did not *learn* Christ in this way." Learning is a process that changes the mind, and a changed mind alters our behavior. God wishes us to reflect on the right thoughts so that we will walk as we should. Paul also said in these verses, "You have heard Him and have been taught in Him." The mind is in view again when Paul said what we hear, and what we apply, will control our actions.

Then Paul told the Ephesians, "You will be renewed in the *spirit of your mind*." Here there is both a physical and spiritual element. Change comes to us when both the mind and spirit are in agreement with God's revelation. In contrast, Paul said the Gentiles were futile in their mind-process and were subsequently "darkened."

It is clear that Paul said there is no way to get to the "new self" without a clear emphasis on how a person uses their mind. When the mind is open to God and His teaching, a person is able to put on the new self. Paul said this new self was "*created*" as righteous, holy, and in imitation of God Himself.

In other words, in the new self is everything we need to be like Jesus, we just need to learn to tap into it.

Paul said to the Romans, "Do not be conformed to this world, but be transformed by the renewing of your mind, so that you may prove what the will of God is, that which is good and acceptable and perfect" (Romans 12:2). When we choose not to be conformed to the dictates and demands of the world, we are free to be "transformed." The Word of God working on our minds brings about this transformation. We provide an atmosphere of acceptance, but the Holy Spirit makes the changes through the power of the Word of God.

Opening Life Channels

How then are we to allow God to transform us as Paul said in the "spirit of our minds?" This is where it gets simple! As we stated at the outset of this chapter, the very presence of Jesus causes revival. We are to give Him access.

Transformation comes from entering the presence of Jesus and applying His words. The best way that we can do this is by reading, studying, and meditating on the Scriptures, and by fellowship with Him in prayer. There are other activities that we must not neglect—such as corporate worship, service, and fellowship with the saints, etc.—however the primary way of transformation must be in our private devotional time with our Lord.

I call these "Life channels" because the mind operates in channels. Faith and doubt cannot operate in the same channel in our minds, for one or the other will prevail. If doubt is predominant then faith is weak. If faith is ascendant—here is good news—doubt must fly! Faith is stronger than doubt, contrary to what we might have thought. Therefore, our devotional time is when we "channel" our hearts and minds to welcome faith by delighting in the presence of God. I should add that the very process of working through our doubts could cause faith to increase, so even doubts have a good purpose when faith is applied.

The devotion we are seeking is simple because we try not to add anything to it to get God's attention or attract His grace, for we must know His grace and His attention are already fully ours. When we seek God in prayer and the Word, we have all the power of Heaven with us. The power in our devotional time is His and not ours. We choose well when we learn to approach the Lord with sincerity and simplicity, removing anything that would hinder our union with God.

For years, spiritual instructors have wisely recommended the "Quiet Time." (My quiet times are sometimes anything but quiet as they are filled with the noise of private spiritual battle and heartfelt appeals.) This quiet time is when we separate ourselves during the day to concentrate on prayer and the Bible. This should be more than just a reading of a prepackaged devotion and closing with a quick prayer. There must be spontaneity since we are meeting the person of the Holy Spirit who has His own plan. Rote readings or prayers will not serve us here.

I recommend a quiet time that gives equal attention to Bible reading and prayer for an hour or more each day. If that is too big a bite to chew at first, then a person could begin with thirty minutes and work up to an hour. If a person is regularly able to go beyond an hour in this time, that is even better! When we discipline ourselves, this habit has the wonderful effect of channeling the grace of God in our lives to effect permanent change.

This kind of devotion is like the valve on the mighty dam that lets the water through on occasion. Behind the wall of the dam is the latent power of the enormous weight of all that water. When you open the valve then the power in reserve comes rushing through the opening. It is the same with our devotions. The resources and power of God are astounding, but we must open the valve regularly to enjoy this power.

Some people say they are just too busy to spend daily time in devotion. Then they are just *too* busy! We might need to take activities out of our schedule but it should never be our time alone with God. R. A. Torrey reminds us, "Apparently the busier Christ's life was, the more He prayed. Sometimes He had no time to eat (Mark 3:20), sometimes He had no time for needed rest and sleep (Mark 6:31, 33, 46); but He always took time to pray; and the more the work crowded the more He prayed."[1]

Martin Luther prayed at least three hours daily, and when someone asked how he could do that when he was so busy, he said he must pray *because* he was so busy.

There can be nothing in our lives more important than the affairs of God.

Practical Considerations

Good habits can make our quiet time more successful. Following is list of time-honored habits that make the quiet time successful.

Choose a regular time. If we set a regular time for our devotions, we are less likely to miss them. A regular time also has the added effect of predisposing our minds and bodies for this important activity. Occasionally *life* gets in the way, and we will have to meet with the Lord in the evening instead of the morning, etc., but we should try to avoid missing the time altogether. By missing our chosen time, we might be giving ourselves a subconscious message that our devotions are not as important as other events throughout the day.

Nevertheless, we need to keep in mind that our devotion arises out of a "love relationship" with our Savior. When we fail to meet Him, or we meet with Him poorly, we should avoid castigating ourselves. Remember that we are not devoting ourselves to a "time" but to His person. He invites us back to continue in devotion to Him, to our mutual joy.

Choose a regular place. A regular place often helps our spirit adjust to what we are about to do. This chosen place also has the advantage of telling others in our family that we are about to meet with God…alone! We may change the location from time to time to avoid monotony, but we should aim for regularity.

Try to limit distractions. This would mean refuse to answer the telephone except for emergencies (this is what the answering machine is for!). Do not sit outdoors or in a room with a window if you are easily distracted (or close the blinds). You should inform your family that you do not wish to be disturbed during this time. A small memo pad nearby can help so that when the "great idea" comes to mind during the quiet time it can be recorded and handled later.

Read the Bible rather than study. Bible study is important of course, as is the use of study aids like commentaries, dictionaries, and cross-references. We should designate time in our week for this, too. Nevertheless, our devotional time is not the best time for study as it is labor and time intensive and does not give the relational insights of lighter reading. Read devotionally by reading larger sections of the Scripture—maybe a chapter or two—in order to understand the sweep of what God is saying. We are not trying to read as much as possible but we *are* trying to see the forest more than the trees. The Holy Spirit may lead you in one quiet time to spend the entire Bible reading time on one or two verses, and no other person can tell us what the Spirit is leading us to do; however, it is usually best not to get bogged down in intensive study.

I highly recommend the "One Year" Bibles offered by various publishers. They arrange devotional readings in dated sets (usually with an Old Testament passage, a New Testament passage, and a passage from the Psalms and Proverbs each day). In this way, since you are reading the Bible in the order of presentation, you will get a better feel for its redemptive message. These Bibles have the advantage of reminding you if you are behind in your reading, and they avoid the passage-search gymnastics necessary when you follow a reading chart.

Follow a set plan. I would suggest a brief prayer time of a few minutes at the beginning of the quiet time to prepare your mind and heart for Bible reading and prayer (yes, praying about your prayer). Once prepared, I read the Bible for a while and follow with prayer, but my Bible reading is interspersed with prayer and my prayer with Bible reading! I am free to break the scheduled plan, and sometimes do, but having one seems to help.

Listen as well as talk. Søren Kierkegaard said, "A man prayed, and at first he thought that prayer was talking. But he became more and more quiet until in the end he realized that prayer is listening."[2] This is important to remember because we have a tendency to turn our devotional time into regimen, which can drain its life. This devotion is two-way, and we will be better off if we listen to God rather than talk *at* Him.

I am a runner, and when I am out, I like to talk to God. On one run, my concentration in prayer was such that I could see very little around me and hear almost nothing, although I was next to a busy street. Suddenly, gently entering my consciousness, I heard a bird singing. When I began to look for the bird, instead I saw the relaxed sway of the tree against the blue sky. At that moment, other sounds around me rushed to my attention: the cars, children playing in the park beside me. I heard the inner voice say, "Listen to My birds, take in the sights and enjoy your time with Me. Don't miss the beauty. Stop *trying* so hard!"

Use a prayer journal. I keep this journal nearby and jot down special revelations in my prayer. I also list specific prayers and then track them. I cross-reference my journal entries with three symbols (any will do that you can recognize and remember) that I put in the left margin of entries. One symbol indicates a prayer seeking an answer, another shows me the entry is an answer to prayer. The last symbol looks like a little pair of glasses that musicians see in music scores that means, "Look at the conductor!" My little glasses mean, "This is important!" These few symbols help me to keep track of what God is doing through my prayer.

I have found, sometimes, that this journal is my best way to communicate with God. When the weight of some revelation or burden is heavy, I find I do not want just to speak it in prayer; I also want to write it down. Writing our thoughts down not only preserves them, it also helps us to *see* and *review* our progress.

Use the journal with care so it does not take over your quiet time. I rarely write for very long during my quiet time so that I will not take time from prayer and Bible reading, but I spend more time writing in this journal at other times in the day.

Inform your family that this journal is strictly off limits. Otherwise, you might not be honest in your entries, and honesty is what you are looking for.

Review your journal from time to time. It is helpful to see a pattern developing in how God has led you in the past, and what He is saying to you now. In fact, it often leads to more prayer!

Reason for Devotion

As we progress through the pages of this book, we will find that life is not as much what we make it as it is what the Holy Spirit can make it through us. The overwhelming focus of the Scripture is on what God has done for us rather than on what we can do for Him. If we understand what God has done and is doing, then our devotion is a natural response.

In Psalm 50, the psalmist presents a picture of a Holy God who calls both the wicked and the righteous into judgment. God reproves the Israelites, not because they lacked sacrifices, but because their sacrifices were insufficient. He said, "For every beast of the forest is Mine, the cattle on a thousand hills...if I were hungry I would not tell you, for the world is Mine, and all it contains...Offer to God a sacrifice of thanksgiving and pay your vows to the Most High; Call upon Me in the day of trouble; I shall rescue you, and you will honor Me" (Psalm 50:10, 12, 14-15).

God is telling the Israelites He does not need their sacrifices. What He wants is "thanksgiving," which is awareness of His constant provision. God also requires His children to "pay their vows," for when one agrees to follow Him they are agreeing to His every command. We all come to the Lord "Most High" because we must. *His* righteousness is in view in our devotion.

This devotion puts us in the presence of the majesty of God and life-change is the result. Jesus is our defense against the sin that will entangle our lives. Life does not stand still, and our relationship with the Lord should not either. We can encourage Jesus to have more freedom each day as life progresses and we can do this by having a life of simple devotion.

---

1. R. A. Torrey, *How to Pray* (Chicago: Moody Press, n.d.), 94.

2. Søren Kierkegaard, *Christian Discourses,* translation: Walter Lowie (Oxford University Press, 1940), 34.

CHAPTER 3

Obedience as Our Joy

Our society seems increasingly hostile to authority. Words like "obedience" are used rarely today and then in careful context, with loopholes allowed. The word obedience suggests that one person is responsible to another, as a slave would be to a master, and this is more than our politically correct society can handle.

We often hear from politicians, salespersons, and even some religious leaders that the direction of our lives should be determined by what we want. They tell us what we "deserve," and that we should throw off the constraints that others would place on our lives and our dreams. Sadly, this is only part of the truth and it may lead us into an entitlement mentality that leaves absolute authority only up to us, each individual becoming the canon for his own life.

Does Christ rob us of personal freedom?

Actually, personal freedom is fundamental to Christianity. God cares so much about our freedom that He will not demand that we accept Him or follow Him. Nothing in our faith is compulsory. However, the saints throughout the ages have discovered that if we choose Christ, we willingly give up all that we have and declare ourselves "slaves" in His service. We learn how we might "decrease so that He might increase" (John 3:30).

When the unbelieving world looks at Christianity from a distance, they might see a straightjacket existence, a joyless and puppet-like mindless following that intelligent people must reject. On the other hand, what the faithful Christian sees is the absolute joy in surrendering everything they have—their finances, their fulfillment, and their future—to the God they so dearly love. Consecrated Christians do not give up their rights to Christ under compulsion; they give them up gladly, willingly, and hoping for more to give.

How can this be?

Biblical Directives

The best we can do is to begin thinking of obedience in different terms than we have, for obedience is not something negative, but is the highest possible joy! Andrew Murray said, "When shall we learn how unspeakably pleasing obedience is in God's sight, and how unspeakable is the reward He bestows upon it?"[1] Murray comments on a list of Scripture that shows God's desire for obedience, some of which follow.

Obedience is all God demanded in the Garden of Eden, and disobedience is what caused paradise to be lost. God appeared to Abraham at ninety-nine years and said, "I am God Almighty; Walk before Me, and be blameless." To Isaac, God said, "I will establish the oath which I swore to your father Abraham...because Abraham obeyed Me and kept My charge, My commandments, My statutes and My laws" (Genesis 26:3, 5). At Mount Sinai, God said to the people of Israel through His servant Moses, "If you will indeed obey My voice and keep My covenant, then you shall be My own possession among all the peoples" (Exodus 19:5). Just before leading the people of Israel to take the Promised Land, God said to Joshua, "Every place on which the sole of your foot treads, I have given it to you, just as I spoke to Moses...Only be strong and very courageous; be careful to do according to all the law which Moses My servant commanded you; do not turn from it to the right or to the left, so that you may have success wherever you go" (Joshua 1:3, 7).

In the time of the kings, God chose Saul to lead His people, but Saul proved a bad example. At a critical time in Israel's history, Samuel commanded Saul to wait until the prophet came to offer a sacrifice. Samuel arrived late, so Saul offered the sacrifice himself. When Samuel arrived and discovered this disobedience, he said to Saul, "You have acted foolishly; you have not kept the commandment of the Lord your God, which He commanded you...But now your kingdom will not endure...because you have not kept what the Lord commanded you" (1 Samuel 13:13-14). Later, Samuel commanded Saul to destroy the Amalekites. He was to "utterly destroy" everything, but he kept back some of the spoils and spared the life of the Amalekite king, Agag. Because of this God told Samuel, "I regret that I have made Saul king," and Samuel said to Saul, "Behold, to obey is better than sacrifice, and to heed than the fat of rams" (1 Samuel 15:22).

The prophets were clear in their call for obedience. God spoke of His people to the prophet Jeremiah, "But this is what I commanded them, saying, 'Obey My voice, and I will be your God, and you will be My people; and you will walk in all the way which I command you, that it may be well with you.' Yet they did not obey" (Jeremiah 7:23-24a).

By the time of the New Testament, the call for obedience was still predominant. All of the New Testament writers made obedience a central theme in their writing, but we will concentrate on the words of Jesus.

Jesus said, "Truly, truly, I say to you, unless a grain of wheat falls into the earth and dies, it remains alone; but if it dies, it bears much fruit. He who loves his life loses it, and he who hates his life in this world will keep it to life eternal. If anyone serves Me, he must follow Me; and where I am, there My servant will be also; if anyone serves Me, the Father will honor him" (John 12:24-26). It is the very act of dying that opens the way for new life. We are dying to our own will, desires, and plans, so that we might replace them with everything that God commands.

One of my pastors, Dr. Jack Taylor, showed the congregation this principle by taking a kernel of corn from a corncob that had sat dormant on his bookshelf for years. As we watched, he asked one of the children to place the kernel of corn in a small cup filled with moistened soil. A few weeks later, he brought it back to church, and a small plant was growing from the kernel. Dr. Taylor reminded us that inside the kernel was life, but the kernel itself must die in the warmth of the soil before life could begin. The other kernels in the cob on his shelf were dormant still.

Dietrich Bonheoffer famously said, "When Christ calls a man, He bids him come and die."[2] Repeatedly, Bonheoffer asserts that God calls all Christians to radical discipleship. The command to die is for everyone that follows the Savior.

"Jesus said to His disciples, 'If anyone wishes to come after Me, he must deny himself, and take up his cross and follow Me. For whoever wishes to save his life will lose it; but whoever loses his life for My sake will find it. For what will it profit a man if he gains the whole world and forfeits his soul? Or what will a man give in exchange for his soul?'" (Matthew 16:24-26).

Jesus set the standard and it has always been clear: When He calls us to follow; it requires our immediate desire to follow His commands. To take any other route to Jesus is utter futility, for Jesus bids a person "come and die."

Our thinking can change our worldview. We are beginning to understand that obedience can indeed be a kind of dying to our will but it is also the only way to spiritual life awakening. Nothing is lost when we consider that true life is possible in our death. All is gain when we obey!

Jesus Set the Example

Obedience was fundamental to Jesus' work. He was a sacrifice without blemish, totally free from sin, which gave Him the authority to extend forgiveness to us. The cross would have been an ignominious death were it not for this fact.

When Jesus came into the world, it was with the understanding that He was to obey His Father. The author of Hebrews quotes the prophecy concerning Jesus from Psalms 40:7-8, "Behold, I have come to do Your will, O God" (Hebrews 10:7). *The Bible Knowledge Commentary* suggests, "In the 'body' which He assumed in Incarnation, Christ could say that He had come to achieve what the Old-Covenant sacrifices never achieved, the perfecting of New-Covenant worshipers."[3] Therefore, the very foundation of the gospel is built on the bedrock of the obedience of Jesus.

Not surprisingly, Jesus expects obedience from His followers. In the seventh chapter of Matthew, Jesus told the disciples to be aware of false prophets who would be known by their fruit. He spoke these telling words, "Not everyone who says to Me, 'Lord, Lord,' will enter the kingdom of heaven, but he who does the will of My Father who is in heaven will enter. Many will say to Me on that day, 'Lord, Lord, did we not prophesy in Your name, and in Your name cast out demons, and in Your name perform many miracles?' And then I will declare to them, 'I never knew you; depart from Me, you who practice lawlessness'" (Matthew 7:21-23). Jesus showed that no work has validity, great or small, if obedience to God is not paramount in the life of the worker.

Many other verses reflect the importance of obedience to the work of the disciples of Jesus (For example, Matthew 12:46-50, John 14:21-24 and Philippians 2:5-11). In one way or another, we will spend much of the remainder of this book dealing with obedience to Jesus and the resulting effectiveness and power promised. However, in this chapter I would like to concentrate on the benefit of obedience that offers the greatest strength, and that is the joy of obedience.

The Joy of Obedience

I remember a radio personality who used to discuss with on-air callers about their disbelief. He told many of them, who usually had some list of reasons why they could not believe, that the reason they did not want to follow Jesus is simply that they did not want to pay the moral price to do so. This reminds us of the person who says they want to follow Jesus, but not yet, as they first have a few things to do.

As we mentioned, obedience has been given a bad reputation. Some people think that obedience leads to life with creativity snuffed out. Actually, the opposite is true: true obedience awakens the best in us and leads us to life in abundance. What I am suggesting in this chapter is not *primarily* that obedience is evidence of holiness, or even that it is a characteristic of holiness, although it is both of these. What I am suggesting is that obedience is the *precursor* to holiness. Our obedience allows holiness to be cultivated in our lives and the result of this holiness is abundance.

In the twelfth chapter of Hebrews, the author encouraged us to "run the race with endurance." He also reminded us to "Fix our eyes on Jesus, the author and perfecter of faith, who for the joy set before Him endured the cross, despising the shame, and has sat down at the right hand of the throne of God" (Hebrews 12:2-3).

Jesus "endured the cross and despised the shame." The cross was difficult in the extreme, but He "endured" it. In addition, He "despised" (literally "scorned") the shame of His death. How? The "joy set before Him" left Him armored against the negative effects of His death on the cross. Jesus' joy was directly related to His obedience. He chose to follow commands with no reservations because He knew that life uninhibited with His Father would be wonderful despite any cost.

We can consider two ideas that Christ shows us through His obedience. The first is that *we need to have joy in what made Jesus joyful*. What made Jesus joyful was to obey the will of His Father. Our life transforms when obedience becomes its central theme. Doing God's will is like an elixir that heals our spiritual weakness and dissatisfaction. When we understand this as Jesus did, we will reach for God's will with energy.

My car sitting in the garage is an example. It runs on a mid-range gasoline. I have never even tried to put a lesser grade of gasoline in the tank just because I know it would not run as well. I am certain it would not run on kerosene at all!

God has created each of us to "run" on obedience. When we obey Him we are efficient, and our lives take on the vitality of the Holy Spirit in full measure. Jesus said, "He who believes in Me, as the Scripture said, 'From His innermost being will flow rivers of living water'" (John 7:38). Obeying Him evidences our belief, and when we obey, living water is the result. Jesus also said, "The thief comes only to steal and kill and destroy; I came that they may have life, and have it abundantly" (John 10:10). In this verse, the "thief" may be referring to Satan but is certainly referring to something from the dark side. If we deny Jesus and His demands on our lives then we are cooperating with the one who wishes to steal from us, and we are ignoring the One who wishes to give us abundant life!

Jesus is for us. He never subtracts from our lives, He always adds. When the Holy Spirit directs us in some way, then we should remember that abundant life and flowing rivers of living water are in exactly that direction.

I have told people throughout my ministry that I believe we have never given up anything of lasting value for the Lord. When God asks us to remove something from our lives, no matter how much we might think we like it, it is something that is already weakening us. On the other hand, if God asks us to add something to our lives, then it is necessary and it will enhance our spiritual experience and joy.

The second idea to consider is *there is an expectation of joy inexpressible when we obey*. While teaching a series on Satan and his wiles, I did some research on the spiritual armor of Ephesians 6. When I came to a description of the "Helmet of Salvation," I noticed the similarity in this to the "Breastplate of Righteousness." Since I believe God gave the breastplate to us by Jesus' imparted righteousness through salvation, then the helmet of salvation must point to something else. I am in agreement with authors like Warren Wiersbe that the helmet of salvation refers to our future salvation, or specifically, the return of Christ and our final deliverance.[4] Paul says in 1 Thessalonians 5:8, "Since we are of the day (and not 'of the night' as in verse 7), let us be sober, having put on the breastplate of faith and love, and as a helmet, the *hope* of salvation" (emphasis added).

When tried, tempted, or persecuted, it helps considerably for us to look toward the final reward promised when Jesus comes again in power. Our *hope*—which the Apostle describes as something we do not yet see (Romans 8:24-25)—keeps us going faithfully when the going is rough. When we are not obedient our hope wanes; our salvation is secure but our relationship sours. When we are obedient, we find that our hope is resonant since we are right with the Savior.

Jesus endured the cross and despised the shame because of the *joy* set before Him. His joy was not just in the reward, but also in finishing the race in obedience and therefore purchasing our salvation. His joy was obedience. We will transform our understanding of obedience when we see it for the joy that it is, and forever remove from our minds its shading as drudgery.

1. Andrew Murray, *The Believer's Secret of Obedience* (1982), 15.

2. Dietrich Bonhoeffer, *The Cost of Discipleship* (New York: MacMilland Publishing Co., Inc., 1937), 7.

3. John F. Walvoord and Roy B. Zuck, *The Bible Knowledge Commentary: An Exposition of the Scriptures by Dallas Seminary Faculty* (Wheaton, Illinois: Victor Books, 1987), 2:804.

4. Warren Wiersbe, *The Strategy of Satan: How to Detect and Defeat Him* (Wheaton, Illinois: Tyndale House Publishers, 1979), 134.

Section 2: Losing Nothing in Order to Gain All Things

"I Surrender All"

CHAPTER 4

Absolute Surrender

Whenever I tell people that I am going to teach the subject of "Absolute Surrender," invariably a few in the room turn a little pale and their eyes may fly open. Just saying the phrase "Absolute Surrender" is frightening—go ahead and try it!

This is the phrase I have adopted to describe the character of a person's life that has been called "laying all on the altar," "being sold out," or even "letting go." *Absolute surrender* is the term that Dr. Andrew Murray used when he wrote an entire book on the subject, and after reading his excellent book years ago this descriptive term has stuck in my mind.

Surrendering everything to God seems to be what we expect of "Super-saints," as if everyday people like you and me should not be concerned with such things. For some people, this chapter may be the sticking point where they lay this book aside and they go on to what they consider to be more reasonable and profitable pursuits!

There is a reason, however, that this chapter is toward the beginning of the book. Absolute surrender is a first step in walking with our Lord rather than an advanced step. If we do not surrender everything, we cannot follow Him faithfully *at all*. Failure to surrender absolutely to Jesus is the primary reason that most Christians are not walking in Spirit-filling, which is a necessary condition for successful Christian service. (We will look more deeply at Spirit-filling in the next chapter.)

Let me insert something to be clear. I said in chapter 1 of this book that there is a difference between our "resting" at the point of our salvation and "resting" as we work out our salvation. I indicated that this book focuses on the "working out," or what we might call our sanctification. However, our salvation is the first part. We cannot absolutely surrender anything else until we have surrendered ourselves.

Surrender at salvation may be imperfect, simply because we are immature, but it must be surrender nonetheless. We must place our faith in the Lord Jesus and in His ability to save. As I have said, we can bring nothing to the table of salvation but our willingness to accept His gift. He will make up for our immaturity in surrender when we ask for salvation and what we lack He will provide. The Lord will not reject the sincere request of a penitent person. However, our work begins at that point. Salvation is free to us, and permanent, but living according to this freedom is ongoing.

Jesus as Our Example

Jesus is our primary example for all aspects of Christian living. Therefore, it is fundamental for us to understand that He was fully tempted. Although He was God and lost none of the divine nature in the Incarnation, He was a man, fully so, and could have fallen if He had chosen. Theoretically, Jesus could have walked away from the will of the Father at any time. Hebrews 4:15 says, "For we do not have a high priest who cannot sympathize with our weaknesses, but One who has been tempted in all things as we are, yet without sin." This statement would be nothing more than mockery if His divine nature protected Him from disagreeing with the Father. Jesus was fully tempted and even to an extent that no other man will ever suffer.

Jesus chose not to deny the will of the Father. Not once did He choose His way over that of His Father. He proved that it is possible for a man to be free of sin, and His example is proof that we, too, can overcome temptation and live in victory.

We also need to affirm that the Bible is very clear that we are all sinners. The Apostle John even says that we are liars if we claim we have no sin (1 John 1:8). However, a person *could* live without sin, for that is what Jesus showed us. We should also understand that in order for Jesus to live without sin He had to surrender completely to the Father's will. One cannot accidentally be sinless.

Jesus was exceptional, there is no doubt, but while He was on earth, He was showing us what He wanted from His followers. His refusal to sin is a message for us: *Do not sin.* His absolute surrender to the will of the Father reminds us that this is what He requires from believers. Holiness is unattainable without this first step.

Murray was in Scotland when he asked a fellow minister who was responsible for training workers what was the primary need for Christian workers. This man said, "Absolute surrender to God is the *one* thing." He went on to say that if he had workers who were weak, low on skill, halting, or any other impediment, if they had this one characteristic of surrender, he could be sure that they would come to fruition in their work.[1]

The Bible Calls for Absolute Surrender

We acknowledge that God is all in all. He "...is light, and in Him there is no darkness at all" (1 John 1:5). He is life and the source of all life (John 6:51). We believe that all things "emanate" from God, and everything has its being in Him (whether they acknowledge this or not). Since we believe this to be true, how could we live without Him and how could we operate without surrender to Him? If God is God, then rightly He demands our loyalty.

Murray makes the point in his book that all nature surrenders to God. The winds, the trees, the flowers, the fish in the stream, the deer in the wood, and the bird in his nest, all have no possibility but surrendering to the purposes of God.[2]

Jesus told us in Matthew 6:28-29, 33, "And why are you worried about clothing? Observe how the lilies of the field grow; they do not toil nor do they spin, yet I say to you that not even Solomon in all his glory clothed himself like one of these…But seek first His kingdom and His righteousness, and all these things will be added to you."

Certainly, these natural citizens do not have the possibility of refusing the Lord just as they do not have the possibility of actively choosing Him. However, each time the Scripture points them out as examples we should remember that they are entirely in the Lord's hands. Without Him, they will not find provision, and yet they do not worry.

Humankind on the other hand can choose to accept the rule of God or reject it. We have the choice. Having the right to choose should mean we would choose rightly. When we surrender to God we must surrender completely just as does the world of nature, for is there any kind of *surrender* other than one that is absolute?

Jesus gave us examples to show that total surrender is what He wants.

Our first example is the Rich Young Ruler. In Mark 10, starting with verse 17, Mark records the story of the young man who approached Jesus and wanted to know how to inherit eternal life. This young ruler was a good man, possibly better than most of us (we should remember that). Jesus told the man first that He was to keep the commandments, "You know the commandments, 'Do not murder, Do not commit adultery, Do not steal, Do not bear false witness, Do not defraud, Honor your father and mother'" (Mark 10:19). These commandments have man as their focus, and this man could say he had kept these all from his youth. To show what God requires, Jesus said, "One thing you lack: go and sell all you possess and give to the poor, and you will have treasure in heaven; and come, follow Me." This man was to give up everything he had, to place the proceeds in the hands of those who most need it, and having been freed from all restraint would be free to be a follower of Jesus. The young man would not do this and walked away sadly. His conflict was that he wanted to follow Jesus, but his desire for what he already possessed was overwhelming.

The Lord has not told all of us to sell everything we have (maybe we do not need this discipline), but he has asked each of us to *relinquish* everything we have. His love for his possessions prevented this man from following Jesus, and Jesus knew it. Our unwillingness to give up anything and everything, like this young man, is exactly what is keeping us from following Jesus.

Jesus made other statements that apply to the idea of absolute surrender. Jesus told each of us, "If anyone wishes to come after Me, he must deny himself, and take up his cross daily and follow Me" (Luke 9:23). When we "deny ourselves," we give up the self and its desires and replace it with "our cross." The cross cost Jesus everything earthly and it will cost us just the same.

It is remarkable that Jesus was using the terminology of the "cross" before the event of His crucifixion! The cross was a way of life for Jesus long before it was for Him an instrument of torture.

Jesus also pointed to the need for His followers to die in order to live. In chapter 3, we discussed a picturesque statement when Jesus said, "Truly, truly, I say to you, unless a grain of wheat falls into the earth and dies, it remains alone; but if it dies, it bears much fruit. He who loves his life loses it, and he who hates his life in this world will keep it to life eternal" (John 12:24-26). A grain of wheat must be buried and die before it will grow. Before we are to produce the fruit that God desires for us to produce, we must experience a total death. In effect, we must lose everything we have in order to embrace what God has for us.

Just like Jesus did.

How Are We to Surrender Absolutely?

Many people do not surrender to God because they think there are too many things they would have to "give up." They will not usually refuse God, at least consciously, but they will remove the very idea of absolute surrender from their consciousness. They will try not to look directly at surrender so they feel they are not responsible before God.

This is obviously no escape since the idea of our surrendering to God is at the very foundation of our service to Jesus. How can a "slave" (the meaning of the scriptural word *doulos* usually translated "servant") choose what way he is to serve? If God calls for absolute surrender of each servant, and He does, then we cannot look another way.

At the heart of this problem is our view of God. How terrible Christians must think God is to try to hold on to their own will with such tenacity. When God asks for surrender and we hold Him off, we are saying that our plans are better than His are. This cannot be true. If we confess God is our perfect Master, it must follow that we believe Him to be a perfect Life-designer.

God is indeed great, He is powerful and sovereign; yet, His most distinguishing feature must be His love. God *is* love (1 John 4:8). Love is the defining nature of God, and since He is love and His knowledge is complete, how could we want anything less than what He wants? When God demands something from us, we should run joyfully to complete His will.

When God commands us to accomplish some task, He is not distant, and we are not left to our own strength in this matter of surrender. Paul wrote in Philippians 1:6, "For I am confident of this very thing, that He who began a good work in you will perfect it until the day of Christ Jesus." Then in 2:13 he wrote, "For it is God who is at work in you, both to will and to work for His good pleasure." God is interested in our success. He will participate in our growth in every area that He commands. Not only do these verses tell us that He has invested in our progress, but they also tell us that He will change our *will* if we allow Him. To surrender entirely to the Lord is an action that initially must take place in our hearts, but the power of God completes our surrender.

The very act of reading this book shows that there are yearnings in your heart that are not satisfied. God put into our hearts the desire to surrender to Him. Even though we might be afraid of surrender, the possibility still draws us.

You may feel that you would certainly like to surrender everything to God and that you agree that you should not hold anything back in your relationship, but you are concerned about what He might ask you to do! Would not absolute surrender open the possibility of your being sent to Siberian missions? It is possible, but not likely. God leads us according to desires He plants in our spirits, and according to the gifts that He gives us. To fear greatly that God might push us toward something we dislike is a thought that the Devil (or our overheated imagination) plants to get us off track. This is not to say we will *not* be sent to Siberia, it is just unlikely. God will send someone with a heart for those in Siberia, and once God touches them in this way, they would rather be nowhere else on earth.

Many of the things that God has called us to do are challenging. After all, He told us to "make disciples of all the nations" (Matthew 28:19). Such a command will not always fit into our plans for comfort! However, if we love our God and truly believe He is sovereign, our desire to please Him and fit into His plan will weigh far heavier than any fears we might have. This is one of the great joys of absolute surrender: we fear nothing He might ask.

In the Lord's Prayer, Jesus gave us important words that help us know how to pray each day. One part of that prayer, prayed daily, will remind us of His desire for our complete surrender, "Our Father who is in Heaven, Hallowed be Your name. Your kingdom come, Your will be done, *On earth as it in Heaven*" (Matthew 6:9-10, emphasis added). When we pray this, we are surrendering absolutely.

Surrender everything today! Seek God for the will to do it, ask Him to sustain it, and then surrender. I believe that getting to the moment of surrender is the more difficult part; surrendering itself is easy. Pray something like, "Dear Lord, I love You, and I understand the Scripture tells me that You cannot fully use a partially surrendered vessel. I realize now that surrendering my all is what You have always asked me to do. I am willing. Take me, for I surrender and hold nothing back. Use me as you wish and help me to discern each step ahead so as to be glorifying to You."

God Accepts Our Offering

Murray emphasized a point that we would well remember, "God accepts absolute surrender when we bring it to Him."[3] When you yield to God, you may feel that it is inadequate. You might ask yourself, "Is it absolute?" Murray reminded us of Mark 9 when the man had a son who was possessed and he asked Jesus to intervene (Jesus' disciples had already failed). Jesus asked the man if he believed, and the man said, "I believe, O Lord help my unbelief." That was enough. Jesus cast the demon out with no rebuke for the man's unbelief.

When we honestly surrender, though we may feel less than powerful or determined, even in trembling the power of the Holy Spirit will work. Murray said:

Have you never yet learned the lesson that the Holy Spirit works with mighty power, while on the human side everything appears feeble? Look at the Lord Jesus Christ in Gethsemane. We read that he 'through the eternal spirit' offered himself a sacrifice unto God. The almighty Spirit of God was enabling him to do it. Yet what agony and fear and exceeding sorrow came over him, and how he prayed! Externally you can see no sign of the mighty power of the Spirit, but the Spirit of God was there. And even so, while you are feeble and fighting and trembling, in faith in the hidden work of God's Spirit, do not fear, but yield yourself.[4]

You may not feel it, you may not fully realize it, but God will take full possession of you and your future if you will trust Him...Absolutely.

---

1. Andrew Murray, *Absolute Surrender,* rev. ed. (1957; repr., Grand Rapids: Zondervan Publishing House, 1988), 49.

2. Ibid., 49-50.

3. Ibid., 52.

4. Ibid.

CHAPTER 5

Being Filled with the Holy Spirit

If we desire personal holiness, and we understand God as its author, we would assume the Holy Spirit must have an extremely important part to play. Indeed He does. Since God is the author of holiness, then the Holy Spirit would be the scribe who would write in on our lives. He must always have freedom to do this work through us.

There has been much discussion in recent years about the filling with the Holy Spirit. This is good because some churches have possibly been too silent. Excesses in this area by some groups have caused an overreaction, even a stifling of the Lord's work through the Holy Spirit, and discussion is necessary.

I have taken my own long journey in researching the filling with the Holy Spirit and His operation in our lives. I visited charismatic churches while I was in the seminary, thinking that they had secrets to which my own denomination was closed. In those days in evangelical circles, discussion of the Holy Spirit and His gifts was muted. We passed over important passages in the Bible, instead focusing on some people who seemed "unorthodox."

My journey into this study was difficult and long. During these dark days of confusion and discovery, I took what I believe to be several wrong paths and had to make midcourse corrections. I arrived at what I believe is a biblical position that follows in this chapter. However much you agree or disagree with my position, please discover this area with careful biblical interpretation, as we cannot ignore it. There is no substitute for the work of the Holy Spirit in our service. He must be free in our lives and we cannot complete our commission without His presence and power.

Spirit-Filling Is Not a "Second Blessing"

The teaching of the second blessing, what some call the "Baptism of the Holy Spirit," has exploded on the scene since the 1960s in America. The popularity of this teaching coincides with the emergence of the charismatic church, a more mainstream version of the Pentecostals (UPC) of the early part of the century (1906). The Assemblies of God (1914) particularly, and other interdenominational charismatic churches, have emphasized this teaching which teaches that there is a separate event from our salvation where the Holy Spirit baptizes a person so that they can be empowered for service. Many of these believers teach that the gift of tongues is a necessary accompanying sign for this gift. This teaching has moved outside of the original denominations to include parts of many mainline protestant denominations, some evangelical, and in the Catholic Church where the teaching has been authorized by Vatican officials.

Each Christian needs to understand that the Holy Spirit's empowerment for ministry is essential for every Christian. However, it is my belief that even though every person must continue to be filled with the Holy Spirit, there is only one baptism with the Holy Spirit and it is a gift given to us when we are saved. This baptism is never subsequent to salvation, nor is it sought. What we must seek after our salvation is a daily filling with the Holy Spirit.

The Bible does not use or imply the phrase "Baptism of the Holy Spirit." Rather, the experience is always in verb form and translated as being baptized *with* the Holy Spirit. The Holy Spirit is not the one who baptizes, Jesus is. Literally, it would be accurate to say there is a biblical baptism of Jesus *with* or *in* the Holy Spirit, but not a baptism *of* the Holy Spirit (in a possessive sense).

John the Baptist said, "As for me, I baptize you with water for repentance, but He who is coming after me is mightier than I, and I am not fit to remove His sandals; He will baptize you with the Holy Spirit and fire" (Matthew 3:11). John also said, "I did not recognize Him, but He who sent me to baptize in water said to me, 'He upon whom you see the Spirit descending and remaining upon Him, this is the One who baptizes in the Holy Spirit'" (John 1:33).

Peter told the seekers of Acts chapter two, "This Jesus God raised up again, to which we are all witnesses. Therefore having been exalted to the right hand of God, and having received from the Father the promise of the Holy Spirit, He has poured forth this which you both see and hear" (Acts 2:32-33).

Jesus baptizes believers in the Holy Spirit. This baptism is a gift to all Christians. In the second chapter of Acts, those who had gathered were "pierced to the heart," and asked what they needed to do. "Peter said to them, 'Repent, and each of you be baptized in the name of Jesus Christ for the forgiveness of your sins; and you will receive the gift of the Holy Spirit. For the promise is for you and your children and for all who are far off, as many as the Lord our God will call to Himself'" (Acts 2:38-39).

Note Peter said this gift is universal for those whom "God calls to Himself." These words indicate that there are not two groups of Christians: those who have received the full gift of the Holy Spirit for service and those who have not. When a person accepts Jesus as their Savior, they receive all of the Holy Spirit they will ever receive. The full presence of the Holy Spirit is theirs at salvation. Peter said later, "Grace and peace be multiplied to you in the knowledge of God and of Jesus our Lord; seeing that His divine power has granted to us everything pertaining to life and godliness, through the true knowledge of Him who called us by His own glory and excellence" (2 Peter 1:2-3). Peter said in *true knowledge* of Jesus is *everything* we need. To say that we need to receive something subsequent to our salvation in Jesus is tantamount to saying that His sacrifice was insufficient. On the contrary, when we receive Jesus, we receive everything that He accomplished on the cross and through the resurrection.

All Christians are saved to the uttermost and baptized with the Holy Spirit. "For even as the body is one and yet has many members, and all the members of the body, though they are many, are one body, so also is Christ. For by one Spirit we were all baptized into one body, whether Jews or Greeks, whether slaves or free, and we were all made to drink of one Spirit" (1 Corinthians 12:12-13). There are no second-class citizens in the kingdom of heaven, or as John MacArthur calls them, "The Have-nots."[1]

The Filling with the Holy Spirit

Jack Taylor, the Southern Baptist author and my pastor for a time, said the reason we need not just a *second blessing* but also *many blessings* is that "we leak!" Even though we receive all of the Holy Spirit and His blessings at the point of our salvation, from that day we find that we must *remain* in the fullness of the Holy Spirit. There is a tremendous need in evangelical churches for individuals to be filled with the Holy Spirit. We need to understand it, we need to teach it, and we need to stay in it—each one of us.

Once Christ baptizes us with the Holy Spirit at the moment of our salvation He abides within us. We may indeed quench the Spirit, grieve the Spirit, and lose His fullness; but He does not go anywhere, He is just limited within us. When we lack His fullness, it simply means that the Holy Spirit is limited in *operation*. We need not seek anything from outside of ourselves; we just need to remove the limitations we have placed on Him. We should release Him in our lives.

The Apostle Paul wrote this well-known verse, "And do not get drunk with wine, for that is dissipation, but be filled with the Spirit" (Ephesians 5:18). Do you attempt to follow this command and not get drunk with wine? Then do you also stay filled with the Spirit? The translation of this verse from the Greek leaves no question. The verse literally commands, "*Keep on* being filled with the Holy Spirit." This present tense in the Greek means once having begun, you are to continue. It is an ever present *now*.

When Jesus told the parable of the ten virgins recorded in Matthew 25:1-13, I believe this subject is in view. This parable is about opportunities lost, and they can be lost when our lamp is not full.

In this parable, all ten women had lamps and all ten were *virgins*, but they were dissimilar in that five were *wise* and five were *foolish*. Though they were different in wisdom, I believe Jesus is referring to ten saved people. The Bible does not refer to lost people as virgins nor would the theology of the Bible indicate that lost people could have a lamp! What is disturbing about this parable is that after the five foolish virgins who belatedly went in search of oil find the door shut, the Master said, "I do not know you." What does this mean?

Saved people are fully and completely saved. There is no saved person less saved than another, wise or foolish. This parable is reminding us that it is possible to be unprepared for the arrival of the Master, and so miss the feast. What we miss is some opportunity to service rather than salvation. There would indeed be sorrow for those who miss some great calling because their lamps had no oil. How are our lamps filled with oil? We must be filled with the Holy Spirit and we must remain in this filling. Someone said, "The bird of opportunity never lights." If we are not continually filled with the Holy Spirit, we may find some opportunity has come and gone. We are to walk always filled with the Holy Spirit so that our work would be effective and blessed.

As we have said, we are baptized in the Holy Spirit at the point of our salvation. To be baptized means to be completely immersed in Him. The word (*Baptizo*) was used in Greek at that time to indicate the sinking of a ship, the dipping of an animal, or even of preserving a pickle in vinegar.[2] (This last one gives us a whole new view of sour Christians.) In each example, the object is submerged in liquid. In our case, we are completely immersed/submerged in the Holy Spirit. The Holy Spirit touches every part of us with His presence and power.

However, we sometimes limit His work by being disobedient. We might be angry and use unwholesome words and so "grieve" the Holy Spirit (Ephesians 4:30). Sometimes, because we are unbelieving and failing in praise and thanksgiving we "quench" Him (1 Thessalonians 5:19). When we sin, we should understand we cannot be full of Him until we get it right. The Holy Spirit cannot fill an unsurrendered vessel, and sin is contrary to surrender.

Steps to Filling

The filling with the Holy Spirit requires a few steps that I would like to mention. This is periodically necessary for every Christian. As we grow in obedience and awareness of the power and presence of the Holy Spirit, we find that more often than not, we just make corrections to put ourselves in the way of His blessing, and that is all that is necessary. However, consciously requesting this filling is never a bad idea, especially if we are unsure.

Here are the steps that are necessary to being filled with the Holy Spirit:

1. Believe that this filling is possible

The author of Hebrews tells us in the eleventh chapter, sometimes called the *Hall of Faith*, "Without faith it is impossible to please Him, for he who comes to God must believe that He is and that He is a rewarder of those who seek Him" (v. 6). James tells us in his epistle that when a person asks for wisdom, "Let him ask of God, who gives to all generously and without reproach, and it will be given to him. But he must ask in faith without any doubting, for the one who doubts is like the surf of the sea, driven and tossed by the wind" (James 1:5). The Apostle John says, "This is the confidence which we have before Him, that, if we ask anything according to His will, He hears us. And if we know that He hears us in whatever we ask, we know that we have the requests which we have asked from Him" (1 John 5:14-15).

Collectively these verses say that if we are to receive anything from God, we must ask believing that it is possible because He promised us. We should believe that this filling is available through the Holy Spirit. We should not ignore this vital step. If we have a question as to whether this is true, we should research the Bible immediately. When the Word of God has convinced us that the filling with the Holy Spirit is available, then we can go forward.

2. Confess our sins

All sin is in view here. Just as king David said, "Who can discern his errors? Acquit me of hidden faults. Also keep back Your servant from presumptuous sins" (Psalm 19:12-13a). Some of our sins are before our eyes and literally drive us to our knees. Others are hidden, possibly even forgotten. It is a good exercise to bring every sin before the Lord because it makes us aware of our need for His great forgiveness and our own stubborn will. However, we do not need to obsess over sins that are too distant or faint to remember. David understood that there are times when God needs to acquit us of what we have forgotten.

John says we all need to admit that we have sin, and then, "If we confess our sins, He is faithful and righteous to forgive us our sins and to cleanse us from all unrighteousness" (1 John 1:9). We should leave it there, for there is no reason to bring a matter up for forgiveness repeatedly. In response to the sincere confession, God forgives immediately and graciously.

3.   Surrender to God and His will

This is partly the reason for the previous chapter. I believe a lack of surrender is the greatest impediment to Spirit filling. Most Christians do not even know this is a step toward filling with the Holy Spirit. Andrew Murray wrote in *Absolute Surrender*:

> Each of us must examine himself. Some have never thought it a necessity to do it. Some have never understood what it meant when Jesus said that, "If a man come to me, and hate not his father, and mother, and wife, and children, and brethren, and sisters, yea, and his own life also, he cannot be my disciple" (Luke 14:26). Is not this the reason of your feeble life, the reason that the Holy Spirit does not fill your being?—you have never forsaken all to follow Christ.[3]

How can the Holy Spirit fill what is not completely yielded to Him? The very idea of filling would presuppose that the entire vessel is empty or surrendered. We surrender everything to God, and we are ready to proceed.

4.   Ask to be filled with the Holy Spirit

This seems an obvious step but there are those who miss it. *Ask* to be filled with the Holy Spirit. It requires no special preconditions other than those that we have already listed. We are also free from having to *feel* anything particular in response to our request. What may seem weak in the flesh is nonetheless mighty in the Spirit. You can be sure the Father accepts your sincere request. God immediately responds; there is no waiting, no agonizing at the "sawdust trail," no "tarrying." God grants the request immediately that He Himself has commanded.

5.   Thank God for this wonderful gift

When we receive something wonderful, we should thank the one who gave it to us. We are thankful because we realize the value of the gift. We are aware that it was expensive for the giver and we are aware that it adds value to our lives. What gift is more valuable than the fullness of the Holy Spirit?

Thanking God also puts a flourish to the end of our request—it is our saying that we believe we have received this gift and are now ready to advance in His power. When we are told in Colossians 4:2, "Devote yourselves to prayer, keeping alert in it with an attitude of thanksgiving," we are reminded that thanksgiving is natural to the person who faithfully prays. When we pray we should expect to receive what God has promised. No matter how we might *feel* about our prayer to be filled with the Holy Spirit, if we are sincere and have taken the steps previously mentioned, He has filled us. God promised!

Thoughts on Thankfulness

Remember that this gift cost Jesus His life. For Pentecost to happen, Calvary was necessary. Jesus had to resurrect before He could ascend. Since the Scripture has told us that the Holy Spirit is the "down payment" of our salvation, we know that His presence with us is our promise of eternal fulfillment. "In Him, you also, after listening to the message of truth, the gospel of your salvation—having also believed, you were sealed in Him with the Holy Spirit of promise, who is given as a pledge of our inheritance, with a view to the redemption of God's own possession, to the praise of His glory" (Ephesians 1:13-14). Jesus' gift of continued filling is a taste of victory to come, which must also remind us what a terrible price He paid to purchase this victory.

We said that we are thankful because our filling with the Holy Spirit adds value to our lives. Not only are we empowered to be what we have been designed to be, but we also can enjoy the benefits of this freedom. The joy that was evident in the Apostle Paul and Silas as they recovered from their wounds in a Philippian prison is no less than we can have through all of our trials. We have this victory because Jesus fills us with the Holy Spirit.

The Benefits of Being Filled with the Holy Spirit

It seems almost unnecessary to list benefits of being filled with the Spirit when we realize that there is no other way to serve the Lord fully. Nevertheless, this can help us understand that every time that God commands a thing, He has good reason for doing so, and we have good reason to obey. Following are six benefits:

Disobedience Is Costly and Obedience Is Life-Giving. We should start by indicating that since the filling with the Holy Spirit is commanded, we will not be blessed as we could be if we are not filled.

Jesus said, "The thief comes only to steal and kill and destroy, I came that they may have life, and have it more abundantly" (John 10:10). In this verse, Jesus is likely speaking of Satan when He speaks of "the thief," even though He is also directly addressing the Pharisees and those like them (9:40-41, 10:8). If we contrast the two views, Satan wishes *to steal and kill and destroy*, and the Lord wants to *give abundant life*. If we choose to refuse a command of Scripture, even partially, we have also chosen the *steal, kill and destroy* route. This will lead to our disability if not outright destruction. On the other hand, Jesus desires to *give abundant life*. Choosing Jesus' option is the only wise choice; our lives cannot hope to be full unless we choose to be filled with the Holy Spirit.

Our Lives Are Empowered. The spiritual gifts listed in various places in the Bible, those like evangelism, faith, helps, wisdom, administration, etc., cannot work effectively without our being full of the Holy Spirit. God has placed the various gifts in the body, just as He wills (1 Corinthians 12:11), and our gifts are not helping "the common good" unless we are working in Spirit power.

There are other non-ministry tasks that we do—living in peace with our families, working at our jobs, doing household chores, taking care of our finances—that are enhanced with the guidance of the Holy Spirit. Every part of our lives is touched when we are empowered for living.

Our Personalities Are Changed Positively. Tim LaHaye deals with this extensively in his book *Spirit-Controlled Temperament.*[4] We all have God-given personalities that will remain consistent. For example, some people are "enjoying" in outlook, while others are more introspective; some see the world through the lens of activity and others through analysis; some people are social in nature and others are more solitary. With every personality, there are strengths and weaknesses. Spirit filling augments the strengths and diminishes the weaknesses.

Our natural temperament is good, and determined by God, but it can be better when under the control of the Holy Spirit. We may try to expend a great deal of energy to change our basic temperament, but this cannot be. If we will allow the Holy Spirit free reign in our lives we will see the greatness of our individual personality and will have no need to change its basic perfection.

We Are Resistant to Temptation. Sin is our greatest enemy. The Devil and the world might bring us our greatest pressure to sin, but it is our "self" that chooses. Nothing can make us fail except our carnal nature within. When we are filled with the Holy Spirit, we have the strength to make the right choices.

We Will Not Miss Opportunities. We touched on this when we spoke of the parable of the ten virgins. We risk missing some important task when the

Master finds us not walking in the Spirit. What He planned for us may go to someone whose lamp is full of oil. It would be a terrible thing to find one day that we missed many assignments.

God Will Bless Us. We have essentially come back full-circle to the first point! God will reward those who remain faithful (Hebrews 11:6, Revelation 22:12), and we cannot remain faithful unless we are filled with the Holy Spirit. However, something more than rewards are in view. Having the full approval of God is the greatest joy a Christian can have. What could possibly be better than to know God is smiling at us? Life is indeed abundant when we walk unhindered with our Lord.

1. John MacArthur Jr., *The Charismatics* (Grand Rapids: Zondervan Publishing House, 1978), 11.

2. *Enhanced Strong's Lexicon*, 2001 electronic edition, Greek word entry #907.

3. Andrew Murray, *Absolute Surrender,* rev. ed. (1957; repr., Grand Rapids: Zondervan Publishing House, 1988), 4.

4. Tim LaHaye, *Spirit-Controlled Temperament,* rev. ed. (1966; repr., Wheaton, Illinois: Tyndale House Publishers, Inc., 1983), 45.

Section 3: A Trilogy of Release

"On Christ, the Solid Rock, I Stand"

CHAPTER 6

Resting in Heavenly Places

The underlying premise of the next three chapters is that Jesus' victory was perfect, and it is in His victory that we should move. It His victory and the resulting holiness that we want to share. We are victorious *only* because Jesus is victorious, and the remainder of our lives should be a practice of resting in the power of His finished work.

Watchman Nee deals with this subject in his book *Sit, Walk, Stand*, in which he said, "Christianity begins not with a big *do*, but with a big *done!*"[1] What Christ did on the cross and through the resurrection is the *done*. However, we have trouble resting in this finished work and find ourselves more often trying to *do*. We are eager to please our Lord, rightly so, but in our eagerness we often choose that which defeats us. We tend to prove our allegiance by rushing forward, and since we then rely primarily on our strength, we are certain to fail.

The Apostle Paul said he is thankful and praying for the Ephesians:

That the God of our Lord Jesus Christ, the Father of glory, may give to you a spirit of wisdom and of revelation in the knowledge of Him. I pray that the eyes of your heart may be enlightened, so that you will know what is the hope of His calling, what are the riches of the glory of His inheritance in the saints, and what is the surpassing greatness of His power toward us who believe. These are in accordance with the working of the strength of His might which He brought about in Christ, when He raised Him from the dead and seated Him at His right hand in the heavenly places, far above all rule and authority and power and dominion, and every name that is named, not only in this age but also in the one to come. (Ephesians 1:17-21)

Paul's confession is victorious! Jesus is seated with the Father, His work having been accomplished. Paul connects this victory of Jesus to His followers. He said that he wanted the believers in Ephesus to be "enlightened" and to know of the "surpassing greatness of His power" that is given to them to live. Then he develops this further, "God, being rich in mercy, because of His great love with which He loved us, even when we were dead in our transgressions, made us alive together with Christ (by grace you have been saved), and raised us up with Him, and seated us with Him in the heavenly places in Christ Jesus, so that in the ages to come He might show the surpassing riches of His grace in kindness toward us in Christ Jesus. For by grace you have been saved through faith; and that not of yourselves, it is the gift of God; not as a result of works, so that no one may boast" (Ephesians 2:3-9).

Our salvation causes us to be seated with Christ. Our salvation in Him is final, unassailable, and perfect. He said, "For by grace you have been saved through faith; and that not of yourselves, it is the gift of God." Salvation is free to those who accept it, and nothing we can *do* will purchase that salvation. In essence, we bring nothing to the table of salvation except our free choice to receive. Nothing in us is worthy of salvation; all the worthiness is in Jesus.

There is more here that we need to see. Our acknowledging total dependence on God's grace in salvation is no more necessary than *staying* dependent on Him as we seek to serve Him. We cannot go forward successfully if we are not "seated" with Him in the heavenly places. This seems to be a contradiction—being seated and going forward— but in fact, it is not. The Christian life must stay dependent on Christ. Without that complete surrender to dependence on Him we will fail when we *go*.

Naturally, we think that we need to act, work, or think—anything but rest—in order to get something done. This passage in Ephesians tells us we must start with learning to rest in Jesus' work. We cannot walk in Jesus until we sit down with Him. Once we have sat down with Him, we should never get up.

As a preacher, I have learned to preach and teach while resting in Christ's work. I prepare faithfully. I study hard. I also make sure that my life fits the text I am presenting. I do all I can throughout the weeks preceding my sermon to stay on God's path and learn from Him. However, when I stand to speak, I release everything to His sovereign will. At times, I have seen much of my preparation derailed to follow a certain direction that God wants to take. Mostly, His will follows how He has prepared me (the Holy Spirit works through our preparation, too), but there are times when He leads me in a direction that I did not choose. I sense just as much power in not knowing where God will take me as in knowing. I aim to be completely dependent on His leadership.

Nee uses a vivid illustration in his book. If you were to stand now, wherever you are, then sit in a chair; recognize what happens to your body as you sit. When we stand, our muscles are tensing in a hundred different motions unknown to us, but when we sit, we are resting our entire weight on the chair. It is working for us. The strain no longer falls on the nerves, muscles, sinews of our body, as it is falling on something outside.[2]

This is also true in our spiritual selves. Everything is to be resting, remaining seated in Christ. We should first learn to rest in Christ before we do anything else.

Paul wants us to have our eyes enlightened (1:18) so that we understand these two powerful truths: God caused Christ to sit, and He wants us to sit *with* Him.

When Were We Crucified?

For further clarification, we should ask the question, "When were we crucified with Christ?" Crucifixion for Jesus meant that He had finished His work, and it followed that He rose in victory. Crucifixion for us would indicate that what we were, died, because crucifixion involves total death. It would follow that we would have to be resurrected in a different form in order to go on living. When did this happen?

Paul said to the Romans:

Therefore we have been buried with Him through baptism into death, so that as Christ was raised from the dead through the glory of the Father, so we too might walk in newness of life. For if we have become united with Him in the likeness of His death, certainly we shall also be in the likeness of His resurrection, knowing this, that our old self was crucified with Him, that our body of sin might be done away with, that we should no longer be slaves to sin. For he who has died is freed from sin. (Romans 6:4-7)

It is clear that our spiritual "crucifixion," "death," and "resurrection" all happened simultaneously at the point of our salvation (and potentially even before that at God's foreknowledge of our salvation before the foundation of the world: Ephesians 1:4, Revelation 13:8). The work that Christ was going to do, He has already done! We have eternal life *now;* we need not wait. Indeed, though we will have to see the death of our physical body, what causes us to be eternal is already present within, and just as death could not hold the Savior, so it will not hold us.

Just so, the power that we need to be what God wants us to be resides in the Life of Christ within us. What keeps us from victory in Christ is our own disbelief and uninspired self-effort. God *gave* us the ability to "walk in newness of life."

The Benefits of Resting

God desires to give us many things, but we are often so busy working for Him that He cannot help us. Our efforts sometimes inhibit *His* working.

God is benevolent, and that beyond what we can imagine. He had to remind the Israelites of His willingness to give in Psalm 50. They were trying to give sacrifices to please Him, and He said, "I do not reprove you for your sacrifices, and your burnt offerings are continually before Me. I shall take no young bull out of your house nor male goats out of your folds. For every beast of the forest his Mine, the cattle on a thousand hills. I know every bird of the mountains, and everything that moves in the field is Mine. If I were hungry I would not tell you, for the world is Mine, and all it contains" (vv. 8-12). God reminds them, "Offer to God a sacrifice of thanksgiving and pay your vows to the Most High; Call upon Me in a day of trouble; I shall rescue you, and you will honor Me" (v. 15). Clearly, in these verses God is telling the Israelites that all wealth is His, and it is available for His children. He meets our fevered attempts to please him with cool resistance. God wants us to call on Him, and to look for His provision so that we might honor Him.

Jerry Bridges said, "Salvation is by grace and sanctification is by grace,"[3] and "There is no such thing as salvation from sin's penalty without an accompanying deliverance from sin's dominion."[4] It is not necessary for us to work so hard when God is working for us. Our salvation is complete, finished in Heaven, and that is where our sanctification rests. When we rest in the power of this finished sanctification, it is then that we can walk in holiness.

When I was in college, I earned a Water Safety Instructor certificate as a part of my degree requirements (I was a Recreation major; No…*really!*). We had to go through lifeguard training and then the WSI. One of the skills we had to learn was how to save a person in trouble in the water who was either active or passive. The passive person was just floating (unconscious), so they were relatively easy. However, the active drowning victim is dangerous. This is why you hear of people drowning trying to save someone: even a child filled with the adrenaline of panic can drown a full-grown man who is untrained.

We were taught that if we did not have a life-saving buoy on a long rope—which is always the best choice with an active victim—the best approach to save the victim was technically called "a deep water approach to a chin level off with a cross-chest carry." This meant we had to learn to dive deeply, note their position, sneak underwater right behind them and explode out of the water to slip our hand over their chin. Then we were to level them off with the force of our elbow behind their upper back, throw our other arm across their chest and lock our arm around them with our hands clasped underneath their side, and do all this in one smooth motion while releasing the chin!

In this position, our hip was in the small of their back, and we were able to kick them into shore while they rested on top of us. If they began fighting us, which almost invariably happens with a panicked person, then we were trained to flip them over and ride them while they were under water. Then we would pull them back up and calmly and as firmly *as we could,* say, "I am a trained lifesaver; you are going to need to calm down and stop fighting me or I will have to leave you." If they tried to fight again we repeated the "flip and counsel" until they calmed down. If they were too strong for us and would not calm down, we were trained to kick them off and leave them to avoid drowning us both.

When I apply this illustration, I am not inferring that God is trying to drown us! However, sometimes in our struggles we might come close to drowning ourselves. It is also clear that God may "hold us under" for a bit, so that we would learn that He is trying to help, *and He is the only One who can.* He waits for our store of strength to dry up, and once we have ceased to struggle, He can then carry us to safety.

We should embrace the power that resides in us to make us holy. The power that we have received for eternal salvation is ours regardless of our subsequent attitude; but the power that God offers to us for our sanctification is fruitful *only* when we understand it and when we cooperate. We should be attentive, as we can limit the Holy Spirit's freedom to make changes.

God desires to see each of us succeed in service to Him. We should remember that He loves to give and He is wealthy beyond imagination. We must learn to rest in His finished work and allow His working power to work in us.

---

1. Watchman Nee, *Sit, Walk, Stand,* rev. ed. (1957; repr., Fort Washington, Pennsylvania: Christian Literature Crusade, 1970), 12.

In these next three chapters, I am indebted to this book. My chapter themes are much like Nee's chapters *sit, walk,* and *stand,* and I would recommend the reader to read his book as well. Though the work herein is my work, I want to acknowledge the influence of Nee on the direction of these chapters.

2. Ibid, 13.

3. Jerry Bridges, *The Discipline of Grace: God's Role and Our Role in the Pursuit of Holiness* (Colorado Springs, Colorado: NavPress, 1994), 73.

4. Ibid, 69.

CHAPTER 7

Walking in Christ

We need a word of explanation to begin this chapter, as this chapter is one of those that require more than usual concentration. We will need to dig deeply.

Years ago, one of the many jobs I took while going through Seminary was to sell high-end jewelry. I worked in "guild" stores, which sold some merchandise such as brooches and necklaces worth hundreds of thousands of dollars. In training, they reminded us that the cost of jewelry relates, at least in part, to its rarity. The most valuable gems are the hardest to acquire, and being rare—are expensive. For example, one rough carat of diamond requires the mining of approximately 250 tons of earth.[1]

We should remember this when we study the Word of God. It requires workers to bring out the truth (2 Timothy 2:15). The gems of the Scripture are mined through much labor. Please take the time necessary to reflect and meditate on this chapter. It is important to understand these concepts if we are to fully understand the steps we have already taken, and the ones we plan to take through the rest the book and for the remainder of our lives.

We must learn to rest in the finished work of Jesus, and then we must stay there. We must learn to rest before we can walk, as we learned in the last chapter, and then we must practice walking *while* resting.

For our purposes, we will define "walking" as how we work out our service, or carry forward the perfect work of Jesus. Walking is where we show what is within. In the illustration of the vine and the branches of John 15, this is the fruit.

Spiritual fruit *and* spiritual gifts are in view here, but for our purposes, we will concentrate on the spiritual fruit.

Spiritual Fruit
Paul gives us this wonderful list of the fruit of the Spirit in Galatians: "But the fruit of the Spirit is love, joy, peace, patience, kindness, goodness, faithfulness, gentleness, self-control; against such things there is no law" (Galatians 5:22-23). I particularly like that last phrase, "against such things there is no law"! Certainly, we should desire them.

Before we look at these spiritual fruit, however, we need to cast a wary look at the fruit of the flesh, "Now the deeds of the flesh are evident, which are: immorality, impurity, sensuality, idolatry, sorcery, enmities, strife, jealousy, outbursts of anger, disputes, dissensions, factions, envying, drunkenness, carousing, and things like these, of which I forewarn you, just as I have forewarned you, that those who practice such things will not inherit the kingdom of God" (Galatians 5:19-21).

As if this list is not bad enough, it ends with that fearful warning that people who "practice" these things will not be a part of the kingdom of God. To practice these means to live in them. A person who habitually and consistently shows these characteristics does not have an inheritance in God's kingdom, and this inheritance is the only way we are part of the kingdom. True Christians may display these actions on occasion, but they will be miserable until they repent and return to righteous living.

In trying to discern between the righteous and the wicked, Jesus said twice in the seventh chapter of Matthew that we will "know them by their fruit." The kind of fruit a person produces will indicate what kind of plant they are. Jesus said, "A good tree cannot produce bad fruit, nor can a bad tree produce good fruit" (Matthew 7:18). What we *are* determines what we will do. If we still have a carnal and unregenerate nature that will show in our behavior. On the other hand, a regenerated person will manifest spiritual fruit.

We need to inscribe on our hearts that the fruit of the Spirit is generated by the Holy Spirit, and not by us. Paul calls these the "Fruit of the Spirit," not the "Fruit of the Christian." We can imitate these fruit, but not very well. The *"deeds* of the Flesh," which we just listed, can be *practiced* (v. 21), because *we* produce them when we are influenced by evil. However, the Holy Spirit must produce spiritual fruit.

We rightly want these fruit but we have erroneously thought that we can "add" them to our lives, or that we can "work on" them. There is no reason for us to add them as they came as a package with the gift of the Holy Spirit, and we need not work on them so much as work with them. We focus on our daily walk with Jesus and remove any inhibitions to the Spirit; the Spirit produces His fruit.

I remember working for years on these fruit, to very little effect. I would work on patience (which seemed to be a recurring problem), and as I worked on this I would see self-control slipping. I would work on self-control and patience would weaken. Then harshness would become a problem and I would have to leave my work on patience and self-control to work on gentleness.

Occasionally I used to watch "Late Night with Johnny Carson." Every once in a while Johnny would have as his guest a man who would balance plates on wooden poles that were six to seven feet tall. He would put a plate on top of a wooden pole, and then he would turn the pole with the palms of both hands so the plate would begin spinning. He eventually got about six plates started in the same fashion, one after another. The plates would spin, balanced, and he would run up and give a pole a turn or two to get the plate back to full spin from a wobble, then on to the next wobbly plate. He could keep six or so plates spinning simultaneously without falling!

I always thought this was a remarkable feat, and I was delighted with everyone else to watch him do this. I had no desire to learn to do this, however, because my life had enough stress already! My spiritual life was much like this, always spinning poles to keep wobbly plates going, except half of mine were always on the floor, broken.

This is not as God intended, but this is exactly what happens when we try to produce the spiritual fruit. We can only imitate the fruit but it is only a fair imitation. The Holy Spirit can keep the plates spinning, as it were, without effort and without fail. If we learn to free Him to His proper role in our lives, we find that we can be what we are commanded to be. For example, when we find ourselves becoming impatient it means there is a "disconnect" in our lives with the Holy Spirit. We should not "work on patience," we should reconnect.

Biblical Testimony

Paul said, "Therefore I, the prisoner of the Lord, implore you to walk in a manner worthy of the calling with which you have been called, with all humility and gentleness, with patience, showing tolerance for one another in love…that you walk no longer just as the Gentiles also walk, in the futility of their mind…and that you be renewed in the spirit of your mind…and walk in love, just as Christ also loved you and gave Himself up for us, an offering and sacrifice to God as a fragrant aroma…for you were formerly darkness, but now you are Light in the Lord; walk as children of Light…trying to learn what is pleasing to the Lord" (Ephesians 4:1-2, 17, 23; 5:2, 8, 10).

What we are seeing here is the need to "walk" in the way of the Lord. In the last chapter, we spoke of "resting." Now, we *walk while resting.* This walking in the Lord has for its potency the Spirit of God, but we must cooperate.

We cannot leap to perfection, nor should we stop our effort, but we must grow in understanding of "what is pleasing to the Lord." Too often we are giving our effort to what will not produce the works of God (trying to create spiritual fruit that is already created?), and not giving effort where we *should*, that is in learning to allow Jesus' finished and completed work to have its effect on us.

Other words from the Apostle Paul further substantiate this. I believe the last half of Romans 7 is often misinterpreted. We should look at this chapter carefully to understand what Paul is saying, specifically verses 14 through 23:

For we know that the Law is spiritual, but I am of flesh, sold into bondage to sin. For what I am doing, I do not understand; for I am not practicing what I would like to do, but I am doing the very thing I hate. But if I do the very thing I do not want to do, I agree with the Law, confessing that the Law is good. So now, no longer am I the one doing it, but sin which dwells in me. For I know that nothing good dwells in me, that is, in my flesh; for the willing is present in me, but the doing of the good is not. For the good that I want, I do not do, but I practice the very evil that I do not want. But if I am doing the very thing I do not want, I am no longer the one doing it, but sin which dwells in me. I find then the principle that evil is present in me, the one who wants to do good. For I joyfully concur with the law of God in the inner man, but I see a different law in the members of my body, waging war against the law of my mind and making me a prisoner of the law of sin which is in my members. (Romans 7:14-23)

Some interpreters see Paul bemoaning his weakness in these verses as the words of a man who is losing his fight with sin and the flesh. I have heard people say something like, "Paul is talking to me in these verses, because I struggle with sin *just like he does*." This is a distortion! Viewing these verses in context brings out another interpretation entirely.

In order to understand these verses, we should look carefully at some of Paul's statements in chapter 6. Following are a few verses with my emphasis added:

How shall we *who died to sin* still live in it? (v. 2).
Knowing this, that our old self was crucified with Him, in order *that our sin might be done away with*, so that we will no longer be slaves to sin, for he who *died is freed from sin* (vv. 6-7).
For *sin shall not be master* over you, for you are not under law but under grace (v. 14).
But now *having been freed* from sin and enslaved to God, you derive your benefit, *resulting in sanctification*, and the outcome, eternal life (v. 22).

These verses tell us how life in the Spirit should be. Paul is presenting a life of grace free from the tyranny of sin. This is not a contradiction to the last half of chapter seven; rather it is a clue to understanding what Paul is really saying.

In chapter 7, verses 4-6, Paul said, "Therefore, my brethren, you also were made to die to the Law through the body of Christ, so that you might be joined to another, to Him who was raised from the dead, in order that we might bear fruit for God. For while we were in the flesh, the sinful passions, which were aroused by the Law, were at work in the members of our body to bear fruit for death. But now we have been released from the Law, having died to that by which we were bound, so that we serve in newness of the Spirit and not in oldness of the letter."

Paul said in verse 4 that we *were made to die* to the Law so that we might be reborn through Jesus, in order *to bear fruit*. The action of "rebirth" instantly put him in another category; he is no longer a slave to the old passions under the law but is now free according to the "newness of the Spirit" (verse 6). These verses are not the words of an oft-defeated man writing to defeated people, as some would interpret. Paul is proclaiming his victory provided through Jesus.

Even for a regenerate person there may be a very real battle between the old nature and the new nature, but Paul is telling us there is a way of victory. We will not find this victory in our strength, but in the Spirit's free control of us.

Coercion is how the law gets one to submit, but grace inspires us. Paul could write both Philippians 3:6 and Philippians 3:12-14. According to the law, he was blameless (v. 6). He kept the law to the letter, in its rules, etc., but this was only in the eyes of man. Verses 12-14 express what Paul knew himself to be in the eyes of God, that he had not "laid hold of it yet." The difference? The law gives us satisfaction in external role keeping but no satisfaction as to our eternal state. God's grace, on the other hand, gives us all we need for salvation, and so, *drives* us forward ("I press on") so that we might live according to God's power.

Jesus does not eradicate our sinful self when He saves us; He contains it, controls it, and defeats it when we live according to the Spirit. The old desires are still latent but they can be held in check.

Interpretively, there is some disagreement on the second half of Romans 7. For our purposes, we do not need to go too deeply into this discussion but we should touch on it. Generally, the argument centers on whether verses 14-25 are pre or post conversion experiences of Paul. Were they his former struggles while he was living according to the law, or current struggles of the apostle while living according to grace?

I personally believe these verses showed exactly what Paul experienced while under the law as a Pharisee, but were also *potential* for him when he wrote these words as a believer. Paul was writing about the struggle from the viewpoint of a regenerated man, otherwise, why would he despise the acts of the flesh, which he clearly does not "want to do" (vss. 15, 16, 19, 20). Paul was not superhuman. He matured just as we do. When he was converted on the Damascus road and spent that time with Jesus as his teacher in the wilderness, certainly he must have struggled with the flesh and surrender. He was not instantly mature.

However, most commentators agree that Paul was not living under the bondage expressed in verses 14 and following while he wrote these words. The old nature, or flesh, is always ready to take over and all of us must determine if we will live according to spiritual dictates or that of the flesh. What we should take away is that it is not the normal Christian experience to be under such bondage. Paul had been freed from the body of death and lived accordingly.

There are not two natures working at one time! When the new nature operated on by the Holy Spirit is ascendant, sin and its power is condemned, and the result for us is living freedom. Therefore, Paul was able to answer his own question, "Wretched man that I am! Who will set me free from the body of this death? Thanks be to God through Jesus Christ our Lord!" (Romans 7: 24-25).

The eighth chapter of Romans clearly presents this new freedom. We will look at the first ten verses.

> Therefore there is now no condemnation for those who are in Christ Jesus. For the law of the Spirit of life in Christ Jesus has set you free from the law of sin and of death. For what the Law could not do, weak as it was through the flesh, God did: sending His own Son in the likeness of sinful flesh and as an offering for sin, He condemned sin in the flesh, so that the requirement of the Law might be fulfilled in us, who do not walk according to the flesh but according to the Spirit. For those who are according to the flesh set their minds on the things of the flesh, but those who are according to the Spirit, the things of the Spirit. For the mind set on the flesh is death, but the mind set on the Spirit is life and peace, because the mind set on the flesh is hostile toward God; for it does not subject itself to the law of God, for it is not even able to do so, and those who are in the flesh cannot please God. However, you are not in the flesh but in the Spirit, if indeed the Spirit of God dwells in you. But if anyone does not have the Spirit of Christ, he does not belong to Him. If Christ is in you, though the body is dead because of sin, yet the spirit is alive because of righteousness. (Romans 8:1-10)

Paul is advocating a new life filled with victory because of the Spirit within. Our rescue from sin's dominance is not in conformity to the law but in the freedom of the Holy Spirit. F. F. Bruce said, "Christian holiness is not a matter of painstaking conformity to the specific precepts of an external law-code; it is rather a question of the Holy Spirit's producing his fruit in one's life, reproducing those graces which were seen in perfection in the life of Christ."[3]

Hupernikomen!

One of my favorite Greek words came to my attention by happenstance one day. My father is a minister, and he gave me most of his library when he knew he would not use it as much as I would. I was reading a commentary written by Dr. Kyle Yates, who was my father's pastor when he served as the Minister of Music at Second Baptist Church in Houston, Texas. In the front of the book, Dr. Yates had written, "Hupernikomen" (in Greek, ὑπερνικῶμεν), just that word, nothing else. I looked it up. This single word translates into the phrase we know so well, "We are more than conquerors" (Romans 8:37). "Nikomen" is translated "we are conquerors (or champions)," but "Huper" (pronounced *hoopare*) added to the front is the preposition meaning "over," "above," or "beyond." We are conquerors! Even more so!

Paul did not write, "We *will* be more than conquerors," or "We *should* be more than conquerors," or even worse, "One day we might be more than conquerors if we try hard enough." On the contrary, he said, "We ARE more than conquerors." Simply having Christ as our savior and the Holy Spirit as our companion has put us in that elite group. We can choose to live accordingly.

Walking While Seated

Theoretically, we may be on the way to prove our point, but we do not live in theory. How do these truths apply to our walk in Christ? *How* do we "walk while resting"?

The first step we must take is *believing* that Jesus has finished His work in power and that He has offered that completed victory to us. The author of Hebrews wrote, "Without faith it is impossible to please Him, for He who comes to God must believe that He is and that He is a rewarder of those that seek Him" (11:6). Meditate on these verses that we have presented in these last two chapters (and the many others that state the same theme), be sure in your heart that God promises this in His Word, and walk forward in confidence knowing that Jesus has offered you a way out of defeated living.

Second, I want to bring together two things we have said. In Matthew 11:39, Jesus said, "Learn from Me...you will find rest for your souls." And in Romans 8:1, Paul said, "There is now no condemnation for those who are in Christ Jesus." Jesus says we should "learn," and Paul says it is "in" Jesus that we are now free. Once we have determined that Jesus has provided the way out of defeat, we *learn* to be *in* Him for rest. The power is all there, we just must grasp it.

We must return to our discussion of the spiritual fruit. A person who is showing the spiritual fruit in their lives is a person that is walking in the Spirit. Our behavior (which we cannot make too much of) is a "barometer" that shows whether the Holy Spirit has freedom in our lives. And the deeds of the flesh that we have named—"immorality, impurity, sensuality, idolatry, sorcery, enmities, strife, jealousy, outbursts of anger, disputes, dissensions, factions, envying, drunkenness, carousing" (Galatians 5:19-21)—are antithetical to the Holy Spirit. Paul says in verse 16, "Walk in the Spirit, and you will not carry out the desire of the flesh."

If we find this concept true and apply it, and find later that we have exploded in anger, or have been unlovely in thought, etc., we should not abandon this truth. Our failure is only proof that what is wrong is within; our life is somehow not covered by Jesus' life, for our behavior shows it. We must learn to rely on the finished work of Christ in order to produce spiritual fruit—to walk while resting with Jesus "in the heavenlies."

Our forgiveness, our kindness, our love, our patience—all of that which makes us different—is found not in ourselves but in Christ within, present in the Holy Spirit. We must learn to walk, while resting in Him. Everything else is just acting, and acting like the Spirit is devastating to our spiritual selves. Counterfeit grace only leaves us still in need of the real thing. Worse yet, this lulls us into thinking our life is pleasing to God, when it cannot be because the flesh generates it, and "nothing good dwells in me, that is, in my flesh" (Romans 7:18a).

Once I was struggling with how to picture this to a study group I was going to teach. I was jogging at the time and it came to me that I do not cause cellular replacement or cellular regeneration in my body. Nor can I make my veins and arteries more efficient. I cannot speed or slow my heart, make my lungs healthier, or cause the other organs to operate well. What I *can* do is eat right, exercise, spend time outside, get plenty of rest, and avoid dangerous situations. In other words, I can provide the right *environment* for health, but it is up to the Lord and the body He designed to do the rest.

If this is true of the body, which we can reach and touch, is it not also true for the spiritual part of us, which we cannot see or handle? We can provide the right environment for spiritual growth, but only the Holy Spirit can cause the growth. It is for this reason that the purpose of this book is to explore ways to provide this healthy environment, which will give the Lord freedom to change us.

What comes from the Holy Spirit is true and sufficient. He abides in us, in part, for this purpose: to show God's works. Listen to other verses that drive home this point:

For we are His workmanship, created in Christ Jesus for good works, which God prepared beforehand so that we would walk in them. (Ephesians 2:10)
To whom God willed to make known what is the riches of the glory of this mystery among the Gentiles, which is Christ in you, the hope of glory. (Colossians 1:27)
For this purpose also I labor, striving according to His power, which mightily works within me. (Colossians 1:29)

Paul said in Philippians 2:13, "For it is God who is at work in you, both to will and to work for His good pleasure." Do you see that? Not only does God give us the power to *work* (*"Energeo"* to be energized, to produce), He will provide the *willing* (*"Thelo"* or the "want to")!

We are not automatons, without a will of our own, simply letting God take over. Neither is the life of maturity instantaneous. Rather, it is our place to "learn" of God's power through His gift of the Holy Spirit. Our part is to get everything out of His way so that He can work the works. We brought nothing to our salvation except faith to receive it, and we release God's work in us with faith. We strive, yes, but according to *His* power that works within us.

We used spiritual fruit as our focus, but we must say that spiritual gifts work the same way. Everything the Lord has required us to do is found in the power afforded us by the finished work of Jesus, whether it is related to our behavior (fruit) or our effectiveness in ministry (gifts). All that we need to be, Jesus is already. We need to set Him free in our lives.

---

1. Houston Museum of Natural Science exhibit advertisement. "Diamonds: Not Just Another Pretty Facet." [Online] Available http://www.facebook.com/note.php?note_id=198181485098, internet post by blogger ErinC., May 6, 2009.
Other interesting diamond facts from this article: Since they are great conductors of heat therefore cool to the touch, they have the nickname "ice." Formed at tremendous pressures from somewhere between 93 and 420 miles below the surface of the earth, diamonds are transported to the surface (or at least near the surface) by magma flows. The majority of diamonds are approximately ¾ of the earth's age.

2. F.F. Bruce, *The Letter of Paul to the Romans.* Tyndale New Testament Commentaries, 2nd ed., (Grand Rapids: William B. Eerdmans Publishing Company, 1985), 146-147.

3. Ibid., 153.

CHAPTER 8

Our Stance in Spiritual Warfare

We move now to the Bible's admonition for us to fight the Devil. In Watchman Nee's book, he points to a progression that follows the pattern of sit, walk, *conflict!*[1] Fighting is not something we enjoy thinking about, but it is as fundamental as being seated in the victory of Jesus and then walking in that victory, for we were saved and equipped for a purpose. Fighting the Devil is a large part of this purpose.

Holiness causes a person to be separated to God. In fact, holiness *means* separation, just as God is separated in righteousness from everything else in heaven and earth. He stands apart. By His gracious choice, we who have accepted His reign stand apart with Him. Therefore, we have become the "holy ones," or "saints," set apart to God's blameless purpose.

Having been separated to God, we have become clear enemies of darkness. Satan and his followers will be dead set on destroying us and ruining our testimony in order to bring dishonor to our Father in Heaven. These dark forces have unstoppable power, when faced in the flesh, but when we face them in the power of the Holy Spirit—well, that is another matter.

Paul said:

Finally, be strong in the Lord and in the strength of His might. Put on the full armor of God, so that you will be able to stand firm against the schemes of the Devil. For our struggle is not against flesh and blood, but against the rulers, against the powers, against the world forces of this darkness, against the spiritual forces of wickedness in the heavenly places. Therefore, take up the full armor of God, so that you will be able to resist in the evil day, and having done everything, to stand firm. Stand firm therefore, having girded your loins with truth, and having put on the breastplate of righteousness, and having shod your feet with the preparation of the gospel of peace; in addition to all, taking up the shield of faith with which you will be able to extinguish all the flaming arrows of the evil one. And take the helmet of salvation, and the sword of the Spirit, which is the word of God. With all prayer and petition pray at all times in the Spirit, and with this in view, be on the alert with all perseverance and petition for all the saints, and pray on my behalf, that utterance may be given to me in the opening of my mouth, to make known with boldness the mystery of the gospel, for which I am an ambassador in chains; that in proclaiming it I may speak boldly, as I ought to speak. (Ephesians 6:10-20)

Three times the phrase "stand firm" is used, in verses 11, 13 and 14. In the original Greek that is literally "stand toward" or "stand against." For example, when a high wind hits a person they naturally lean into it. Their feet are firmly placed, and they place their weight against the wind. This is the idea of "standing firm." Not once in these verses are we asked to attack or to take the offensive. Every word and every bit of armor is defensive in nature and we are to firmly stand against the onslaught of evil. We will say more about this later in this chapter.

Remember the progression of what we have shown in the last two chapters: we are to rest in what God has provided through His victorious Son, then we are to walk while resting in this completed work. Finally, while relying on this finished work we are to stand against evil.

Look again at verse 10, "Finally be strong *in the Lord* and the *strength of His might*" (emphasis added). What does this mean? To get started, we need to lay some groundwork.

Refusing to Take the Enemy Lightly

I am often concerned about what I hear coming from some churches and biblical teachers who speak a great deal of "rebuking the Devil," etc. I think this is the result of a dangerous misunderstanding of our standing in spiritual warfare.

Jesus often "rebuked" the demons when He faced them, but never once is this word used by the disciples or other Christians in this way. The disciples always stood in the strength that Jesus provided in their warfare, for they knew that they were easy targets outside of His strength. Appropriately, when they spoke a command to a demon, it was in the name of Jesus (Acts 3:6, 9:34, 16:18).

Two passages of Scripture will help us understand. The first is rather humorous, and is in Acts 19:11-16. Seven men, all of a family, had some reason for going out and challenging demons. Possibly, as Jews, they wanted to refute what was being done on the Christian side. They were exorcists and their father was a chief priest, so they had something to prove. Like poor Don Quixote, off they "sallied" and "tilted at windmills."

What we see is a clear case of a lack of authority. When they spoke to a man who was possessed, they said, "I adjure you by Jesus whom Paul preaches." It is interesting that Jewish men were naming as their authority the Christian focus of power. In this case, it was the *Jesus* preached by Paul. Also note the word "adjure" (*Horkizō*) they used literally means these men were putting this man (and the demon) under oath. They were exercising authority which they obviously did not have, for the man who was possessed jumped on them and beat them so badly that all seven ran from the house naked and bruised! Obviously, just the words and believing in the words alone have no power for the demon himself told these men he was not impressed (v. 15).

Some would immediately point to the fact that these seven sons of Sceva were not saved and so it would not apply to Christians. However, we should not look at this story from the perspective of the exorcists but from the perspective of the demon. Words or actions in challenge to the demonic without the right authority are dangerous in the extreme.

For further clarification, we can look at another view of demonic warfare in Jude 8-10. In this passage, we have some people who are "dreamers," "despising authority," and are "reviling angelic majesty." They are taking spiritual powers lightly, both angelic and demonic. Verse 10 shows again that naïve people may imperil themselves by their own ignorance: "But these men revile the things which they do not understand; and the things which they know by instinct, like unreasoning animals, by these things they are destroyed."

Jude tells us when Michael the archangel faced the Devil he was much more reserved! We must first establish that there is no Christian on earth with the power and standing of Michael. Certainly, the Bible tells us that we will one day judge angels (1 Cor. 6:3), but as long as we are on earth the angels greatly exceed us in power. Michael is the strongest of the angels, yet, when he faced Satan in this strange case of an argument over the very body of Moses (Jude 9), Michael did not directly rebuke Satan at all. He said, "The *Lord* rebuke You!" If Michael approached the Devil with this caution by covering himself with the power of the Lord, so much more should we. Outside of what Jesus provides, we have nothing.

Paul did not take this conflict lightly, "Our struggle is not against flesh and blood" (Ephesians 6:12). He knew that Satan and his subordinates are trying to derail everything we do in the name of Jesus. They are hard at work in our schools, our governments, our neighborhoods, and our families. According to this Scripture, the dark forces that we cannot see are responsible for the trouble that we do see and they are vastly powerful. We cannot hope to be successful in fighting them unless we stand in the Lord's power.

Holding His Ground

We must understand that we are to stand on the ground that was already won by the Savior. When we stand in God's finished work through the Son we share His power because it is in His work that we are trusting, not our own. We will lose when we start an offensive skirmish and step out of the defensive posture that God commanded.

Our warfare is defensive because Jesus warred offensively! Christ was on the offensive in His warfare and He carried the battle to the enemy. Because of His work, we defend what He has already taken. Warren Wiersbe said, "It is this victory of Christ that gives us a safe and solid standing as we fight the Devil. Wherever we walk, we stand on victory ground!" Later, he quotes George Duffield's hymn, "Stand Up, Stand Up for Jesus:"

> Stand up, stand up for Jesus,
> Stand in His strength alone;
> The arm of flesh will fail you—
> Ye dare not trust your own.
> Put on the gospel armor,
> Each piece put on with prayer;
> Where duty calls, or danger,
> Be never wanting there.[2]

When we grasp this truth, it will bring a great sense of relief. We are nowise causing the work to be done nor do we have to put great energy into the work so that we might win. Rather we learn to rest in the work that is already finished so that we might advance.

His burden is indeed *light*!

Picture in your mind a map with land marked off with a clear boundary. Your assigned work is within that boundary. Your spiritual skills must be kept up to date in order to do it, but you simply operate within that victorious boundary and send any invaders packing. In James 4:7 we are reminded to, "Submit therefore to God, resist the Devil, and he will flee from you." The word "submit" means that we are sure that we are under the protection of God. We are to be willing, spirit-filled, and free of known sin. The word "resist" is the same word we discussed in Ephesians chapter 6, which means to "stand against" or "hold your ground." Jesus purchased the land we are holding, so when we resist, the Devil will "flee." The word *flee* literally means that the Devil will "disappear quickly." He and his henchmen will disappear quickly when a person submitting to God stands against him. They have no power in response to God's overwhelming might. Remember, there is an infinite distance between any kind of power and omnipotent power.

Our warfare is defensive. We have already been given stewardship of the kingdom (God's) and we are to hold it.

We must take another step, because there is an element in our warfare that takes us forward. In other words, is it right for us to say all of our warfare against the dark forces is defensive since we have clear marching orders?

Going Forward in Jesus' Name

In order to understand the *active* form of our *defensive* warfare, we should look at the necessity of moving forward in Jesus' name.

The name of Jesus is powerful beyond comprehension. When Paul told the Philippians of the righteous sacrifice of Jesus, even "to death and that on the cross," he concluded with these famous words, "For this reason also, God highly exalted Him, and bestowed on Him the name which is above every name, so that at the name of Jesus every knee will bow, of those who are in heaven and on earth and under the earth, and that every tongue will confess that Jesus Christ is Lord, to the glory of God the Father" (Philippians 2:9-11).

It is Jesus' name and His authority that will cause all knees to bow and tongues to confess.

In Acts, Peter and John were going to the temple at the hour of prayer, and at the gate called Beautiful they encountered a lame man. The man was asking for alms but he got so much more. Peter said, "I do not posses silver or gold, but what I do have I give to you: in the name of Jesus Christ the Nazarene—walk!" (Acts 3:6). He walked.

Later, in response to this healing, a gathering of the disbelieving including the High Priest, rulers, elders, and scribes asked Peter and John, "By what power, or in what *name*, have you done this?" (Interpretation: "Why didn't you ask *us*?"). Peter answered, "let it be known to all of you and to all the people of Israel, that by the name of Jesus Christ the Nazarene, whom you crucified, whom God raised from the dead—by this name this man stands here before you in good health" (Acts 4:10).

It takes no effort to speak the name of Jesus. When faithful people speak this name according to God's will, things happen. The man who was lame was not partially healed he was gloriously and totally healed. Peter was careful to point out that the power that caused this healing was in the name of Jesus.[3]

"What's in a name?" we should ask. The power of the name of Jesus is not in the simple verbal repetition of the word. This is nothing like magic. Rather, the name is representative and carries the *authority* of the Lord.

In the Bible, the name of a person represented their character and their standing:

> They believed there was a vital connection between the name and the person it identified. A name somehow represented the nature of the person...The connection between a name and the reality it

signified is nowhere more important than in the names referring to God. The personal name of God revealed to Moses in the burning bush—"I AM WHO I AM"—conveyed something of His character (Ex. 3:14). According to Exodus 34:5–6, when the Lord "proclaimed the name of the Lord," He added words that described His character. The name of the Lord was virtually synonymous with His presence: "For your wondrous works declare that your name is near" (Ps. 75:1). To know the name of God is thus to know God Himself (Ps. 91:14).[4]

In spiritual warfare, the boundaries of the map of the Lord's victorious territory are fluid. They move with the Holy Spirit. In other words, the finished work of Jesus is also evident when we go forward into uncharted territory. Since we go forward in His name, then His kingdom is with us and our work in His name is effective, just as He is effective. Our efforts must be submissive to His claimed *and changing* territory.

A clear example is the area of evangelistic work. Before Jesus gave us the commission to "Go therefore and make disciples" He reminded us that "All authority has been given unto Me" (Matthew 28:18-19). Peter and John called attention to this authority when they said to the examining council, "There is salvation in no one else; for there is no other name under heaven that has been given among men by which we must be saved" (Acts 4:12).

When we witness to a person then we can rest in the fact that if God's boundary is extended to include this person, it will not be our work that will cause this to happen. We are only His messengers. Jesus' work will take this person and include them in the map of His kingdom.

This is not to say our work is not important, for "how shall they hear without a preacher?" We are clearly to go, and as we go, we are to remain faithful. However, this work that seems to be part of an offensive warfare is actually defensive. Jesus does the work and gives to us the task of defending His claim. He draws the boundaries.

Whether we are discipling, growing our churches, ministering to the suffering, counseling, or any of the other facets of our calling, we will be effective only when our work is not only "touched" with the grace of God but has in fact become the very grace of God itself. We are to be free conduits of His power. Our bodies may tire, our minds weaken, we may face attacks from the Evil One, and we may struggle with emotional battles—but the spiritual work is effortless. When we use human effort to cause spiritual work, we are not effective. In spiritual matters, Christ alone is effective.

Can Jesus Give His Name to You?

It is clear that Jesus has sent us to do the work. He has called us and equipped us with the Holy Spirit. However, the Lord cannot give His name in authority to us if we are not willing to follow His commands, for we must be worthy of His trust.

An idea that is prevalent today is that since a Christian has the name of Jesus—as in salvation—they have authority. But authority is clearly only given in full measure if we are obedient. Jesus is our example, for the New Testament is filled with incidents where observers note His authority. In Mark's gospel, "They were amazed at His teaching; for He was teaching them as one having authority, and not as the scribes...so that they debated among themselves, saying, 'What is this? A new teaching with authority! He commands even the unclean spirits, and they obey Him'" (Mark 1:22, 27).

Obviously, Jesus had innate authority because He was the Son of God and the promised Messiah. However, He was also "tempted in all things as we are" (Hebrews 4:15). He was as fully *man* as He was fully God. On the "man" side He had this tremendous authority because He was "tempted in all things as we are, yet *without sin*" (emphasis added).

Jesus was just as able to sin as we are, yet He never did. As in the Father, "there is no variation or shifting shadow" (James 1:17), Jesus never shifted in His relationship with His Father. We will never have authority in the measure of Christ because we have already failed—we have shifted. However, Jesus offers His authority to us today if we are worthy of His name.

Nee mentions how careful we would be to give the responsibility of our finances to another person.[5] This person would need to have access to the deepest private affairs of our monetary life. We would need to give them access to our bank accounts, our investments, and the requisite authority to make changes and purchases. How careful would we be in choosing such a person? How much would we need to trust them before we trusted them with this authority?

It is the same with God. We often speak of our trust for Him, but He must trust us if He is to give us His authority. There is an example of this in the Old Testament when Hanani the prophet rebukes Asa, the king of Judah, because he lost an important battle. Asa had relied on men and not God. Hanani reminded Asa that he had previously been victorious against great armies when He relied on the Lord only: "For the eyes of the Lord move to and fro throughout the earth that He may strongly support those whose heart is completely His" (1 Chronicles 16:9). Holy people completely give themselves to God, and God has promised to support them.

Remember that the name of Jesus is given to us gladly and freely in reference to our salvation, and this will never change. No matter how we might fail Him, He will not fail us and the name of Jesus assures us His salvation. However, we must see the distinction between His name given for salvation, which cannot be withdrawn, and His name given for works, which can. We have the authority of Jesus to do His works only when we cooperate with Him. He must be able to trust us.

Can God commit His name to us? Is God able to commit His name to our church? Are we authorized to use His authority?

Nee lists four essential features of a person to whom God can commit His name.[6] I have listed them here and have expanded on each thought:

1. The first vital need is of a *true revelation to our hearts of the eternal purpose of God*. Some may pick out a particular thing and label it as most important. Often, some label evangelism/missions as the most important thing, and though it is important, it is one of many tasks. The Son of God should be seen as preeminent; that is as close to God's eternal purpose as we can state it.[7] Jesus is central to all that we say and do. This will involve such elements as evangelism, discipleship, fellowship, etc., however, no individual part is the focus—Jesus is.

2. All work that is going to be effective and blessed must be *planned by God*. If we conceive the idea then there is no assurance that God will bless it. Henry Blackaby showed in *Experiencing God*; that a Christian must find where God is working, and join Him.[8] Several times in Acts, the Holy Spirit forbade a particular work (for example, in 16:6 where we are told Paul and his companions were forbidden of the Holy Spirit to speak the word in Asia). Sometimes, He opened a work as in the "Macedonian call" (16:9). We should learn to be sensitive to God's plans.

3. If the work is to be effective, it must *depend on God's power alone*. We may have not understood power as it is presented in the Bible. It is certainly *not* what we can do alone. When we are most aware of our weakness, God is often able to use us. If we try to accomplish work in our own power, it will lose the mark of the power of God. We may notice that God has been at work in our lives in such a way that our confidence has been weakened. He sometimes chips away at what we have relied on. In such times, He desires to teach us to rely on His unfailing power rather than our shaky efforts.

4. The end of all work must be *the glory of God*. Do you desire ministry to be satisfying to yourself? You may have wondered if your personal satisfaction and fulfillment is not deep, you must not be successful. Nee said, "The less we get of personal gratification out of such a work the greater is its true value to God."[9] I think that may be an overstatement, but it is God's glory that we seek, and that does not *always* bring us personal ease or recognition.

When God commits His name to us, and we walk in His power, then our work will be effective. We do not define victory by whether we win but by whether He wins through us. Our personal defeat can still be His victory.

There are many examples of this in the Scripture, but none more powerful than the crucifixion of Jesus. He was completely obedient, and walked to that final moment in *all* the power of God, and yet He was humiliated before men and suffered what some would see as an ignominious death. That was not the end, of course. Because of the perfect faithfulness of Jesus even to death, "God highly exalted Him, and bestowed on Him the name which is above every name, so that at the name of Jesus every knee will bow, of those who are in heaven and on earth and under the earth, and that every tongue will confess that Jesus Christ is Lord, to the glory of God the Father." (Philippians 2:9-11). The hinge of history is on the crucifixion and resurrection of Jesus; what appears to be a catastrophic failure results in unimaginable victory.

It follows that we should stop defining our spiritual victory by how things go for us. That seems a hard concept to grasp, at first, but as we progress in the power that Christ offers for battle it becomes more natural. Actually, it becomes *supernaturally* natural to say with John the Baptist, "He must increase, but I must decrease" (John 3:30). When we adopt this attitude, our stance in spiritual warfare is unassailable.

---

1. Watchman Nee, *Sit, Walk, Stand,* rev. ed. (1957; repr., Fort Washington, Pennsylvania: Christian Literature Crusade, 1970), 41.

2. Warren W. Wiersbe, *The Strategy of Satan* (Wheaton, Illinois: Tyndale House Publishers, 1979), 131, 136.

3. It is beyond the scope of this work to deal with this subject in detail, but I believe that the miraculous works are much more prevalent when God is laying the groundwork through unbelieving communities. We do not see the miraculous healings or other spectacular works in the same way today. God does work miraculously today, for I believe our *entire* work must be based on His supernatural intervention. However, the reason our works do

not issue in such powerful healings as what we see in these verses is that God wills it so. No application of *His name* can change anything against His will.

4. *Nelson's Illustrated Bible Dictionary,* 1986 ed., 744-745.

5. Nee, *Sit, Walk, Stand,* 51-52.

6. Ibid., 53-57.

7. Ibid., 53.

8. Henry T. Blackaby and Claude V. King, *Experiencing God: How to Live the Full Adventure of Knowing and Doing the Will of God,* (Nashville: Broadman and Holman Publishers, 1994), 74.

9. Nee, *Sit, Walk, Stand,* 56.

Section 4: A Trilogy of Empowerment

"Rejoice, Give Thanks and Sing!"

CHAPTER 9

Choosing to Rejoice

The Apostle Paul gives three "constants" in three verses in 1 Thessalonians 5:16-18. He commands the Thessalonians to rejoice always, pray without ceasing, and give thanks for everything!

Paul here is not reluctant or reticent. He expects nothing less than a total and constant outpouring of faith. These three verses are not the only important verses in this chapter; however, I wish to bring these three commands forward in the next three chapters because they will help build an unshakable foundation. If we are faithful with these three qualities, we can continue to see the Holy Spirit freed to operate in our lives without limitation. Holiness will result.

Since we believe the Holy Spirit inspired the authors of biblical text, it follows that this constant nature of devotion and God-mindedness is not Paul's idea. Our Father in Heaven is reminding us there is an *unceasing* element to devotion that He encourages in each of His disciples.

The qualities of rejoicing, prayer, and thanksgiving are interdependent. Charles H. Spurgeon said when we hear Paul say, "Rejoice always," we may stagger and ask how such a command is possible. As if in answer, the verse follows immediately, "Pray without ceasing." Spurgeon adds, "When joy and prayer are married their first born child is gratitude."[1] How closely these great activities are connected!

We will start with the first command, Paul's admonition to "rejoice always." This is the shortest verse in the Bible, in the original Greek shorter even than the famous "Jesus wept" of John 11:35. However, this short verse may be one of the verses we ignore the most.

Rejoicing is not new to the careful Bible reader. To give joy or rejoice is constantly encouraged. I believe that rejoicing is evidence of holiness; however, like the other activities of the chapters of this book, rejoicing is also the foyer to holiness. We might say that rejoicing *results* in holiness. When we truly rejoice, we have given Jesus free reign of our hearts, and the result of His unhindered presence is always holiness.

Merriam-Webster defines the word *joy* as "the emotion evoked by well-being, success, or good fortune or by the prospect of possessing what one desires: DELIGHT," and "the expression or exhibition of such emotion: GAIETY."[2] Biblical joy takes this further and "rises above circumstances and focuses on the very character of God."[3] The Bible pictures joy as the natural result of serving a Savior who cares for us unquestioningly, and who has the power to back this care with benevolent acts. We have purpose in life when we serve Jesus, and it shows in our outlook on life.

Jesus said, "He who believes in Me, as the Scripture said, 'From his innermost being will flow rivers of living water' " (John 7:38). I have always thought this passage pictures, at least in part, the presence of joy in the life of a follower of Jesus. Just as my worries and fears seem seated in the belly (and may even *gnaw* there), when I am joyful the feeling of confidence is there as well. I even imagine that joy brings healing to my "belly."

The other word used often in the Bible is the one used in our focal text: *rejoice!* Paul said in another famous verse, "Rejoice in the Lord always; again I will say, rejoice!" (Philippians 4:4). *Re*joice, our best translation of the Greek χαιρω (Kairō) is a heightened form of the word *joy*. It actually indicates a double dose of joy. Therefore, this passage actually has Paul encouraging the believers in Philippi to, "Give joy twice in the Lord, always, and now repeat that— twice again!" Of course, what he is saying is to rejoice all the time and with all our strength.

The word *joy* occurs some 182 times in the Bible. *Rejoice* occurs 234 times. These important words reveal a mindset that a Christian should be certain all things are well, even when they appear not to be. Paul uses an imperative verb in 1 Thessalonians 5:16 (and in verses 17 and 18), because he wants us to be sure it is not optional to rejoice always; we are commanded to remain in this attitude.

Obviously, when things are going badly it is harder to rejoice. Nevertheless, this might be when we most need to rejoice. When we fail to rejoice in hard times, we have in effect removed God from the throne of our lives and replaced Him with the worry of the moment. Worries make horrible Masters! God is better, and we enthrone Him in our hearts when we make every other event, thought, and word subordinate to His reign.

The Apostle Paul told the Philippians, "Not that I speak from want, for I have learned to be content in whatever circumstances I am. I know how to get along with humble means, and I also know how to live in prosperity; in any and every circumstance I have learned the secret of being filled and going hungry, both of having abundance and suffering need. I can do all things through Him who strengthens me" (Philippians 4:11-13). When Paul wrote these words, he revealed the reason for his contentment in verse 13: "all things" are possible because "He strengthens me." God's strength is always there, undiminished, no matter how we might feel about it. Through every trial, there is reason to rejoice for we are undefeatable in Him!

If we are to rejoice at all times, then this must also mean we are also to rejoice when everything is going *well*. We often take God for granted when we are prosperous. Joseph's greatest challenge through all of his great sufferings was possibly when he lived in prosperity in Potiphar's house

(Genesis chapter 39). When Potiphar's wife presented herself to him for an illicit relationship, he was vulnerable. In the five verses preceding this event (vss. 2-6), Moses is careful to note in each verse that Joseph and everything he touched prospered. Joseph was riding high! However, he remained faithful because he was alert, and because his joy was in God rather than in personal success.

When everything is going well, some people respond by indulging— they may pop a cork, spend money, or throw a party. Believers should respond first in sober rejoicing because we know all good things come from the Father in Heaven (James 1:17) and rejoicing connects us to this source of victory.

What Reasons Do We Have for Rejoicing?

Those who follow the Lord have good reasons to rejoice.

The first is our *eternal salvation*. Receiving a gift of this magnitude should certainly qualify for rejoicing. If someone were to approach any of us and give us some large gift—say a million dollars—we would be ecstatic! We would want to tell everyone that would listen. So why should the significantly greater gift of eternal life bring a tepid response?

What keeps us from rejoicing is clear: we have not recognized the greatness of God's gift. We should cultivate the attitude that realizes and responds to the great gift in Jesus. We should walk each day in an atmosphere created and sustained by eternal promises. A person who truly grasps that they have the promise of eternal bliss will live joyfully.

A second reason for rejoicing is that *our lives are purposeful*. When Rick Warren wrote his "Purpose-Driven" books, he struck a chord worldwide and the massive sales should tell us that everyone wants purpose.

Every child of the King has purpose. Jesus commissioned us. He said "Go therefore and make disciples of all the nations, baptizing them in the name of the Father and the Son and the Holy Spirit, teaching them to observe all that I commanded you; and lo, I am with you always, even to the end of the age" (Matthew 28:18-20). To be called out to participate with Jesus in building His kingdom, to help add people to the "Lamb's Book of Life" (Revelation 21:27) so that they might enjoy eternal life, and to teach them how to walk fully in the presence of God; this constitutes a purposeful life worth rejoicing.

What Is the Result of Our Rejoicing?

The first result of rejoicing is that *it gives us strength*. In the eighth chapter of Nehemiah, Ezra read the law to the people of God and they began to weep. Their sins seemed heavy as they listened to God's holy word read all through the morning. Nehemiah, Ezra, and the Levites told them not to weep because, "The joy of the Lord is your strength" (v.10). The people had just observed the Day of Atonement and Nehemiah was reminding the people that the awareness of sin leads to confession and God's cleansing, and God's cleansing (forgiveness) leads to rejoicing. After the Day of Atonement in the Jewish feasts came the Feast of Tabernacles which was set aside for seven days of joyful celebration (Leviticus 23:33-44). The order, then, is confession, cleansing, and celebration.

We should understand the glorious result of atonement more than Nehemiah's audience did. Our rejoicing is in answer to what Christ has done on the cross and through the tomb, and it brings into our lives the strength of the Savior. Rejoicing is not only a reaction to God's provision; it *releases* God's provision. We rejoice because we are strong in the Lord and we rejoice in order to be stronger.

Proverbs 17:22 simply says, "A joyful heart is good medicine, but a broken spirit dries up the bones." When we are ill, medicine is wonderful to have near. However, medicine can also be pre-emptive as it wards off any attack of disease. Our rejoicing heals *and* prevents our diseases.

When Paul tells us to "rejoice always," he is reminding us of another result of rejoicing, which is *a continuous focus*. Rejoicing must have its focus in the Lord. If we rejoice in abundance, happiness, health, wealth, our children, our spouses, ultimately we are rejoicing in the Savior who provides all these things. When give our hearts to rejoicing, we focus on our Lord. When we do this continuously each day, we find the circumstances that would normally pull us down have no ill effect. Our steadfast God and His ready salvation get our attention rather than the barometric reading of earthly events.

Most significantly, when we rejoice *we receive God's favor*. We have a tremendous example in Job. He suffering was great, and we might have understood if he had grown angry with God. However, at the consummation of his many calamities when his wife told him to "curse God and die," Job said, "Shall we indeed accept good from God and not accept adversity?" The biblical record states, "in all this Job did not sin with his lips" (Job 2:9-10). In fact, Job responded to calamity by rejoicing in God:

Naked I came from my mother's womb,
And naked I shall return there.
The LORD gave and the LORD has taken away.
Blessed be the name of the LORD. (Job 1:21, emphasis added)

Job sinned when he cursed, not God, but the day of his birth. He began in chapter three to lament his suffering and God's silence. When God rebuked him Job responded by retracting and repenting of his words (42:1-

6). Nevertheless, at the end of Job's ordeal, God spoke to his friends and said He was angry with them (especially the young Eliphaz who was the most condescending) and that they had not spoken what is right about God as Job had. The punishment was swift with the three "counselors." They were to offer sacrifices for atonement in Job's presence, and he was to pray for them. God bestowed His favor for all to see on His servant Job as He blessed all that he had twofold more than he had lost (42:10).

Job was blessed because he blessed the Lord! Where he failed is when he stopped blessing the Lord. However, because of his life of praise, he was counted as worthy of God's favor.

Paul was another excellent testimony to constant rejoicing. At the end of his letter to the church in Philippi, Paul reminds them to, "Rejoice in the Lord" (Philippians 3:1). Here is a man in prison telling free people to remember to rejoice! You would think it would be the other way around. Many times Paul encouraged others to praise God when his personal situation was difficult.

The Philippians undoubtedly remembered Paul and Silas, while shackled in their city prison, belting forth in hymn singing. The other prisoners heard their singing and praying, but so did God. He caused chains to fall off the prisoners, doors to open, and the resulting salvation of a lost family (Acts 16:25-30). God rejoices in the rejoicing of His people.

I have always desired God's favor. When I was a child, I remember reading in the Beatitudes, "Blessed are the pure in heart, for they shall see God." I did not know exactly what that meant but I definitely wanted to *see* God.[4] Having the pure heart of a faithful child, we should wish to please our Heavenly Father. Others may scoff, but we should rejoice in all circumstances. God will favor us because we trust Him as loving children.

Avenues of Rejoicing

I would like to suggest a few ways that we can find expression for rejoicing.

One method that will help our constant awareness in rejoicing is to *sing hymns or spiritual songs*. If we commit simple songs to memory, we can sing anytime and lift our spirit to heaven. Each day as I drive to work, I sing praises to God. This positive spiritual mindset is likely to continue throughout the day, and I am able to face any challenge.

I suggest learning simple songs or even parts of songs for this purpose. I can sing, "Praise to the Lord, the Almighty, the King of Creation! O my soul, praise Him, for He is thy health and salvation! All ye who hear, now to His temple draw near; Praise Him in glad adoration." Sometimes I mix up parts (or make up parts) accidentally, but I do not think God cares nor does it limit my joy.

If you know choruses, then sing them. Some of the choruses today are very catchy and easy to remember. We should be certain that any hymns or choruses that we sing are biblically based and have spiritual substance. We dishonor God in rejoicing, I think, when we sing anything that is erroneous or silly. King David said, "Let the words of my mouth and the meditation of my heart be acceptable in your sight, O Lord, my rock and redeemer" (Psalm 19:14).

I sing my *prayers* sometimes, like a monk who did not learn the chants and made it up as he goes along. This is okay too, as this is not so much about making music as releasing it.

God's people sing! (Even though I am aware, some of them sing badly.)

Christian radio is a resource. If you have the radio on then you can absorb the positive spiritual message wherever you are. Christian radio is accessible in most places, and it is a tremendous resource to support constant spiritual rejoicing. CDs, DVDs, or other sacred recorded media are helpful as well.

Rejoicing should be a part of what we do when *we attend church*. Instead of concentrating on the inadequacies of our Sunday school class, the worship service that "just doesn't work right," or the less-than-stellar sermon from our pastor—why not praise God for all of these things for the gifts they are. Freedom to assemble for worship is a privilege. Those throughout the world who do not have this privilege would be glad to tell us how to rejoice since we *do*. When our attitude changes, we will find that our perception changes, and then we can honestly praise God for these gifts.

When we see these three verses lined up next to each other in the fifth chapter of Thessalonians, we need to remember that rejoicing is expressed in our *prayer and thanksgiving*. It is impossible to separate these without harming all of them. When we pray, rejoicing gives it power; and when we rejoice, thanksgiving adds harmony. They are interdependent and mutually supportive.

Finally, we can also *rejoice in difficulty*. When we least feel like praising God this may be one of the best times to rejoice, for our rejoicing in difficulty sanctifies our circumstances. Joy "defangs" our troubles. What seemed impossible before, when bathed in the praise of God becomes manageable, even beneficial, and can turn difficulties into expressions of holiness.

Suffering Is Real

Before I close this chapter, I want to consider the reality of suffering. We will study this subject and its relation to holiness in depth in chapter 16. For now, remember that rejoicing does not attempt to hide what we feel when we suffer. When a person loses their child to accidental death, for example, the emotional load would be devastating. The burden of loss would seem too great to carry. Would rejoicing at such a time be too much to ask?

We should remember that rejoicing sometimes has nothing to do with what we are feeling. We can rejoice even when it seems to be a ridiculous thing to do. When we are under extreme pressure or hobbled with mind-bending sorrow, remember that joy is simply our response to what is true. What is true is that Jesus loves us, He knows how we hurt, and has promised, "God will wipe every tear from their eyes" (Revelation 7:17). The prophet Isaiah tells us, "The ransomed of the Lord will return and come with joyful shouting to Zion, with everlasting joy upon their heads. They will find gladness and joy, and sorrow and sighing will flee away" (Isaiah 35:10). The Lord also promised through the prophet Joel, "Then *I will make up to you* for the years that the swarming locust has eaten, the creeping locust, the stripping locust and the gnawing locust, my great army which I sent among you. You will have plenty to eat and be satisfied and praise the name of the Lord your God, who has dealt wondrously with you; Then My people will never be put to shame" (Joel 2:25-26, emphasis added).

Jesus is not callous and does not ask us to overlook great suffering. In fact, He keeps pace with us when we stumble. He understands when we hurt deeply. However, regardless of our current situation, whether in prosperity or pain, the right response is to rejoice. This is a statement of our faith in a benevolent and ever-present God.

---

1. Charles H. Spurgeon, *Sermons on Prayer* (Grand Rapids: Zondervan, 1959), 159.

2. *Merriam-Webster's Collegiate Dictionary,* 11th edition, s.v. "Joy."

3. *Nelson's New Illustrated Dictionary*, s.v. "Joy."

4. Today, I believe this means simply to have a heart that is "unmixed." Our pure hearts are full of devotion to God, without reserve. The result is that our awareness of God is augmented, and we "see" Him in everything.

CHAPTER 10

Prayer Without Intermission

Many of us are proud to be called a people of the Book, or people who are committed to the principles of Scripture. However, there are parts of the Scripture that we do not really know, so we certainly cannot act on them with any consistency. One such verse is 1 Thessalonians 5:17, where Paul told the church in Thessalonica to "Pray without ceasing." This verse can be interpreted, "Pray without intermission." Paul is admonishing these believers to pray, and not to stop. Praying constantly, or praying "without intermission," may be a largely neglected discipline in Christendom and I believe it is behind much of our ineffectiveness and lack of joy.

This verse of Scripture itself is usually not in dispute. Most interpreters believe it is a clear command to pray without ceasing. The question arises, however, as to what *is* praying without ceasing. Regardless of our possible disagreement as to particulars, once we are comfortable with a definition it is important to make the habit of unceasing prayer a part of our lives.

We should recall that this short verse is in command form, or the *imperative* mode. Unlike commands from your computer, which can often be ignored without consequence (sometimes), commands from Scripture should never be ignored. All of us are accountable to what Paul said.

One of my Seminary professors liked to say the best commentary on the Bible is *the Bible*.[1] If we want to understand a verse; we must understand it in its context. We should see the verse in context to the verses surrounding it, the chapter, book, and Testament in which we find it. We should also try to see its place in the entire Bible. What other Bible passages help us understand the continuing and incessant prayer that Paul has commanded?

We can begin by studying other verses written by Paul. He told the Ephesians, "With all prayer and all petition pray at all times in the Spirit" (Ephesians 6:18), and he said concerning the Colossian Christians that he and his companions were "praying always for you" (Colossians 1:3). Paul, together with Timothy and Silvanus, said in 2 Thessalonians 1:11 that they always prayed for the believers in that city. And when Paul wrote to Timothy, his "child in the faith," he said, "I thank God, whom I serve with a clear conscience the way my forefathers did, as I constantly remember you in my prayers night and day" (2 Timothy 1:3). Incidentally, this last verse indicates praying constantly is one way we can serve with a *clear conscience*.

Paul often used strong language, but he did not exaggerate. He was praying for all of the people he mentioned all the time, which indicates a continued intercessory chain of concern.

Paul is not alone in teaching constant prayer.

Jesus gave us the wonderful prayer parable in Luke 18:1-8. You may know it as "The Parable of the Importunate Widow," *importunate* meaning troublesome and persistent! Luke introduced this parable by saying that Jesus was "telling them (the disciples) a parable to show that at *all times* they ought to pray and not to lose heart" (emphasis added).

This widow needed protection from her adversary, but had no one to stand in for her in a court of law. She appealed to the only power she had, an "unrighteous" judge who seemed to be uninterested. The parable says in verse five that she bothered the judge and he thought she might wear him out, so he relented and gave her legal protection.

Jesus makes the point that if an unrighteous judge relented and answered an appeal like this, how much more a righteous God will answer the prayers of those He loves when they pray! Note however, that Jesus did not suggest that prayer is effortless, but said in conclusion that God will not delay *long* over his righteous ones who *cry to Him day and night*.

Jesus wonders aloud in verse eight whether when He returns He will find faith on earth, and faith is defined here as God's people being persistent and expectant in prayer.

It Is Possible!

Once we seriously view 1 Thessalonians 5:17 as a command, we are apt to ask, "How is it possible?" Can a person pray all day long, every day? Are there reliable living examples?

In several of the churches I have pastored, we mentored men in our churches. As we advanced in the mentoring process, we tried to teach each man how to pray without ceasing. When I was explaining this topic to one of the deacons, he began nodding knowingly. He said, "I have prayed without ceasing for as long as I can remember"!

Dr. Billy Graham is another vivid example.

We consider Dr. Graham honest and forthright. We also consider him humble and self-aware, and in response to an interview in 2003, he says that he has never stopped praying.

Jerry Jenkins, the co-author of the *Left Behind* series with Tim LaHaye, was invited to help Dr. Graham write his memoirs. Jenkins inquired about Graham's personal spiritual habits, and Graham replied, "It's certainly not a secret. It's not hidden from us. There's no secret key in the Bible. There are two things that we're instructed to do: That's pray without ceasing and to search the Scriptures."

Jenkins followed up with the question "Do you pray without ceasing?" Dr. Graham said, "I pray without ceasing...I have every waking moment since I became a believer as a teenager." Later in the interview Jenkins asked how Graham resumes his Bible reading routine after missing one or two days, and Graham answered, "I don't think I've ever done that…It's my spiritual food. I don't want to miss a meal."[2]

There is no doubt in my mind that there is a direct connection between Dr. Graham's commitment to prayer and the Word, and the mighty way God has used him throughout the years.

What Is Praying Without Intermission?

Since there is confusion here, we need to wrestle with what Paul and other biblical writers *meant* when they said we should pray continuously.

It certainly is not being in constant *conscious* prayer. Our conscious minds will be taken with many activities during the day, and we will not necessarily be praying consciously at such times. In fact, I would heartily encourage some Christian drivers to pay attention to their driving and hold their prayer if they cannot do two things at once!

As we have mentioned, the Apostle Paul said many times that he and others were praying without ceasing for the saints in various churches (Romans 1:9; 1 Corinthians 1:4; Ephesians 1:15-16; Philippians 1:3-5; Colossians 1:3; 2 Thessalonians 1:2). It would be impossible to pray effectively for all these people at once so constant prayer must mean that Paul and his companions were praying cyclically without stopping. We might say they were always praying for these they mentioned, or they were always getting ready to.

Furthermore, praying constantly obviously requires no particular attitude of body, such as kneeling, closed eyes or folded hands. Neither is location a determinant for constant prayer or it could not take place everywhere, and at any time.

Constant prayer is being in an unbroken state of communication with heaven, a God-awareness you might say that sometimes calls for words and at other times simply does not. I have heard it compared to being in a car with a close friend, both would talk at times but neither would talk all the time (or they might choose other friends). Two close friends may travel miles without saying a word and yet fellowship does not wane in the silences.

I think it is valuable to see what a few respected leaders say about this important practice of constant prayer.

John MacArthur said, "To 'pray without ceasing' basically refers to recurring prayer, not nonstop talking. Thus it is to be our way of life—we're to be continually in an attitude of prayer…It is living in continual God-consciousness, where everything we see and experience becomes a kind of prayer, lived in deep awareness of and surrender to Our Heavenly Father."[3]

Thomas Kelly said, "There is a way of ordering our mental life on more than one level at once. On one level we may be thinking, discussing, seeing, calculating, meeting all the demands of external affairs. But deep within, behind the scenes, at a profounder level, we may also be in prayer and adoration, song and worship and a gentle receptiveness to divine breathings."[4]

Philip Yancey said, "Our minds have the potential to attend to more than one thing at once, and I have found it possible to give God attention even when doing something else: to pray *simultaneously* as other activities are going on. I simply try to direct Godward the inner dialogue that is taking place all the time. To pray without ceasing taps into the mind's multitasking ability."[5]

Neither does constant prayer interfere with other worthy activities. When Spurgeon discusses unceasing prayer, he suggests we not "sully one activity with the blood of another," or do not constantly be running away from study or labor to pray. We can pray when the activity ceases. During any activity he suggests we can send "little darts and hand grenades of godly desire" without interrupting our work.[6]

It is interesting that those who write on this subject use terminology like "atmosphere," "spirit," and "attitude" to describe this continuing state of prayer. This is not to say that we are somehow passively suspended in this state, on the contrary, we must make a conscious effort to pray. However, we should be careful not to turn this practice into legalistic, life-stealing, nonstop *labor*. Although continuous prayer requires our attention, it should also be natural and refreshing, since prayer is the result of an attitude of reverence more than its cause.

Practical Considerations
When we mentored people in the discipline of incessant prayer, we encouraged them to begin their day in prayer, and then continue to pray throughout the day. The daily quiet time (discussed fully in Chapter 2) is foundational to continuous prayer. G. Campbell Morgan said:

No man will pray always who neglects the formation of the habit of regular prayer. The disciple who regularly observes a place and time and method will gradually find the habit learned in the secret place is binding through all the public life. A confirmed habit of regular prayer will create regularity and constancy amidst all irregularities of time and place and method. Prayer in secret will create a spirit which will obtain in all public places. Fellowship with God as an activity will issue in fellowship with God as an attitude.[7]

If we give our attention to God at the beginning of the day, then we will not be drawn away unless we ourselves allow the concentration to lapse. As we said, there are many activities throughout the day that take our full attention, and during those moments we may not be aware of conscious prayer; but if we are in a spirit of prayer, we will be prayerful nonetheless. I have found it helpful to judge that when those moments of concentration on some task end, and my heart is immediately drawn to my Father and either through words or thoughts I acknowledge Him and worship Him, it indicates I am praying without ceasing.

Kelly said, "By quiet, persistent practice in turning all of our being, day and night, in prayer and inward worship and surrender, toward Him who calls in the deeps of our soul. Mental habits of inward orientation must be established...it is a simple art...but it may be long before we achieve any steadiness in the process."[8]

We encouraged the people that we mentored in unceasing prayer to grade themselves as they progressed. With the understanding that constant prayer is not always *conscious* prayer, we would ask them, "What percentage of your day did you pray constantly?" If a person can approximate the time they believe they were praying constantly (50%, 80%, 100%), then they can stay focused on this discipline and congratulate themselves as they improve!

Practically, if any of us were to pray for what we *need* to pray for we will be well on our way to prayer without intermission. For example, if you are tempted to lust: you should *pray*. If you are cut off in traffic and the anger rises: *pray*. If you fear an upcoming job interview: *pray*. If your spouse comes to mind: *pray*. If you are concerned about your child: *pray!*

Pray when you think of your parents. Pray when you are concerned about your national leaders. Pray when you are concerned about the direction of the country you live in.

Your church and denomination need your prayers. Your pastor, church leaders, and denominational leaders need your prayers. In fact, the advancement of the Kingdom of God is dependent on your prayers.

Pray when things are going well and pray when things are going badly. Just pray.

I have found that constant prayer, contrary to what some think, does not become dry or wearisome. Just as extensive Bible reading (done correctly) does not lead to boredom, so constant prayer does not become drudgery. One of the blessings of the spiritual disciplines is that the more you practice them, the more joy they produce.

We must add a very important point, and that is if you fail in constant prayer, keep trying. I am not like Dr. Graham, in that praying constantly is still a struggle for me. Just remember that we are praying unceasingly because we love the Savior. He is not going to reject us for failing the serious effort—neither should we reject ourselves. When you fail, refuse to be remorseful and allow your failure to drive you to begin again.

When you measure your success in constant prayer and it seems low, compare it to when you were not trying at all! The more you work on this, the more effective it becomes. Kelly said that at first the practice of this prayer is an alternation between the outward reality and the "Inner light." But as we grow in its practice, the two become one, and we are able to live with prayer and worship undergirding the whole of life, with no alternation at all. Some abandon the practice too early without persevering and enjoying the result.[9]

Positive Results

As you can imagine, there are worthwhile results to praying constantly.

When constant prayer becomes a habit, we are able to *live effectively*. It produces the imminence of God's presence that relieves unnecessary stress, gives us power to defeat temptation, makes us effective intercessors, and gives us the ability to minister to our hurting world with the available grace of God's kingdom. Prayer is effective because God designed it to be that way.

An added benefit to always praying is that we are able to *handle the occasional emergency*. Jack Taylor said that when we are praying as we should and we encounter an emergency then prayer will be the result rather than *panic*.[10] Trying to find spiritual armor in the heat of battle is bad timing, it is always better to be outfitted before the battle begins!

Constant prayer also assures that we are *participating in the work of Heaven*. The Bible tells us that Jesus has taken His place at the right hand of God, and that He is constantly interceding for the saints (Romans 8:27,34; Hebrews 7:25). When we pray we participate with Jesus.

Prayer is the activity of the citizens of Heaven. Revelation says of the four living creatures around the throne, "day and night they do not cease to say, 'Holy, Holy, Holy is the Lord God, The Almighty, Who Was and Is and Is to Come" (Revelation 4:8). It is clear that the twenty-four elders who surround the throne and all of the angels as God's emissaries and ministering spirits *do not cease* to praise Him. When we are not prayerful, we are missing the work of the ages, which is constant attention to the Lord of Lords and asking for His intercession.

Continuous prayer can also serve as a *barometer of our spiritual condition*. Charles Spurgeon said, "Have nothing to do with that which you cannot ask God's blessing upon, have nothing to do with it, for if God cannot bless it, you may depend upon it the devil has cursed it. Anything that is right for you to do you may consecrate with prayer, and let this be a sure gauge and test to you, if you feel that it would be an insult to the majesty of heaven for you to ask the Lord's blessing upon what is proposed to you, then stand clear of the unholy thing."[11]

Conscientious prayer will keep us from willful sin and will alert us to our present spiritual condition. It is impossible to be in a state of true prayer and participate in what we know is evil. Therefore, our constant prayer will keep us in direct communication with the holiness of heaven, and it will cast a light on what is unholy so that we might avoid it.

How shall we remain holy? The thesis of this book is that only Our Lord is holy and so we look to Him for the effects of holiness. Prayer is one tool He has given us to maintain this link. What the Lord calls us to do He will equip us to do. He has called us to unflinching, fervent, and incessant prayer. We should ask that the Holy Spirit will create this desire in us to pray without intermission, and with our sincere effort, He will give us the ability to do so.

---

1. I do not remember which professor said this; however, Bible College and Seminary students should be encouraged to realize that many of the statements or teachings in classes stay with us the rest of our lives. To this day, I quote many wonderful statements that have had a great impact on me, and many of them came from my formal education.

2. David Roach, "Jenkins: Chronicling Graham's Life a Transforming Experience." [Online] Available http://www.bpnews net/bpnews.asp?id=16851. October 13, 2003.

3. John McArthur, *Alone With God: The Power and Passion of Prayer* (Wheaton, Illinois: Victor Books, 1995), 17.

4. Thomas R. Kelly, *A Testament of Devotion* (New York: Harper and Brothers, 1941), 35.

5. Phillip Yancey, *Prayer: Does it Make Any Difference?* (Grand Rapids: Zondervan, 2006), 316.

6. Charles H. Spurgeon, *Sermons on Prayer* (Grand Rapids: Zondervan, 1959), 165.

7. G. Campbell Morgan, *The Practice of Prayer* (Alexandria, Ls.: Lamplighter Publications, nd), 112.

8. Kelly, *A Testament of Devotion,* 38.

9. Ibid., 40.

10. Jack Taylor, *Prayer: Life's Limitless Reach* (Nashville: Broadman Press, 1977), p. 131.

11. Spurgeon, *Sermons on Prayer,* 161.

CHAPTER 11

Giving Thanks in Everything

Jewish tradition tells of two angels sent to earth, the Angel of Request and the Angel of Thanksgiving. Each angel had a basket and was to bring the prayers they gathered back to heaven. The Angel of Request immediately filled his basket, and returned to heaven with it overflowing. The Angel of Thanksgiving returned to heaven with only one prayer in his basket for God's many mercies.[1]

To neglect thanksgiving is a serious sin. Paul writes in the first chapter of Romans of those who in "ungodliness and unrighteousness...suppress the truth" of God's existence (v. 18). He said that God was evident to them through creation, but "even though they knew God, they did not honor God or give thanks...their foolish heart was darkened" (v. 21). The people who chose not to believe, neglected thanksgiving at their peril, and then to their utter loss.

Christians are not in danger of losing their salvation because of thanklessness, but this sin is magnified in light of how much we have been given. Sadly, thanksgiving for many of us is not a regular practice.

Some may find they habitually give thanks only before meals, or at special events like the Thanksgiving holiday. Others find that thanksgiving is immediate when they are in public worship, but it simply does not come to mind at other times throughout the week. Biblical thanksgiving, however, is much more pervasive—for being thankful is the natural state of the redeemed person. It encompasses all of life.

Remember that we choose to be thankful! Conversely, we are also thankless by choice: we do not think it is important enough or are not thankful through simple neglect. Holiness cannot fully develop unless it is planted in the soil of thankfulness, for only when are thankful are we in a true state of mind.

Imagine for a moment that you were somehow transported back in time, and while standing among Old Testament believers *you* were invited by Jesus to see the most sacred parts of Solomon's temple. Jesus leads you past all the waiting penitents in the outer courts. He ushers you still further past the priests, who stand by in the Holy Place, awed that you are being honored in this way by the one they recognize as the Messiah. Jesus then takes you past the High Priest, beyond the huge olive wood and gold doors and the ornate curtain hanging there, into the Holy of Holies itself. Here only the High Priest goes once a year on the Day of Atonement under strict guidelines. Can you imagine that you would slouch around as Jesus showed you the Ark of the Covenant and the fifteen-foot high cherubim guarding the ark with their fifteen-foot wings? Do you think you would be disinterested while you stood in the very presence of Almighty God Himself who inhabits this place? On the contrary, I think awe and gratitude would overwhelm you.

This of course is a parable, but perhaps it does not go far enough to express what has happened to us when we accepted Jesus as our Savior. God has not only invited us into the inner sanctum, we ourselves have been remade as the Holy of Holies. In a mysterious union, the Triune God has chosen to abide within us giving us unhindered contact with His holiness. Gratitude naturally flows from our awareness of this truth!

In Thessalonians 5:18, Paul said, "In everything give thanks." As in the previous two verses, this is in command form. Not a suggestion, this is an unyielding word spoken with the authority of the Apostle: "Give thanks...*in everything!*"

My father used to gather the family around at special occasions and ask us to go around the circle and tell one thing for which we were thankful. We were thankful if we could remember something before it was our turn (Think, *THINK!*), because Dad would always remind us that it should not take long to remember something for which to be thankful. Reasons for thankfulness are all around us. Our shame is in not seeing.

The Bible Knowledge Commentary notes that the two previous verses deal with time ("always" and "without ceasing"), but this verse deals with circumstances.[2] Paul said to give thanks in every circumstance. Not because we believe everything is good, for some things are thoroughly bad. However, just as we *rejoice* when things go badly, and just as we *pray* when the heavens seem to be brass, we also *thank* God in everything because we recognize that He redeems all things.

The role of a redeemer is to restore or to buy back what is lost. In Deuteronomy 7:8, Moses told the children of Israel "The Lord brought you out by a mighty hand and redeemed you from the house of slavery." In 2 Samuel 4:9, David said the "Lord redeemed my life from all distress." Job said, "I know my redeemer lives," even when he suffered greatly (Job 19:25). The psalmist reminds us "Oh *give thanks* to the Lord, for He is good, for His lovingkindness is everlasting. Let the redeemed of the Lord *say so*" (Psalm 107:2, emphasis added).

In the previous chapter, we discussed praying without ceasing. As we learn to pray this way it is a natural progression to give thanks in everything for prayer and thanksgiving are connected. Paul reminded the Philippians, "Be anxious for nothing, but in everything by prayer and supplication with thanksgiving let your requests be made known to God. And the peace of God which passes all comprehension, will guard your hearts and minds in Christ Jesus" (Philippians 4:6). We are thankful because we have always seen God's benevolent hand before and we expect to see it again. As a result, God promised peace when we are praying and seasoning our prayer with thanks. In fact, thankless prayer may lack God's blessing because it does not take into account the reciprocal nature of God's benevolence.

Once when I was about to enter seminary for another semester my pastor was mentoring me. I was stone-broke and did not know how I would be able to go back to school since the seminary required matriculation fees up front. The date for panic was fast approaching, and somehow my pastor found out about my need. He asked me how much I thought I needed to return to seminary and I named a figure. He said he wanted to give it to me so that I could stop worrying about it. I was gratified, but I managed to say, "Well, thank you very much, but I don't believe I can receive it because..." Before I was able to finish the sentence he said, "I see you have your pride speech all worked up." *Then* I was speechless. He said something I have never forgotten, "Show me a poor receiver and I will show you a poor giver." He explained the reciprocal nature of giving. When someone gives in a worshipful way, he understands that abundance is a gift of God. We are sometimes up and sometimes down. Giving and receiving is God's way of keeping the balances going. If we are poor receivers, then we may be showing that we do not understand the nature, and the need, of giving at all.[3]

Prayer and thanksgiving are part of this cycle of giving. They are reciprocal. We pray because we have a need, and we give thanks because we understand the One who possesses all material and spiritual wealth loves to give it away.

Thanksgiving Is a Clear Command of the Scripture

We need to look at a few other verses that are clear in this matter of giving thanks. In Colossians 3:15-17, Paul wrote, "Let the peace of Christ rule in your hearts, to which indeed you were called in one body; and be thankful. Let the word of Christ richly dwell within you, with all wisdom teaching and admonishing one another with psalms and hymns and spiritual songs, singing with thankfulness in your hearts to God. Whatever you do in word or deed, do all in the name of the Lord Jesus, giving thanks through Him to God the Father." This passage is overflowing with thanksgiving. It is clear that thanksgiving is a natural response to Jesus, but it is also clear that thanksgiving is necessary as a *chosen* discipline.

Choosing to be thankful in Paul's mind is completely keyed in on all that a person has in Christ. "Whatever you do," Paul said in verse 17, be sure that thanksgiving in the Lord is part of it. Paul is not suggesting so much that we try to be thankful as to realize that the reasons to be thankful are already evident. The bounty that God gives us is enough to keep us giving thanks. It follows that if we are unthankful; something needs alteration in us.

The Bible never hides the difficulty of this life. In fact, it is daunting sometimes in its honest portrayal of the challenges of the life of faithfulness. Therefore, it is not as if Paul did not understand that there are real sorrows and heartbreaks, even for the faithful and maybe especially for the faithful, but he understood clearly that our victory overwhelms all sorrow. He said, "For I consider that the sufferings of the present time are not worthy to be compared with the glory that is to be revealed to us" (Romans 8:18). There you have it: sufferings are nothing next to glory! That may be hard to believe when you are suffering, but this is where faith comes in for it gives substance to hope (Hebrews 11:1).

Another encouragement to thanksgiving is in Hebrews, "Through Him then, let us continually offer up a sacrifice of praise to God, that is, the fruit of lips that give thanks to His name" (Hebrews 13:15). I have always liked that phrase, "the sacrifice of praise." It is tied to a grain sacrifice in Leviticus 7:12 where praise was offered with the loss of something, in that case fine grains and the labor used to prepare the "cakes." Sometimes we offer thanksgiving with sacrifice. Thanking God when things are tough, even *for* the things that are tough, is a statement of faith. When we do this we are showing that we believe in the promises of God more than what we see or feel.

Reasons to Be Thankful

The list of what we can be thankful for could be very long, but I will mention just a few obvious reasons.

Salvation is at the top of the list. Remember that we said in chapter 9 that when we rejoice, our salvation is first in our minds. This is true for thanksgiving as well. Paul spoke in 2 Corinthians 9:15 of the gift of God's Son, "Thanks be to God for His indescribable gift!"

Thanking God for our salvation is a legitimate response *for* the gift rather than a dependence on any feeling *about* the gift. We are thankful because we are aware of the greatness of our salvation whether our feelings are touched or not. It is only doubt of the gift of salvation that causes it to lose its luster in our hearts, for the gift itself is beyond our comprehension. Paul calls it *indescribable*, which may be why we have trouble describing it. However, we can grasp it with our hearts and thanksgiving is the result.

Another reason for thanksgiving is our *life of victory*. Paul wrote to the Corinthians, "Thanks be to God, who gives us the victory through our Lord Jesus Christ" (1 Corinthians 15:57). Later he said, "Thanks be to God who always leads us in triumph in Christ and manifests through us the sweet aroma of the knowledge of Him in every place" (2 Corinthians 2:14). Life in Christ is a perpetual victory! The better we comprehend this truth, the more our thanksgiving flows.

Our *future victory* also generates thanks. We saw in chapter 6 in relation to our place in Jesus that the Father "raised us up in Him, and seated us with Him in the heavenly places in Christ Jesus" (Ephesians 2:6). Jesus finished His victorious work and since we were "seated" with Him, our work in Him is finished in victory even as it continues today. In other words, we work *from* the position of victory rather than toward victory. This victory is transformational and our present circumstances will take on luminance when we choose to live with great hope.

Finally, we should be thankful because *we are commanded to do so*. I have always thought that a simple command from God should be sufficient reason to do something. The Holy Spirit inspired Paul to write the clear command we have studied: "In everything give thanks." This command (and the many other similar verses in the Scripture) reminds us that it is beneficial to thank God for all things.

Some Benefits of Thankfulness

Everything God calls us to do is beneficial. I would like to look at a few benefits of thanksgiving, although just being obedient to God's command should be enough!

When we are thankful, our *mindset is positive*. What we think has a great deal to do with how we feel, how we act, and ultimately which way our lives progress. When we are thankful—truly thankful—we have a God mindset. Somewhere I picked up the term, "God-inside-mindedness." The God-inside-mind is both the cause and the result of being thankful. Because we believe God, we are thankful; and since we are thankful, we are open to God.

Romans 8:28 reminds us, "God causes all things to work together for good to those who love God, to those who are called according to His purpose." When we believe these words, we grasp that God is working everything out. When we stay focused on His victory rather than on our troubles or failures, we are naturally positive.

Thankful people are *filled with wonder*. I love my garden and my trees. I often spend part of my daily prayers wandering through my yard giving thanks to the Creator. The wonder of our world is evident to me more when I am thankful.

Jesus said, "Unless you are converted and become like children, you will not enter the kingdom of heaven" (Matthew 18:3). One characteristic of children is their sense of wonder. Children are fascinated by everything because to them everything is new. As adults, we have lived long enough to receive many hard knocks while unraveling the mystery of life, and we have become hardened. We have often replaced our wonder with cynicism. Nothing restores our natural wonder more than thankfulness. Furthermore, I believe that a mature person can experience wonder more deeply than a child.

I was looking to add a tree to our large back yard and had been interested in the Bur Oak. This oak tree has increased in popularity in recent years. I knew they grew large, and I had been looking alongside the road for a large specimen as I drove here and there (much to the consternation of my passengers). One day I saw what I thought was an enormous bur oak, and we had to turn around to approach the roadside park. It was indeed a bur oak and we soon stood under the eighty to one hundred foot tall specimen that could have been over 250 years old. The massive black limbs reached to the sky set on a trunk that must have been over four feet in diameter. As I looked up, I felt like a small child again gazing at something that astounded me. Thankfulness to my Creator was the happy result and all my worries melted away, as I stood, lost in wonder!

Finally, thankfulness in one person *encourages thanksgiving in others.* Clovis Chappell spoke of a person who increased "the melody of the world."[4] A thankful person possesses inward harmony, which is highly contagious. A gentle and thankful person can soften hardened and embittered hearts. Just like when someone says, "I am in a great mood, and no one is going to ruin it;" it is hard to disturb a thankful person and his or her calm in the midst of challenges is infectious.

---

1. Peter V. Deison, *The Priority of Knowing God: Taking Time with God When There is No Time* (Grand Rapids: Discovery House Publishers, 1990), 44.

2. John F. Walvoord and Roy B. Zuck, *The Bible Knowledge Commentary: An Exposition of the Scriptures by Dallas Seminary Faculty* (Wheaton, Illinois: Victor Books, 1987), 2:709.

3. In this case, after prayer I turned this offer down because of extenuating circumstances that are not important to mention. I still learned the lesson: when I returned home, with matriculation at the seminary only days away, I asked God for the same amount this pastor had offered to give me (I did not say anything to anyone about this). The next day a letter was in the mail from another source. Remarkably, I *knew* whom the letter was from before I took it out of the mailbox, and I *knew* there was a check in it for the exact amount I had prayed (so it proved). I remember that my hands were shaking as I took the check out of the envelope.

4. Clovis Chappell, *Sermons on Biblical Characters,* rev. ed. (1922; repr., Grand Rapids: Baker Book House, 1970), 65.

Section 5: What We Are Given to Do

"Living for Jesus a Life that is True"

CHAPTER 12

Action through the Spiritual Disciplines

As we continue in this book to learn how we are to share the holiness of God, we will find the subject of this chapter of great importance. As we have stated, there is no need to produce holiness when God offers it, but we also need to know what it is that we are to do to stand "in the way" of His grace. The chapters we have already studied show us certain actions to take that will increase the freedom of the Holy Spirit in our lives, and therefore result in our holiness. However, there is still more to do.

It would not surprise me if you were thinking at this point, "I thought you said His burden is LIGHT! This looks like a lot of work." First, remember that we said in chapter one His burden is light, but it is *still a burden*. God has not called us to easy living but to fruitful and empowered living. Second, remember that the labor of the few things that we do that are outlined in this book cannot compare to the blessings of holy living. Our rewards are immediate *and* eternal when we live holy lives. Finally, this burden really is not heavy when the Lord carries it for us. The power to be like God—which can be found nowhere else in the universe—can be enjoyed simply through His unhindered presence in our lives. In the light of these things, the few disciplines that we are learning to practice are as light as a feather.

What Can We Do?

So, what has God given us to *do* to be like Him? The answer would have to include the spiritual disciplines. The spiritual disciplines are actions that we regularly practice that connect us to the hand of God (see Psalm 123:1-2). Whether you call them spiritual disciplines, or as Rick Warren prefers, habits[1], it only matters that you practice them. All the steps we are taking in this book are important, but there may be nothing as *concrete* or *proactive* as the spiritual disciplines.

Ever since Richard Foster's book *The Celebration of Discipline* appeared on the scene in 1978, Christians discipline has been reborn in our churches. *Spiritual* discipline, in particular, is that which attempts to "stir up" the gift within us, that which was given to us when we were given the gift of eternal salvation. Our eternal salvation inherently offers sanctification; what we might call *daily* salvation. This gift is within us but we must act in order to keep it fluent.

A Verse to Remember

The Apostle Paul had this innate power in view when he wrote to the Ephesians, "Now to Him who is able to do far more abundantly beyond all that we ask or think, according to the power that works within us" (Ephesians 3:20). Notice that the power to do these great works is "within us," not floating around somewhere in the spiritual stratosphere.

Notice also what this unleashed power can do. If you were to read this in the original Greek, you would find that we have dismissed a "beyond all" in translation. Literally, this verse translates, "Now to Him who is able *beyond all* to do *abundantly beyond all* that we could ask or think." That seems repetitious, but it is the Greek way of adding superlative upon superlative to get to an exalted meaning.

We should make this personal. If I were to ask, "Would you like to be able to do *far more* in your life?" I think you would say, "Please, yes." If I asked, "How about *far more abundantly?*" you might wonder how something could be far more than abundant, but would certainly agree to find out. Then if I were to say, "Well, then, would you like to do *far more abundantly, beyond all that you could even dream or ask for?*" You would be overwhelmed but would immediately say "yes." The Apostle Paul is saying exactly that. GOD is able to cause you to do beyond your wildest imagination of abundance, through the power that is resting in you, *right now*. All that is necessary is for you to stir it up. The spiritual disciplines help us to tap into this power.

Before we continue, I think we need to note something about the word "power" when used in this verse and in the New Testament. Many people view power as an explosive, even spectacular display that is by nature impressive; and since we *want to be impressive*, we naturally seek this kind of power. Michael Horton, editor of the book *Power Religion: The Selling Out of the Evangelical Church?* said in his introduction, "Power has become a familiar word in Christian circles. Unlike the small church down the street we used to go to, the new megachurch in a neighboring town has *powerful programs*, and its buildings often compete with corporate office buildings for the impressive architecture of power. Or, the healing service last week was *powerful:* we all felt the power."[2]

I believe we are wrong when we view spiritual power in this way. It is unfortunate that Alfred Nobel named his discovery *dynamite* after this Greek word, because dynamite is explosive, and the word power (*dunamis*) is not interpreted this way in the Bible. The root of this word literally means, "to be able" or "to be capable." The power that we should look for in God does not make us superman, but gives us this exceeding power to be *everyman*. He gives us the power to live quietly in this world, while quietly effective. God's power may indeed be spectacular but usually manifests itself ordinarily. We should keep in mind when Paul speaks of the "power that works within us," he is primarily speaking of that which makes us able to be effective in God's service.

The Benefit of Discipline

The author of Hebrews said, "Therefore leaving the elementary teaching about the Christ, let us press on to maturity" (Hebrews 6:1a). After giving a warning to his readers of the dangers of falling away from grace he said, "Beloved, we are convinced of better things concerning you, and things that accompany salvation...and we desire that each one of you show the same diligence so as to realize the full assurance of hope until the end, so that you will not be sluggish, but imitators of those who through faith and patience inherit the promises" (Hebrews 6:9,11-12).

The author said that maturity leads to "better things" which "accompany" salvation. The word *accompany* comes from a word in Greek that means to "belong to" or "hold nearby," as we would say of things that are closely linked together. Therefore, the better things are derived from salvation, and in order to release them, the author said the person should show diligence and avoid being sluggish. On the other hand, the author exhorts them to inherit the promises by faith and patience.

Here are many words that may lead to our confusion, but we can simplify it. What this passage is saying is that inherent in the gift of salvation is the power to live in maturity. However, our diligence and work activates this "power". When we continue to apply our discipline in the right area, the result is better living. In this particular case in Hebrews, it manifested itself in love for God as shown toward other believers (v. 10). However, *all* true Christian acts are generated through God's power, which is released through our discipline.

Yet this passage makes clear that this "discipline" or "work" is not that which we do as an effort to please or produce goodness, but as result of the grace given to us. Even though we are encouraged to *press on* and *be diligent*, we should also wait with *faith* and *patience*.

In this chapter, I am not trying to be exhaustive in covering the spiritual disciplines. There are good books that do this well and I would encourage the reader to pursue this topic further (I recommend Richard Foster's *The Celebration of Discipline* and Dr. Donald Whitney's *Spiritual Disciplines for the Christian Life*). What I want to do in this chapter is to highlight a few of the disciplines, and give them introductory attention. My purpose is to remind you of their importance so that daily we might be in contact with the grace of God.

I have chosen briefly to touch on the "Seven Deadly Sins" as I think it adds to our discussion. Next to each spiritual discipline, I will list the sin(s) in parentheses that the discipline effectively neutralizes. Where it is helpful, I include a description of how the discipline works against the sin. In other cases, the parenthetical listing is sufficient.

Seven Deadly Sins

The sins in this historical list are deadly, but we must add the caution that all sins are deadly. There are no small sins in God's eyes as He is rumored to hate them all. These seven serve only as a convenient list that group some of our greatest spiritual threats. The sins included in this list vary historically, but today usually include *wrath, greed, sloth, pride, lust, envy, and gluttony.*

Wrath indicates both unholy anger and its result: strong vengeance and malice.

Greed is a grasping pursuit of wealth, status, and power. Usually associated with wealth, it is the desire to have more than is needed.

Sloth points to a lethargic approach to life that is the result of pure laziness or discouragement.

Pride has for its Latin root, *Superbia,* which means haughtiness and can be manifested by superiority. Many consider this the greatest of the seven sins, and even the source of the other sins. This is a competitive sin which causes one to desire to be more important or necessary than others.

Lust in Latin is *Luxuria* and means extravagance. It becomes evident in excessive desire for other people, particularly those desires that lead to sexual enslavement.

Envy is the inordinate desire for what another has. Envy is like greed, but the envious person goes further and is unsatisfied that another person has what they *lack.*

Gluttony is primarily the over-consumption of food and drink, but may include the use of anything that results in waste.

Celebration (vs. Sloth, Envy)

Chapter 9 was entirely devoted to rejoicing and chapter 11 to thanksgiving, and yet I suggest that this discipline of celebration—though it uses elements of both rejoicing and thanksgiving—is somewhat different. The discipline of celebration would go as far as embracing all things in a new way. Through the lens of joy that God gives us, we celebrate those parts of life that have been neutral until now.

We can celebrate life, the simple fact that our physical processes are continuing and we are alive another day. We can thank God—at least for now in America—that we have been born in one of the finest nations in the world, where freedom is real, and we are able to live our lives as we desire. We *choose* to notice the sunrises and sunsets and the beautiful days or to see the mighty hand of God in the crashing storms.

In Jesus' parable, when the prodigal son returned to his father and family, the father said, "...bring the fatted calf, kill it, and let us eat and celebrate" (Luke 15:23). They had a reason to celebrate and they did! (The older brother chose *not* to celebrate.) In Leviticus 23, God gave seven feasts (i.e., Passover, Unleavened Bread, First Fruits, Pentecost, Trumpets, Day of Atonement, and Tabernacles) to the children of Israel for celebration for a certain purpose and in response to various events. The children of God were to *choose* to remember in these feasts what bounty they had in their lands, their harvests, and their spiritual abundance—all from the hands of their benevolent God.

It is obvious that there are good things to celebrate, but there are also "bad" things to celebrate! Jesus spoke shocking words in Luke 6:22-23: "Blessed are you when men hate you, and ostracize you, and insult you, and scorn your name as evil, for the sake of the Son of Man. Be glad in that day and leap for joy, for behold, your reward is great in heaven. For in the same way their fathers used to treat the prophets." It is obvious that choosing to celebrate life in service to God does not diminish when we are mistreated. Jesus said that our mistreatment at the hands of disobedient people is indicative of how we are blessed. Celebrating in difficult circumstances does not come naturally. It takes discipline. We choose to be glad!

We must add the caution that celebration should be real. It should come from our hearts. Richard Foster warns that we should not pretend to celebrate when the true spirit is not in us, "If we pretend an air of celebration our inward spirit is put in contradiction."[3] He suggests that we will not truly have this celebration until we learn to be, as Paul said it, "Careful for nothing" (Philippians 4:6).

The "deadly sin" of *Sloth* (Latin: *Acedia*) literally means "discouragement." Celebration certainly counteracts discouragement for how can we be discouraged when we are celebrating. Peter Deison tells the parable of the Devil going out of business. The Devil put all his tools up for sale, like bitterness, wrath, jealousy, lust. However, there was one he wanted to keep and would not sell. When asked what it was he said it was discouragement, because it works on anyone, at anytime, and is his most effective tool.[4]

Celebration reverses discouragement, and is God's effective tool for us. In celebration, we choose to see everything with grace-tinted glasses. We are careful for nothing.

Fasting (vs. Pride, Gluttony)

Probably this discipline is the most misused by either neglect or misapplication. There are many of us who understand the benefit and the proper use of fasting, and yet rarely do it; and there are others who do it, but for the wrong reasons. Those who understand it correctly and do it regularly might be a small group.

We can define spiritual fasting as limiting the intake of food or drink for spiritual reasons. Its primary purpose is to train the spirit while training the body. When we fast, our natural man screams for attention, and this can remind us to give our spiritual attention to God.

Fasting fine-tunes our body and spiritual senses. I have found that when fasting, my body seems to grow increasingly alert and efficient. The neglect of food seems to remove toxins from my system so that I feel better than before. However, these natural effects are not as important as what is happening to my spiritual man. When I fast, my spiritual "sense" is tuned. My prayers are more consecrated, my worship more free, and my awareness of God's purifying action on my weaknesses is vivid.

Fasting does not bring spiritual benefit because we are punishing ourselves. God is not interested in our self-abuse. Rather, fasting enhances our spiritual perception because we have removed the desire to constantly feed our appetite.

It is alarming that even though the Bible refers to fasting often as a normative part of the sanctified life, we have neglected it in theory and in practice. We should remember that Jesus said to His disciples, "When you fast..." (Matthew 6:16-17), which indicates that He believed it should be a practice for all of His disciples.

The practicing Jew in the First Century often fasted once a week. The proud Pharisee of Jesus' parable in Luke 18 announced "unlike other men" he "fasted *twice* a week" (Luke 18:12)! Even so, there is no biblical evidence for a specific number of times to fast. The Lord has left that to our discernment. What we hope to do in this brief section is define the fast scripturally, and then set out a guide for its practice.

One remarkable facet of fasting is its change in meaning from the Old Testament to the New. In the Old Testament, fasting was linked to mourning. There was an element to it that was sacrificial, and so, expectant of blessing. For example, because of King David's illicit relationship with Bathsheba, their child lay dying. David's response was to fast and mourn, "David therefore inquired of God for the child; and David fasted and went and lay all night on the ground" (2 Samuel 12:16). However, the child died as God had promised. When David found this out, contrary to his servant's fears, he did not fall further into mourning but released himself from his spiritual duty, "So David arose from the ground, washed, anointed himself, and changed his clothes; and he came into the house of the Lord and worshiped. Then he came to his own house, and when he requested, they set food before him and he ate" (2 Samuel 12:20). His servants were confused and asked why once the child died he did not continue mourning and fasting, and David said, "While the child was still alive, I fasted and wept; For I said, 'Who knows, the Lord may be gracious to me, that the child may live.' But now he has died, why should I fast?" (2 Samuel 12:22-23a). Therefore, fasting was an attempt to purchase God's favor, which was sanctioned for the Old Covenant believers.

However, Jesus showed that the meaning of the fast changed with His work. In the Sermon on the Mount, we have a clear teaching on this subject from the New Covenant perspective:

> Whenever you fast, do not put on a gloomy face as the hypocrites do, for they neglect their appearance so that they will be noticed by men when they are fasting. Truly I say to you, they have their reward in full. But you, when you fast, anoint your head and wash your face so that your fasting will not be noticed by men, but by your Father who is in secret; and your Father who sees what is done in secret will reward you. (Matthew 6:16-18)

Here Jesus was speaking against the improper practice of fasting in His day, which had been corrupted from its Old Testament roots of self-sacrifice to bring about God's favor; to something sinister: self-sacrifice well placed to bring about sympathy and respect for public piety. In these words, Jesus showed us first that fasting should not focus on the one who is fasting. Even though He promised a reward to those who fast secretly, it seems only secondary to the hidden spiritual meaning of the fast. This act of worship focuses outward.

Jesus also showed that fasting had changed in *meaning*, and especially so with His coming death and resurrection. When John's disciples came to ask Him why Jesus' disciples did not fast like them or the like the Pharisees' disciples did, Jesus replied:

> The attendants of the bridegroom cannot mourn as long as the bridegroom is with them, can they? But the days will come when the bridegroom is taken away from them, and then they will fast. But no one puts a patch of unshrunk cloth on an old garment; for the patch pulls away from the garment, and a worse tear results. Nor do people put new wine into old wineskins; otherwise the wineskins burst, and the wine pours out and the wineskins are

ruined; but they put new wine into fresh wineskins, and both are preserved. (Matthew 9:14-17)

The "new wine into the fresh wineskins" is tantamount to a transformation in the meaning of a sanctified life, and therefore a change in the meaning of fasting. In these verses, Jesus was pointing to the victory He would purchase for all people of faith, and since the Bridegroom is gone—and He is ever victorious—our fasting now has a powerful element of rejoicing. We are no longer under the old covenant of recurring sacrifice for sin, but under the new covenant, which offers full and final redemption. Our fasting should always reflect this victory, and we fast for the greater progress of the gospel, and for the benefit of those who labor in His name.

This is not to say that we do not mourn, because we mourn for our sinful selves and because our lost world rejects our Savior. We will mourn other things, such as the loss of loved ones or tragedies in our lives. It would be a good idea to include these ideas of mourning in our fasting. However, even with an element of mourning in our fasting, we must remember that our victory is coming *and* the solution for our tragedies is with us. For after the coming of the Holy Spirit at Pentecost, the Bridegroom is present.

We cannot spend a great deal of time on the actual practice of fasting as that is beyond the scope of this book. However, I would like to touch on a few things that I believe will help.

First, we should be sure that we have a medical "green light" before we fast. That is, we should have no preexisting conditions that might make fasting a danger to our health. (Hunger does not count as a preexisting condition!) For example, diabetics and heart patients should probably avoid fasting altogether. If you think you might need to check on your physical condition, your doctor may be able to give you a recommendation. If you are generally healthy, you could probably proceed with a short fast, maybe by skipping a meal while drinking juice, and monitor your health from there. If everything goes well, then you could extend your fast the next time.

Second, we generally need to feel a burden to fast. Regular fasting can be done without this burden (as the Jews did once a week), but usually fasting is best if we have a burden about some matter that needs spiritual attention. I try to fast about one specific need—e.g. family finances, another person's needs, kingdom advancement—and conclude the fast when the burden is lifted. The answer may not come, but the burden is the key. Attention to a burden in fasting avoids fasting too often (which can harm our health) and fasting without purpose.

Third, we should choose the kind of fast before we begin. There are three kinds of fast: the absolute fast, the partial fast, and the normal fast. The *absolute fast* is that where the person does not eat or drink anything. This fast is biblical (Exodus 34:28) but it is entirely supernatural and I personally do not believe it is called for today. The *partial fast* is that where the person refrains from some food or drink, for example eating only vegetables, or not eating at all and drinking only fruit juices. Daniel practiced the partial fast on several occasions (Daniel 1:1-13, 10:3). Finally, the *normal fast* is that which refrains from all food and drink except water.

It is probably best when you are new to the discipline of fasting to begin with a juice fast for a short duration. For example, you could skip one meal and drink nutritious juices as well as water.

My most common fast is the 24 hour normal fast. This would mean I eat one meal on the first day, breakfast for example, and then do not eat until breakfast the next day. During this time, I drink only water.

Fourth, the duration of the fast is flexible. I have personally never had a need to fast longer than three days or 72 hours. If you feel a strong call to a longer fast, you should probably coordinate this with your doctor so you can have regular checkups during the fast.

A longer fast is not necessarily a better fast, but it is sometimes called for because the burden is greater. For example, our fasting in response to some besetting sin may require a longer period to break its power. Another time we may feel that the spiritual work is not finished after we have gone the time originally planned, and feel it necessary to extend the fast. At all times, we should let the length serve the purpose of the fast and avoid falling into legalism.

Finally, New Testament fasting should involve celebration and worship. As we mentioned, the victory that Jesus purchased for us should always be a consideration in our fasting, and so the "gloomy face" (Matthew 6:16) is not called for. We may have often heard the phrase, "Fasting without prayer is just going hungry." This is true, but to neglect rejoicing in our fasting can even make our prayer ineffective.

Prayer (vs. All Seven Deadly Sins)

We will not say a great deal about prayer here because it has been the subject of several chapters already, but prayer is a very high work and worthy of our attention. Prayer is communication with heaven, and since we are heavenly creatures, it connects us to what is our lifeblood. Since Christ lived in the world of corruption and yet completely avoided all taint of corruption, it is to Him we must go to be free ourselves. Communication with Him, connection to Him, will give us victory in this wicked realm.

Foster said that all who walked with God, in the Scripture and out, made prayer the main business of their lives: "For all of these and many more, prayer was no little habit tacked on to the periphery of their lives—it was their lives."[5] People who walk with God find prayer an intricate part of their existence.

It has become clear in this book that I advocate both the "Quiet time" and constant daily prayer as two parts to the whole. We should spend time concentrating on prayer without distractions and we should walk in fellowship with the Lord throughout the day *despite* distractions. Our prayer will not always be perfect but we should stay "connected," for when we are on spiritual autopilot, we have *dis*connected. An unselfish saint has never prayed a bad prayer. Prayer, undertaken seriously, is received perfectly in heaven even when offered by broken vessels. John Calvin said, "Nay, even our stammering is tolerated by God, and pardon is granted to our ignorance as often as anything rashly escapes us: indeed, without this indulgence, we should have no freedom to pray."[6]

Our prayer should be strong or energized (James 5:16). Our prayer is not lackluster, but compassionate and involved. We should not think in facing the challenges of the entire spiritual kingdom that bland piety will be effective. Rather, the subject of our prayers should move us. On the other hand, we should not think that insincere emotion or theatrics are necessary. Emotion alone does not move God, but our faith and righteous concern does.

Paul said simply, "Devote yourselves to prayer" (Col. 4:2a). The Greek verb he used tells us to stay constant, or to persist in prayer. We should heed this command.

Study (vs. Sloth)

Study is important to spiritual maturity because it channels the mind in the right direction. It also helps refine our service to God because it "sharpens our sword." Devotional Bible reading has its place, and as we said in chapter 2 is probably best for the daily quiet time, but we should find time for study, too. If we were to compare Bible reading to skiing, then Bible study would be more like scuba diving.

Many passages of Scripture will need our study to understand fully. When we read the Bible, it will be normal to find some passage that will pique our interest. We should write the reference down, and come back to it when we have time. What we will do with the reference is an *exposition* of the Scripture, and is the main ingredient of all good sermons. We can use concordances, Bible dictionaries, commentaries, cross-references, and the many other Bible study tools available to help. Diving deep into a passage or passages is an adventure in discovery, for when we begin looking deeply, more avenues that are interesting open to our interest.

Sometimes, it is best to do a *topical* study, which is where we seek out a subject (topic) and find all the information about it that is possible. For example, if you have wondered why the Scripture speaks clearly against divorce, you could chase down related Bible references to it. When you get a feel for God's connection of sacred marriage to the fidelity that Christ has with the church, you will begin to understand the seriousness of the subject. You might want to understand love for humankind more deeply, so you could begin with 1 Corinthians 13, and work out from there to the many Bible references to love and its characteristics.

In any case, our discovery should lead to life-change, for that is why we study. We do not study only to gain knowledge, though that is a fine goal. Our gain in knowledge should lead us to follow God more faithfully and ultimately to be equipped to lead others in this same way.

At other times, we would find it helpful to do an in depth study of a *passage*. For example, we might do an extended study on the contrast of the deeds of the flesh and the fruit of the Spirit found in Galatians 5:19-23. This might lead us to want to study further the definition of each of the deeds and fruit listed.

Bible study can take other forms, for example: *word study, language study, background study*, etc. Our interest will increase, and we may find the problem has shifted from not wanting to study, to not having enough time or resources to study all that we wish!

Paul requested that Timothy, his "child in the faith," visit him while he was in prison. He said, "When you come bring the cloak I left at Troas with Carpus, and the books, especially the parchments" (2 Timothy 4:13). Paul needed the cloak to fend against the cold, but we get the impression that this was only secondary to his having his valuable papyri and parchments so that he might spend his time enjoying and producing through the Word of God.

Simplicity (vs. Greed, Lust)

The discipline of simplicity counters the counsel of this world that we need more *things*—that constant accumulation is a normal way to live. All three synoptic gospels (Matthew, Mark, and Luke) record Jesus cautioning the disciples as He sent them out, "Do not acquire gold, or silver, or copper for your money belts, or a bag for your journey, or even two coats, or sandals, or a staff; for the worker is worthy of his support" (Matthew 10:9-10). This instruction is exclusive to the disciples in certain ways, as we are not all commanded to go out with such meager possessions. However, the underlying command is for all of us, "Do not find your substance in anything of material substance!"

Today, we are bombarded with the message that we need to have anything new, with updated bells and whistles, and we need it *now*. In my home, we use our material possessions until they *die*. Our cars, for example, are worth very little when we finally sell them; we use them until they are costing us too much to maintain. We do not replace them in order to keep up with the current models or to impress others. This principle applies to all material things, as Foster says to the perceived need to stay fashionable with our clothes, "Hang the fashions."[7] When we are payed well in our jobs, it is wise to use that to keep our clothes in good repair and updated, but this is different from following the fashions.

We can show simplicity in more than our material possessions. An unadorned life, economy of speech, and generosity with the abundance we already have are expressions of this discipline. As we practice simplicity, our desires begin to change. We no longer *need* the things that so drive other people. No longer enslaved by the things we possess, we find ourselves to be the free creatures God designed us to be.

To be simple people in a world that prizes complexity will cause tension. We may feel alienated from the mad rush to be "worried and bothered about so many things" (Luke 10:41). We need to remember that we have chosen the better part. Furthermore, if you are living simply, some well-meaning folks may want to give you their used clothes (leaving you to wonder if your clothes have aged too much!). If appropriate, accept the gift graciously. On the other hand, if a person criticizes your choice to simplify, gently remind them that you find joy in simplicity and you are entirely satisfied with what you have.

Submission (vs. Pride, Envy, Wrath)

In his imaginative book *The Screwtape Letters*, C. S. Lewis has a senior demon by the name of Screwtape teaching a subordinate demon named Wormwood the finer points of temptation. Once Screwtape tells Wormwood to try to get the Christian he is targeting to begin thinking about his humility, even to actually catch himself in an act of humility, and therefore have *pride* in his humility![8] Sadly, we all tend to be proud of our humility. The idea of *submission* is less subject to distortion for either we are submissive or we are not.

The spiritual discipline of submission requires our willingness to let others be first. This can only happen when we desire to be pleasing to the Lord and so put *Him* first. True submission to others can begin only with our submission to our Father in heaven.

Furthermore, submission must be a way of life rather than an occasional effort. To learn submission we must apply it at all times. If not, we could be using it as a tool for promotion or praise.

Foster says that every spiritual discipline has a corresponding freedom, and that of submission is "the ability to lay down the terrible burden of always needing to get our own way."[9] We discover new life when we end the hard quest to be treated rightly.

All of us will face oppression. When other people hurt us, it is often unintentional. At other times, it can be vicious. In either circumstance, I have found it helpful to *visualize* submissively bowing my head (we can actually do this with our heads up). For example, we should bow our heads in submission when others are unkind. We can bow our heads before the difficult circumstances of life. We bow our heads when we must follow morally suspect earthly governments. We should always begin by bowing our heads before the sovereign will of God. We are promised that when we are patient before mistreatment, that God Himself will not only take care of it, He will take care of *us* (see Joel 2:25-26; Psalm 23:5; Matthew 5:11-12; 1 Peter 2:23).

There are limits to submission. Submission itself can be sinful. When submitting would become destructive, we should humbly refuse to submit. The prophets are the best example, as they simply would not do what wicked people wanted them to do. At times, we advance the progress of the kingdom of God by our *refusal* to submit. We should be careful here not to resist according to our selfish needs, but only according to discernment as to what is right in God's eyes.

Service (vs. Pride, Envy, Sloth)

There are not many words synonymous with our Christian calling more than *service*. It defined our Master's work, it defines our relationship to Him, and it is what He called us to do in reference to others.

Jesus said of Himself, "The Son of Man did not come to be served, but to serve, and give His life a ransom for many" (Matthew 20:28). He provided a template for everything we do. He exemplified a life of seeking people in need of ministry.

First, we are *His* servants. The word most often used in the New Testament to describe our service to God is *doulos,* sometimes *sundoulos,* which means respectively "slave" or "fellow slave." It may not be politically correct to say that we are *slaves* to Jesus, but it is biblically correct. Service must start with glad service to our Lord. Donald Whitney said, "It was the unwillingness to serve God that once turned some angels into demons."[10]

Second, when we consider service to humankind we find the word most often used in the New Testament is *diakonos*, which is the word from which we derive the English word *deacon*. The word in different forms appears some 36 times in the New Testament and is rarely used for the church officer that we are familiar with, but most often to describe the regular Christian. The word means, literally, "through dust." This probably refers to the dust that caked the servants feet (because of open-toed sandals), or is a reference to the dust that was raised in their travels. In the Greek world, the servants so named were often table-waiters. Their occupation was to help others in more exalted positions.

It has been said, "A man wrapped up in himself makes a very small bundle." Serving, which focuses outward, is one of the best ways to enlarge us. Our serving can take many forms and is as varied as the needs of others around us, but we should always think of our service as first to God and then to our fellow man (Matthew 4:10).

Worship (vs. Pride)

Worship is part of everything we do. Once we have become followers of Jesus, our moments are to be filled with the adoration of God.

True worship has many benefits. It weakens our tendency toward self-preoccupation and self-adoration. It will give clear insight (relief?) into the things that we hate and fear, just as it will temper our view of the things we *love* (including such wholesome things as our devotion to our families or careers). As worship permeates our spirits and we breathe divine air, we become balanced, centered, right.

Worship can be defined simply as honoring and adoring God. It is the activity of the spiritually observant. Consider the passage in Revelation where the Four Living Beings, who most likely represent all living creatures and the created order, together with the twenty-four elders, who may represent all of the saints of the ages, bow before the throne of God in heaven saying, "Holy, Holy, Holy, is the Lord God, The Almighty, Who was and Who is and Who is to come" (Revelation 4:8). They do not cease to give God this praise. If this, then, is the activity of heaven, it should be our activity, too.

Worship not only gives praise where praise is due, it draws the worshiper into eternal music. When we worship we respond to God, for it is He that "seeks" worshipers (John 4:23). So, all beneficial worship begins in God's heart as He draws us.

It is perhaps necessary to say that worship should be happening for each of us everywhere and at all times, not just when we gather in church. If our worship were to be limited to when we gather, then we are impoverished—

even as a community of worshipers—for worship should be continuous and individual just as it should be occasional and communal.

Our faithful worship throughout the week will enhance our worship together. Worship is at its most powerful moment when God's people gather. Jesus told us that He was in our "midst" when we gather, and that if we agree together in prayer, what we ask "will be done" for us (Matthew 18:19-20). The Lord also reminds us to gather in "His name." This is what moves the hand of God. When a church is obedient and seeking God's glory in worship, He will answer in power. When the church gathers to pray for the advancement of the kingdom, or the increased holiness and protection for the gathered saints, mighty answers are expected! Were the church to gather to pray for selfish reasons, there is no guarantee of God's blessing.

Giving (vs. Greed, Envy)

The institutional church has received a bad rap. Some people, usually those who do not go to church, think that churches are "just after my money." Some churches and televised ministries give credence to this because they are often making appeals for financial help. It takes money to operate any ministry (just as it does for other organizations that people do not gripe about so much), so appealing for funds is necessary. Nevertheless, Christian organizations ought to seek to be aware of the impression they are making and trust more to God's provision than to impassioned pleading.

Having said that, we need to be reminded that giving is a spiritual discipline. We need to learn to be willing to give of our financial means to good causes, and especially for the advancement of God's kingdom work.

The Bible unapologetically calls for God's children to be ready to give. When Jesus pointed out the widow and her giving her small amount to the temple treasury, all she had to live on, He praised her. It seems at first glance to be irresponsible for her to give everything she had, but Jesus commended her action (Mark 12:41-44). It should leave an impression on us that Jesus elevated her gift over all the other wealthy people because of the *sacrifice* she made. Her small gift might have meant very little to the treasury of the temple but it meant everything in revealing the treasure of her heart.

Paul wrote to the Corinthian church, "Now this I say, he who sows sparingly will also reap sparingly, and he who sows bountifully will also reap bountifully. Each one must do just as he has purposed in his heart, not grudgingly or under compulsion, for God loves a cheerful giver" (2 Corinthians 9:6-7).

Giving of our resources certainly helps the churches, benevolent organizations, or needy persons to whom we give, however, the greatest advantage might be to us. When we give, we release our hold on what holds us, for our material possessions can be tyrannical in their control. For example, we should remember how much that financial setback—the large car repair bill, the storm damage, the falling stock market—*devastated* us. We hold on very firmly to what we possess.

When we give, we are giving God controlling interest in all that is ours. We are releasing our hold on what we have, actually declaring personal freedom, and at the same time are sharing with someone else who will be blessed by receiving it. That seems like a win-win proposition.

There is more! God "loves a cheerful giver!" We will reap when we give. We do not know how it will come, but we do know that our cheerful giving will result in bounty.

We also need to remember that our giving includes more than our finances. Our talents, our skills, our knowledge—everything is to be used by God. One commodity that we feel we have so little of yet we need to be ready to give is our time. Whitney says, "If we are going to be like Jesus, we must see the use of our time as a Spiritual Discipline. Having so perfectly ordered His moments and His days, at the end of His earthly life Jesus was able to pray to the Father, 'I have brought you glory on earth by completing the work you gave me to do' (John 17:4)."[11]

Since our time is valuable, we are often selfish with it. Think of the father who can lavish money on his children but cannot give himself to them. We must free ourselves from this oppressive control of the minutes of our days. Our time is not always our own, we need to release it and give it in service to God and man.

Purity (vs. Lust)

Job said, "I have made a covenant with my eyes; How then could I gaze at a virgin?" (Job 31:1). I have not seen purity included as a spiritual discipline, although I think it should be, even more as today as the presence of impurity is so prevalent. I am amazed at the rank levels to which our society has fallen and the excuses we make for exploiting sexual appetites for business or pleasure. For example, one of the primary "conservative" news websites in America has its click-through galleries every news day with salacious pictures. Today, I checked (without clicking!) and found these *news* items: "Playboy Pose Gets Jailer Fired," "MTV Video Vixen Round-up," "How to Pleasure a Woman," "Blushing Bikini Brides," with clickable photo galleries, of course. I only wish this kind of display was an exception, but it is not.

The word from which we get the word "lust" of the seven deadly sins is *luxuria*, and it literally means "extravagance." The discipline of simplicity deals with this tendency overall; however in the sexual realm, the discipline of purity is the best weapon.

There are body parts of members of the other sex—who are not our spouse—that we should not purposely look at and certainly not *gaze* at. Since dress tends to immodesty today, it is a discipline for us like Job to "make a covenant with our eyes." If someone is revealing more of their form than they should (right before our eyes), then we should concentrate on something else.

We should also be sure our own personal attire is modest. In this way, we give no fuel for someone else's fire. We have all seen people dressed in our churches in a way that leads to the sin of almost every innocent person in their path (lust for some, jealousy for others). Who has the greater sin: the one who fell into it accidentally or the one who perpetrated it, however unintentionally?

We should also guard our purity in what we read, what movies we see, and what recreation we pursue. There is no area of life untouched by this discipline.

Purity is a way of life. If we learn to stay prayerfully alert and unwilling to compromise, we have gone a long way to guarding ourselves against sexual sin.

In conclusion, we can explain the benefit of the spiritual disciplines in two simple ways: they put us into God's purview, where God's nature can become our nature; and they take us out of the arena of the flesh, where Satan, the world and the flesh can weaken our spiritual resolve. Since nothing can be done perfectly on man's side, we are trying through these disciplines to allow the Holy Spirit to work His perfection in *us*.

For this reason, I am a little uncomfortable with the phrase "spiritual disciplines," since it is not man's side that is in view, but God's. This phrase seems to suggest our discipline is the focus, and it is not. We might consider these the "spiritual avenues," "spiritual doorways," or some such thing, so that we remember that they put us in the realm of the Lord where He changes us. The word *discipline* has an austere ring to it, and though I am comfortable with discipline, we would be wise to see the spiritual disciplines as *opportunities*. When we grasp the wonder they introduce us to, we will be throwing these doors open more frequently, with joy.

---

1. Rick Warren, *The Purpose-Driven Church: Growth Without Compromising Your Message & Mission* (Grand Rapids: Zondervan, 1995), 348.

2. Michael Scott Horton, ed., *Power Religion: The Selling Out of the Evangelical Church?* (Chicago: Moody Press, 1992), 14.

3. Richard Foster, *Celebration of Discipline: The Path to Spiritual Growth* (San Francisco: Harper and Row, Publishers, 1978), 166.

4. Peter V. Deison, *The Priority of Knowing God: Taking Time With God When There is No Time* (Grand Rapids: Discovery House Publishers, 1990), 124.

5. Foster, *Celebration of Discipline,* 31.

6. John Calvin, *Institutes of the Christian Religion* (Edinburgh: Edinburgh Printing Company, 1845), 2:475.

7. Foster, *Celebration of Discipline,* 79.

8. C.S. Lewis, *The Screwtape Letters,* rev. ed. (1960; repr., New York: Macmillan Publishing Company, 1982), 63.

9. Foster, *Celebration of Discipline,* 97.

10. Donald S. Whitney, *Spiritual Disciplines for the Christian Life* (Colorado Springs, Colorado: Navpress, 1991), 112.

11. Ibid., 126.

Section 6: What We Can Overcome

"Faith Is the Victory"

CHAPTER 13

Loosing Worry's Grip

Alfred E. Neuman, the poster child of *Mad Magazine*, was occasionally pictured in ignorant bliss saying, "What, me worry?" The inference is that intellectually lazy people do not worry. Actually, it is a sign of intellectual and spiritual *vigor* to control worry. (Not counting Mr. Neuman.)

The Word of God makes it abundantly clear that worry is a nonessential, ineffective means of thinking. The late Zig Ziglar who was called "The Prophet of the Sunny Outlook", said negative thinking is "stinkin' thinkin'."[1] It can color other thoughts with a black crayon. Worry strips us of what is essential to effective living; it saps our strength, paralyzes us, and makes us illogical. It is a parasite, but one that we seem to cultivate—a pest that we invite into our lives.

Holiness is possible when the Holy Spirit has freedom to rule in our lives. It should be obvious that when worry is ruling us, the Holy Spirit is not. Worry is a sin because it limits what is beautiful *in* us, namely, God, but also because it inhibits His freedom to work *through* us.

It is possible that we are unclear on what worry is, and so, fail to know when it is dangerous to us. We often use the term in a way that is not what the Bible condemns. I might say, "I worry about my son's education." I could mean that I am *concerned,* or even that I am *planning* to make ends meet for his education. This is not the sin of worry. Joel Gregory said the Bible does not prohibit "foresight...but *foreboding*, not necessary preparation and planning, but constant, useless anxiety."[2]

The sin of worry is like when we used to say a dog "worries" a sock. The dog would take the sock from room to room in the house, bite it, paw it, and bark at it. The dog could spend a long time subduing that sock! It gave much more attention to the sock than deserved. For a dog, this is harmless fun, but when we deal with our troubles this way it is destructive.

A Biblical View of the Sin of Worry

A memorable example of the wrongness of worry is recorded in the Gospel of Luke, the only Gospel to mention the event. Jesus knew His time was near, and that He would go to Jerusalem to begin the end (Luke 9:46). On their way, He and His companions stopped for a rest:

Now as they were traveling along, He entered a village; and a woman named Martha welcomed Him into her home. She had a sister called Mary, who was seated at the Lord's feet, listening to

His word. But Martha was distracted with all her preparations; and she came up to Him and said, "Lord, do You not care that my sister has left me to do all the serving alone? Then tell her to help me." But the Lord answered and said to her, "Martha, Martha, you are worried and bothered about so many things; but only one thing is necessary, for Mary has chosen the good part, which shall not be taken away from her." (Luke 10:38-42)

The village in this story was Bethany. It seemed the house was Martha's, and she had invited Jesus to stay. Though Martha was doing a good thing in making preparations, as Jesus was a guest, Mary was doing what was better—she sat rapt in attention to the Master's teaching. To Martha's request that Jesus command Mary to help, Jesus gently—using the introduction, "Martha, Martha"—suggested that Martha stop bustling and *relax*.

Jesus cautioned Martha that she was "worried and bothered." The word *Merimnao* translated here as "worried" means to take thought or be anxious. "Anxious expectation" might be a good definition. Max Lucado says that since this compound word literally means to *divide the mind*, "the result is half-minded living."[3] The second word *Thorybazō*, translated here as "bothered," means being encumbered or upset. These words together present the biblical idea of worry: being burdened with anxious thoughts, which often result in nervous deeds.

Mary was listening to the words of the Master, who would be on earth only a short time; Martha was taken with household chores. In all fairness, we might be more like Martha, as our thoughts of disaster (even household disasters) often cause us to miss the very presence of God. Mary was a good example as she focused on what was important.

Jesus showed an even stronger contrast to Martha's anxiety. Though He knew as He headed to Jerusalem His great suffering would soon begin, He had the time and presence of mind to communicate the need for joy in the moment. He pointed out that Mary, in listening to the teaching of what is eternal, was on the right track. Commentators have noticed that though Jesus had the enormous task of bringing redemption to the entire world, He was never in a hurry. There is no place in the Scripture where He was rushed, on the contrary, He often stopped to help people when others seemed pressured to meet schedule (See Matt 14:13-21, Matthew 20:29-34, Mark 10:13-16).

When we worry as Martha did, we are anxious, hurried, inefficient, and we even miss the joy of the journey. Watchman Nee tells a fable in his pamphlet, *Self-knowledge and God's Light*:

There was a centipede talking with a toad. The toad asked the centipede, "You have so many legs, how do you walk? Which leg do you move forward first when you walk?" The centipede then tried to determine which leg moved forward first when it walked. No matter how hard it tried, it could not set its feet right. Afterward, it became tired and said, "I don't care, I'm leaving." When it started to go, it again thought of which leg to move first and this inhibited it from taking any step. After a while, sunshine came through the clouds. When the centipede saw the rays, it became very happy and ran toward the sun, forgetting all about the stepping order of so many legs. Thus, it was able to move once more.[4]

Worry can get us looking at our feet, so to speak.

Why Worry?

Though we all seem to be good at worrying, we ought to ask ourselves why we should. The following passage of Scripture may be one of the best known and least practiced of the Scripture. Jesus spoke these words in the Sermon on the Mount:

No one can serve two masters; for either he will hate the one and love the other, or he will be devoted to one and despise the other. You cannot serve God and wealth. For this reason I say to you, do not be worried about your life, as to what you will eat or what you will drink; nor for your body, as to what you will put on. Is not life more than food, and the body more than clothing? Look at the birds of the air, that they do not sow, nor reap nor gather into barns, and yet your heavenly Father feeds them. Are you not worth much more than they? And who of you by being worried can add a single hour to his life? And why are you worried about clothing? Observe how the lilies of the field grow; they do not toil nor do they spin, yet I say to you that not even Solomon in all his glory clothed himself like one of these. But if God so clothes the grass of the field, which is alive today and tomorrow is thrown into the furnace, will He not much more clothe you? You of little faith! Do not worry then, saying, "What will we eat?" or "What will we drink?" or "What will we wear for clothing?" For the Gentiles eagerly seek all these things; for your heavenly Father knows that you need all these things. But seek first His kingdom and His righteousness, and all these things will be added to you. So do not worry about tomorrow; for tomorrow will care for itself. Each day has enough trouble of its own. (Matthew 6:24-34)

Jesus is telling us that when we are anxious, our very devotion is at stake. He said, "You cannot serve God and wealth" (v. 24). Our worry will cause us to serve what is material, and God is not material. Some themes emerge from these verses:

First, *Worry Is Unprofitable*. When Jesus spoke these words in Matthew, He was aware of the vulnerability of His disciples. It would not be long before they would have the threat of persecution as well as all other concerns over their heads. Therefore, He drew their attention to the birds and the flowers of the field. They, too, are vulnerable. Yet they do not worry, for their Father in Heaven takes care of them. Elizabeth Barrett Browning wrote:

> The little cares that fretted me,
> I lost them yesterday
> Among the fields above the sea,
> Among the winds at play.

Why does the presence or thought of natural things relieve us so? There is a natural sedative in seeing that nature, which is on such an enormous scale, goes on seamlessly in an eternal rhythm. This reminds us of the impermanence of our problems. We gain perspective.

Jesus uses the palette of nature to teach us of the deceptiveness of worry. It will not add to our safety. Verse 27 says, "Which of you by being anxious can add a single cubit to his lifespan?" Can worry lengthen our lifespan? Might it shorten it?

Jesus shows that *worry is unprofitable in nature*. If a robin could speak would it say, "Worms, worms, worms. How can I be sure I will find worms? I have found them every day of my life; but today?", or the flower, "The more I think about it, this blue in my petals just doesn't *go* with all of this green. What will the other flowers say?"

When applied to these natural creatures, worry seems ridiculous. It has no point, and is not necessary.

Jesus shows that *worry is unprofitable in us*. Ultimately, God has not even left the power of provision in our hands, any more than He left it in the hands of the lilies. We will never dress as well as the lilies, and that is the point. Jesus shows that we are greater than the lily—which "tomorrow is thrown into the furnace"—but since the lily always surrenders to the provision of God, He is free to dress it in splendor.

Worry profits nothing! It is not doing us any good. We are accustomed to getting rid of costly things that are not bringing any profit to our lives, so, we should start with worry.

Second, *Worry is Defeating.* Worry is more than unprofitable, it *is aggressively defeating.* An old proverb says, "The bow that is always bent will soon break." Just like the bow, a person that stays under constant tension will eventually break into many pieces.

Worry defeats us because it *dishonors reality.* For example, concerning food, how many of us had parents that starved? Grandparents? Great-grandparents? Can we think of anyone in our family line that starved? Do we know of this happening to anyone in someone else's family line? Certainly, starvation is a very real problem for many people in the world, but for most of us it is so remote, that our fear of not having enough food is not worth the thought.

Worry creates an unshakable negativism; it adds a dark lining to every silver cloud, and can make the glass half-empty, just before it immobilizes us.

Do you remember when you first learned to drive? I do. I was miserable and probably made everyone around me miserable. I would drive down the road thinking: "Watch out for that ditch on the right"; "Oops, a little close to the lane on the left"; "I've got to keep my eyes on three mirrors at once"; "What was that sound?"; "How much do I press this brake pedal?"; "What do you mean I'm going too slow!"

Now, I drive and do not think a thing about it. The reality of driving is much more fun than anxiety about it.

Worry is defeating because it *dishonors God's power.*[5] Jesus asked in verse 25, "Isn't life more than food?" He who created us and purchased our redemption, can He not be trusted to secure our food? When we are anxious, it saddens our Lord for we are looking doubtfully at His ability to provide.

Worry defeats us because it *dishonors God's love.* In verse 26 when He spoke of the birds of the air, Jesus said, "Are you not worth much more than they?" The birds fly about without concern about the future. They instinctively know God cares for them.

I remember when I was young I visited a farm with a group of other children on a school field trip. I remember nothing about the trip except for one vivid event. The farmer told all of us to get inside the stalls in the barn and shut the doors. We could just see over the half-doors for our makeshift theater. He picked up one of the piglets that were running around. That little thing put out much more noise than something that small should. Then we heard a thundering noise and four or five sows each weighing about 300 to 400 pounds were tearing our way. The farmer let the pig go and hopped into a stall. The sows ran into the barn snorting and pacing, willing any of us to step out of our stall. We did not *move.*

If a creature made by God is this alert to the cries of its young, do you think our Creator (who cares for us so much more), will be available when we need Him?

Worry is defeating because *dishonors God's presence*. When we embrace the worries of the future, in effect, we add them to today. Therefore, tomorrow takes over today (v. 34). Jesus is showing us that preoccupation with tomorrow is impractical and shows distrust. He showed us that today has *enough* trouble, and He will take care of tomorrow.

For those who are parents, it is like our children fretting about their future and welfare while we are in the room. If our repeated assurance of our protection were not to relieve them, it would reflect on us. It would be heart breaking. It must be so for God, who is so much more able to take care of us.

How can we stay on the right path in this journey of holiness if we banish God from our consciousness? Only God can bring holiness to bear on our lives, and since worry effectively resists Him and stifles His Spirit, how shall we continue in holiness if we choose to be anxious?

Third, *Worry is Conquerable*. Now for the good news! We can defeat worry with God's help. The Master told us in verse 33 to, "Seek first His kingdom...and all these things will be added unto you." He promised to provide everything we need. He said, "Seek His righteousness."

Livermore said, "Other things being equal, the good man prospers better in worldly affairs than the bad man. All vices are expensive and losing, as all the virtues are gainful and thrifty."[6] Even if we did not believe, biblical truths would cause us to live well. When we add belief to virtuous living, it becomes markedly better; for when we believe in God's power and providence we have true faith, and an awareness of greater resources. We will need strength to face all of life's challenges, and by faith, we can choose to keep the energy that worry would steal.

Jesus said, "Observe how the lilies of the field grow" (v. 28). Human power can artificially dress kings, but God dresses the lilies who surpass the richest and most glorious king who ever lived. Who would we want to dress our life?

Spiritual Vision Is Needed

A true absence of worry is possible when we are completely relaxed in the hands of Jesus, but it will require our positive imagination.

Why did Jesus rebuke the disciples on the Sea of Galilee? We remember the story from Matthew 8:24-27, where the disciples were sure they were going to perish when a storm blew up, threatening to swamp them. They saw the effect of the winds; they heard and felt it. Every physical sense they had (and we might include "good sense") told them they were in danger. When they shook Jesus awake—who was fast asleep!—He asked them, "Why are you afraid, you men of little faith?" What is Jesus pointing to when He speaks of "little faith"?

Many times since the recording of this event, good people have been on ships in a storm. Many have also tragically lost their lives, and it must have been terrifying. Is Jesus saying that it shows little faith to fear such a catastrophe, even while it is happening? I do not believe so. What Jesus was speaking to was specific: the disciples had *the Master in the boat*. He was not finished with His work on earth, and they should have known that. Nothing would take Jesus until God was ready, because of this—the disciples were safe *with Him*.

When the Master is with us in the boat, there is nothing whatsoever to worry about. We may not be saved in our particular circumstance (ultimately this is not for us to determine), but we can be faithful when we have rested our welfare, quietly, in Jesus' hands.

Did Jesus have weak faith when He walked to the cross? Certainly not, there could be no greater evidence of faith on earth. Even though He walked to His death, faith won out because God was "in the boat," so to speak. Jesus had already dealt with His deep agony in the Garden of Gethsemane. He had given Himself over to the Father's will and the result in this case was suffering, the end of His earthly life, and though Jesus agonized in prayer, He did not fret.

The Apostle Paul wrote in Philippians 4:6-7, "Be anxious for nothing, but in everything by prayer and supplication with thanksgiving let your requests be made known to God. And the peace of God, which surpasses all comprehension, will guard your hearts and your minds in Christ Jesus." If we pray rather than being anxious, we will be able to understand the near presence of the Lord. The peace of God indeed passes understanding, for how often we fear and grow agitated just before we encounter His presence then to become unusually calm. We should agonize in prayer if necessary, while not agonizing over our circumstances.

Consider another biblical example when the enemies of Elisha had him surrounded. The king of Aram had plotted to capture Elisha and he had found out that he was staying in Dothan:

Now when the attendant of the man of God had risen early and gone out, behold, an army with horses and chariots was circling the city. And his servant said to him, "Alas, my master! What shall we do?" So he answered, "Do not fear, for those who are with us are more than those who are with them." Then Elisha prayed and said, "O Lord, I pray, open his eyes that he may see." And the Lord opened the servant's eyes and he saw; and behold, the mountain was full of horses and chariots of fire all around Elisha. When they came down to him, Elisha prayed to the Lord and said, "Strike this people with blindness, I pray." So He struck them with blindness according to the word of Elisha. (2 Kings 6:15-18)

I am not suggesting that we seek miraculous visions like this, because this was God's choice for this specific incident. What I *am* suggesting is that we cultivate spiritual vision that does not rely on what we see in our circumstances, but on what the Word of God tells us. Spiritual *and* physical blindness caused the Aramean army to lose, and they had to slink back home as a result of Elisha's prayer. The armies of God do not fight with sword and shield; they change events and drive terror into the heart of the enemy.

We need to remember that our troubles, very real indeed, tend to overtake our imagination. This leads to our anxiety. We can dream up all kinds of horrible ends! Rather, we need to imagine the love of God, the excellence of His purposes, and the promise that He will provide for us. We unleash our imagination to see His armies camped in the surrounding hills.

Think Simply

To summarize, I wish to close this chapter with two simple prescriptive thoughts from the Bible that, when followed, will never fail to conquer worry.

1. *Seek God.* Actually, this is the subject of this book. Seek God in prayer, the Bible, worship, service, etc. "Thou wilt keep him in perfect peace, whose mind is stayed on thee" (Isaiah 26:3). When we seek God, the object is to know and trust Him. Trust is the opposite of worry, and is stronger than worry. Jesus told us to seek first His Kingdom and righteousness, and that worry is "little faith". We exercise our faith by seeking Him.

2. *Seek God's thoughts.* We must identify and eliminate errant thoughts. It may take some time. We can replace these thoughts with good and positive ones. Paul said, "We are destroying speculations and every lofty thing raised up against the knowledge of God, and we are taking every thought captive to the obedience of Christ" (2 Corinthians 10:5). Jesus pointed the disciples to the birds and the lilies; Elisha pointed his servant to the armies of the Lord. We should learn to see things God's way, even to every thought.

In his commentary on Matthew, William Barclay quotes an experience that happened to Tauler, the German mystic:

One day Tauler met a beggar. "God give you a good day, my
friend," he said. The beggar answered, "I thank God I never had a
bad one." Then Tauler said, "God give you a happy life, my
friend." "I thank God," said the beggar, "I am never unhappy."
Tauler in amazement said, "What do you mean?" "Well," said the
beggar, "when it is fine, I thank God; when it rains, I thank God;
when I have plenty, I thank God; when I am hungry, I thank God;
and since God's will is my will, and whatever pleases him pleases
me, why should I say I am unhappy when I am not?" Tauler looked
at the man in astonishment. "Who are you?" he asked. "I am a
king," said the beggar. "Where then is your kingdom?" asked
Tauler. And the beggar answered quietly: "In my heart."[7]

1. Zig Ziglar, *See You At the Top*, rev. ed. (1974; repr., Gretna,
Louisiana: Pelican Publishing Company, Inc., 1976), 31-32.

2. Joel Gregory, *Growing Pains of the Soul* (Waco, Texas: Word Books,
1987), 33.

3. Max Lucado, *Traveling Light* (Nashville: W Publishing Group, 2001),
48.

4. Watchman Nee, *Self-Knowledge and God's Light* (Anaheim,
California: Living Stream Ministry, 1992), 11.

5. W. Sunderland Lewis and Henry M. Booth, eds., *The Preacher's
Homiletic Commentary* (New York: Funk and Wagnalls Company, 1896),
154-155.

6. Ibid., 156. "Livermore" not identified by a first name.

7. William Barclay, *The Daily Study Bible Series: The Gospel of
Matthew*, rev. ed. (1956; repr., Philadelphia: The Westminster Press, 1975),
260-261.

CHAPTER 14

Disabling Our Doubt

As we have seen, certain attitudes if allowed to have a place in our lives will inhibit God's freedom, and so the working of holiness by the Holy Spirit. There are also attitudes that we can practice that will disable these weaknesses. In this chapter, we look at the foundational necessity of faith, just as we take aim at the hindrance of doubt. In looking at worry in chapter 13, we ended the chapter speaking a great deal of faith. Are we being repetitious?

First, we cannot speak too much of faith, since it is the bedrock for our spiritual journey. We should not forget that faith is essential to our success as spiritual people.

Second, we will take a different view in this chapter. We are looking not so much at the lack of faith that causes us to question God's provision, but that which causes us to doubt His very existence. When our faith falters in this area, we lose hope, we begin to distrust God, and we compromise our spiritual strength.

No Help from this World

We are in a world of disbelief. At this writing, the results of a study published by the American Physical Society state that religion might become extinct in some countries. Citing nations that have a makeup of large percentages that are not "affiliated" with any religion (60% in Czech Republic for example), they contend that there is a good possibility that the trend will continue, and in the years to come religion will not exist at all in some of these nations.

As I watched in the single day after a news outlet posted these results online, there were more than 5000 comments, the majority being negative toward faith. The general feeling seems to be: "Great!—religion is hokum"; "I am so glad to hear this"; "Christians are all Neanderthals and backwards." There seems to be no love lost between the world and believers today. Should we expect much help from the world for our faith? Has the world ever provided this comfort?

I once spent some time on an internet site dedicated to atheists and agnostics. Christians were not welcome there, though they accidentally wandered on sometimes where they were good fodder for the other bloggers. I liked to log on and blog for a certain period each day for approximately six months (before the site was shut down because of their defamation of public people). I wanted to see if I could help some of them see the Lord and His people differently. (I also wanted to hone my apologetic skills!)

The viciousness of most of the bloggers was amazing. *Ad hominem* attacks were *de rigueur*. Christians in general were "Idiots," "Neanderthals," "Boobs," "Hayseeds." Personally, they said I was "stupid," "blind," "refusing to grow up." I dealt with the many comers in the realm of ideas (when you are the only Christian on a site with many online unbelievers, you get many opportunities to converse) attempting to defend against their false assumptions and outright lies about the Scriptures and other believers. When I challenged their thinking, and dealt with their questions with what I thought was enlightened discussion, they would not answer my questions, but instead ridiculed me and fell to calling me names.

There is hardly a greater testimony to the wrongheadedness of atheists and agnostics than their refusal to answer some questions, and their virulent behavior and sarcastic diatribes. Many on the website kept repeating the mantra that there were *no intelligent Christians*; that all Christians, by definition, were dim-witted. Granted, not all atheists think this way, but I believe it is sadly characteristic of many of them. Even if I were not a believer, their name-calling and "blanket" statements about Christians and the Bible would be enough for me to question their views.

To make matters worse, as we try to defend the faith our own hearts fight us sometimes. Someone said, "Unbelief is easy." Indeed, it is. We tend to find new challenges to our faith that seem to shake us for a while, only to let go as we find the sunlight again.

The world attacks, the Devil attacks, and our own doubts add to the chorus. One of our favorite hymns says, "Just as I am, tho' tossed about, with many a conflict, many a doubt; fightings within and fears without, O Lamb of God, I come! I come!"

The Christian and Biblical Perspective of Doubt
Doubt in the Bible is literally being of two minds. In the New Testament, the Greek word (*Diakrino*) is a compound word that means to "judge through," or to make distinctions. In some places in the New Testament, it is translated "to judge," or "to discern." When it refers to doubt, it means we can confuse ourselves by contending with ourselves!

It reminds me of the family at a restaurant when the server approached and stood by with her note pad. Everyone ordered, but the youngest boy was having trouble deciding what to eat. His mother said, "Honey, make up your mind!" He said, "That's easy for you because you have one mind. I have *two*!"

Sometimes, all of us have *at least* two minds.

There is a rigid view that may see all doubt as sin. We may not teach this directly while still implying it. Passages like James 1:5-8 cause us to equate all doubt with wickedness, "But if any of you lacks wisdom, let him ask of

God, who gives to all generously and without reproach, and it will be given to him. But he must ask in faith without any doubting, for the one who doubts is like the surf of the sea, driven and tossed by the wind. For that man ought not to expect that he will receive anything from the Lord, being a double-minded man, unstable in all his ways." We should notice this passage is dealing with the question of someone asking for something from God and doubting His willingness or ability to provide, not doubting God's existence.

In his book, *Wrestling with Doubt,* Frank Rees agrees with Søren Kierkegaard that James' discussion is focusing on, "questions of attitude and personal engagement, not theoretical or intellectual issues." Rees understands the rebuke as not dealing with "outright unbelief," but "prayer without conviction, without 'heart.'"[1] This passage in James does not condemn the Christian that occasionally doubts the faith itself. We must look at this phenomenon differently.

It may seem to be a contradiction, but *we can live faithfully while doubting*. Our fidelity to the Lord need not end when we entertain honest questions. A person can be eternally lost by doubting and subsequently rejecting the Lord, but doubt for a believer is not of the same caliber.

In his book *If God is God*, Richard Koenig discusses three categories of doubt: direct, nihilism, and religious doubt. *Direct* attacks are those where someone, usually an atheist or agnostic, tries to refute the teachings or the reality of the Christian confession, including the existence of God himself. *Nihilism*, which Keonig thinks is our most dangerous challenge, would state, "Who cares? It does not matter." Outright attacks are unnecessary.[2]

Nihilism is definitely a great danger, for indifference is a curse of this age. However, things have changed since Koenig wrote this book, and the rise of what some call the *New Atheists* (e.g., Richard Dawson, Sam Harris, and the late Christopher Hitchens), may indicate that direct and sometimes sneering attacks are trendy.

Religious doubt, Koenig says, is that which Christians face. It is not hostile to faith, even though it may go so far as to question the reality of God Himself.

Doubt is not opposite to faith; *settled unbelief* is opposite to faith. This unbelief has decided where doubt is still working it out. Doubt can be an aid to faith. An unquestioning faith is not even admirable because we base our faith partly on evidence; we do not eschew evidence.

There are Christians who are rarely troubled by doubt. This may be a gift of personality or giftedness more than consecration. However, others are plagued by doubt. Although we would never encourage anyone to doubt as a faith-building exercise, our churches should, with love and grace, embrace the honest doubter. We may have been afraid to admit our doubts to each other. If we cannot learn to be honest with other Christians, with whom will we confide? If we will not support our struggling brother or sister, who will?

We should encourage each other to find our solution to doubt while serving faithfully and continuing to respond to God in belief. In this way, we remain in a state of obedience, and can take any time we need to research or pray to lead to the correct conclusions. The Bible can answer our probing, God is not afraid of our questions, but our faithfulness will protect us from error. Koenig said, "Secure in the grace and mercy of God, the Christian in doubt can learn to employ the technique of keeping certain things in abeyance. The believer does not despair each time he encounters some difficulty in faith. If he cannot answer his questions immediately, the Christian can 'put them on ice,' leaving them until more information or study is available...It means the Christian holds his questions in tension with faith and still functions as a Christian...Much of Christianity is this kind of 'believing unbelief.'"[3]

Hebrews 11:6 says, "Without faith it is impossible to please Him." A doubting Christian may think at first that this means he/she is condemned. However, it is hopeful to read further, "For he who comes to God must believe that He is and He is a rewarder of those who seek Him." Ultimately, all Christians believe "He is." When we doubt, we are struggling *while* "seeking Him."

When Jude, the brother of James, wrote his epistle, he warned against those who were "mockers, following after ungodly lusts, those who cause divisions, worldly minded, devoid of the Spirit" (Jude 18-19). Just a few verses later, he told his readers to "have mercy on some who are doubting" (Jude 22). Here are two classes of people. Those who mock or divide are under judgment, but Jude said we are to extend mercy to the honest doubter.

Overview of the Doubts that Disturb Us

It is obvious that we can only deal lightly with so vast a subject. However, we will attempt to do what we can in this section to deal with a few of the areas of doubt that disturb us. These may also be the categories that are most used as accusations by those who are hostile to belief.

The first four categories that follow we should deal with and then mostly leave alone. Their challenge to our sensibility will not change; neither will their answers. Rather than rehash them, it is best to leave them to God's sovereign will.

The last category, that of "settled" science, will need to be revised as we go; simply because scientific discoveries are not static, so neither will be our response.

Our Suffering World. This of course, is an age-old problem. How do we reconcile a loving and all-powerful God with a world filled with suffering?

First, only to see suffering in a negative light is a narrow view. Without suffering, the world would be bland and unable to mature. Suffering can be cleansing.

Jesus is our best example, who needed to suffer death on the cross and rejection by the very men that He came to save in order to purchase redemption. If Jesus must suffer, and yet the result is redemption of all willing people, then that gives us hope concerning our suffering.

Second, Paul taught that suffering was necessary to complete God's work on earth. Jesus fully completed His earthly work, there is nothing left that He needed to do. However, the work of His followers continues. It is necessary for us to suffer, as Paul did, so that God's Kingdom will advance and others might experience blessing (see 1 Corinthians 4:8-13; 2 Corinthians 13:9; Philippians 2:30, 3:10; Colossians 1:24; 2 Timothy 1:8). Note the wars of the past, both secular and sacred, where many gave their lives, their freedom, or their financial reserves, in order that others might enjoy the fruit of that sacrifice today.

Third, suffering is the result of our sin. Adam and Eve chose to discount God's clear warning in the Garden of Eden, and since sin entered the world, the relationship between God and His creation has been marred. Suffering is the opposite of what God desired, but necessary now that we chose our own way. I said it is the result of *our* sin, in that we are collectively responsible. Adam and Eve's failure started this, but our sins are ever before us.

Finally, since God is the ultimate sufferer (witnessed through His Son), then He participates in some way with all pain on earth. How that happens may not be evident, but if creation "groans," then we can be sure that the Creator must also groan with it.

The Seeming Brutality of the Old Testament and God's Fury. When God commanded, for example, that all of the inhabitants of Canaan be destroyed, including those we would consider innocents—small children and animals—our "civilized" souls revolt. In this particular case is a possible answer for all such cases.

In Genesis God told Abram (Abraham) of future events. He said that after Israel had been enslaved to the Egyptians, and had been released, He would bring them into the Promised Land. Abraham himself would not see this, because "the iniquity of the Amorite is not yet complete" (Genesis 15:16; the term Amorite here is synonymous with Canaanite). There would be a time that the sin of the inhabitants of Canaan will have grown to such proportions, that God would take their land from them. He continued this theme in Leviticus, telling the Israelites to stay far away from sins including bestiality, homosexuality, and child sacrifice, "for by all these [sins] the nations which I am casting out before you have become defiled. For the land has become defiled, therefore I have brought its punishment upon it, so the land has spewed out its inhabitants" (Leviticus 18:24-25).

The extermination of this entire race of people was a judicial act. This is also the only way to settle the Promised Land, to prepare for the coming of the Messiah, who would bring the possibility of salvation to *all men*.

A Navy Seal team killed Osama Bin Laden sometime back, and it would be hard to find good people in the world who are sorry he is dead. (Some have questioned the methods of his end, while still being happy he is gone.) Death seems justified for a man who ordered the death of over three thousand innocents, and hoped and planned for many more. We are thrilled that this man no longer lives to bring degradation to others. These annihilated in Canaan had the same stain of iniquity, deserving of death. God Himself said so.

Remember also that the times were different. If I were somehow transported to the brutal days of warfare in Old Testament times and taught modern laws of civilization and fair dealing, my life would likely be short but probably not sweet. The leaders of that day would view me as an insurrectionist. God worked within the times, and He did not change the times as much as He changed hearts. In the New Testament, it was biblical teaching that destroyed slavery in most nations on earth, even though the Bible did not attack the institution directly. The Bible taught the equality of all men *and* the understanding of women as equal in value to men, but it did not upset the entire culture to do this.

The teaching of the Scripture is largely responsible for our modern concept of civilization. God, who called for the death of many people, for certain purposes in the Old Testament, revealed principles in His Word that causes us to be horrified at the thought today. What can seem brutal to us was business as usual in those days. This is not to suggest that God lowered His moral standards, but that He worked within the order of society in that day to bring His will to pass.

We also need to consider whether our society really *is* more civilized and less brutal. We are guilty of ending many innocent lives in the womb, and worldwide warfare and conflict seems to be our happy habit. It is sometimes not even safe to go to school anymore as children bring weapons and mow each other down. This is our legacy of compassion. Some of the greatest horrors of our cruelty against each other have happened in the last century. God ordered none of these slaughters, by the way, we did them all by ourselves.

Finally, we must take into account the "gap fixed" between our thoughts and those of God whenever we attempt to understand His actions. The wandering ant that crawls up on the pulpit while the preacher preaches to the congregation has no concept, indeed cannot, of the proceedings going on. The ant is only aware of the food he wishes to find, he does not know that the person preaching is testifying of the goodness of God. There is no communication because of the enormous difference in awareness between them. Yet, the gap between the ant and the preacher is miniscule compared to the gap between the preacher and the Creator. Where the preacher and the ant are definable creatures, God is infinite and beyond description. His thinking is beyond our comprehension—even, or especially so, when we try to apply to Him the rules of good behavior.

What is permissible for God is not necessarily permissible for His creatures. It would not be for us to go and make such decisions as the annihilation of an entire group of people. God Himself gave us our sense of morality, and we can be sure He does not violate that even when He shows His fury and commands destruction.

Hell. The concept of hell as presented by the Bible causes difficulty for believers and unbelievers alike. Seekers present a variation of the question, how it would be righteous for God to damn a person eternally for refusing to believe in Him, when He "hides Himself." Some Christians have tried to find an alternative approach like softening hell by turning it into some kind of temporary state, repackaging it as total annihilation rather than perpetual suffering, or simply excluding the idea altogether.

However, God's Word unapologetically presents the reality of hell.

It is hard to know for sure what hell is actually like, except that it is a horrible place. In the Bible it is often described as fiery, or a *lake of fire*. However, this may not be literal, as "fire" often indicates judgment rather than a physical reality (see James 3:6). In Revelation where the references to the "lake of fire" occur, symbolic language is the norm and needs careful interpretation.

This is no comfort, however, as the word for hell that the writers of the New Testament use, and which Jesus uses frequently, is *Gehenna*. This refers to the valley of Hinnom, which was the place where the people of Jerusalem threw their garbage, including dead animals, and where fires were kept burning to destroy the refuse. When the wind blew the right/wrong way, people in Jerusalem would understand the illustration well.

Hell is a bad place.

Keep in mind why it is this way. It is a place where none of the light, life, and goodness of God will penetrate. *Nothing* that is joyful, praiseworthy, and beautiful will exist in this dread place. Furthermore, people choose this place for themselves.

In Romans, Paul tells us, "For the wrath of God is revealed from heaven against all ungodliness and unrighteousness of men *who suppress the truth in unrighteousness,* because that which is known about God is evident within them; for God made it evident to them. For since the creation of the world His invisible attributes, His eternal power and divine nature, have been clearly seen, being understood through what has been made, so that they are without excuse" (Romans 1:18-20, emphasis added). Recall that Jesus said, "For God so loved the world, that He gave His only begotten Son, that whoever believes in Him shall not perish, but have eternal life. *For God did not send the Son into the world to judge the world, but that the world might be saved through Him.* He who believes in Him is not judged; he who does not believe has been judged already, because he has not believed in the name of the only begotten Son of God" (John 3:16-18, emphasis added).

It is clear that God desires all people to be with Him eternally. His love excludes no person on earth; He sacrificed His very Son in order to pay the frightful penalty that separates us from Him. Some, to their peril, turn their back on His generous offer and choose for themselves a permanent existence that is apart from all life, which would necessarily be permanent death. The result is the horror of hell.

To the questions that arise concerning those who "have not heard," we reiterate that the Word of God says they have *no excuse* (Romans 1:20). However, when we still wonder, we have to rest our concerns on the fact that God is fair in a way that we can only imitate. We leave final rulings to Him knowing that He is eternally just.

The Silence and Hiddenness of God. If God wants all to believe, why not just reveal Himself, even a little? He did to the Old Testament saints, why not to us?

It must be true that "blessed are those who have not seen, and yet believe," because it is certainly more difficult. I read recently where someone said what he obviously thought was a withering answer as to why he did not believe in God: he could not believe in what he cannot see or test.

God is frustratingly hidden and sometimes excessively quiet. We need to try to understand why this is so.

I remember when Jesus told how the rich man in torment asked that Lazarus, the man he ignored in life, would be sent to warn the rich man's brothers so they would not end up like him. Jesus said, "If they do not listen to Moses and the Prophets, they will not be persuaded even if someone rises from the dead" (Luke 16:31).

James speaks of the man who looks in a mirror and forgets what he looks like as soon as he turns away (James 1:24). He is applying this in another context, which we will get to in a moment. However, we can apply his illustration here. Try to stop and think right now what you look like! Without a mirror or a photograph, we are only vaguely able to remember our appearance. It is the same with direct intervention. God steps in and we are sure we will never doubt again…but we do.

The Israelites are prime examples. When God revealed Himself, it was in rare occasions of national need, in order to set the future standard. He usually revealed Himself to the leaders of Israel, rather than the "congregation." Still, even when the entire congregation saw miracle after miracle, like through the period of the Exodus, it was only a matter of time before they were sinning again with abandon. God's silence and hiddenness can actually cause our faith to grow in strength. If we were to see more, like the Israelites, we might trust less.

In Psalm 10, the psalmist struggled with the hiddenness of God. He asked God in verse one, "Why do you stand far off, and why do you hide in times of trouble?" This agonized question is often on righteous lips. The psalmist turned his attention to what seems to be the prosperity of the wicked and said, "The wicked, in the haughtiness of his countenance, does not seek Him. All his thoughts are, 'there is no God'…He says to himself, 'God has forgotten, He has hidden His face; He will never see it'" (vv. 4,11). The wicked here do not *want* to see God, and are hoping that He does not see their deeds! However, the righteous psalmist concludes, "You have seen it, for You have beheld mischief and vexation to take it into Your hand…O Lord, You have heard the desire of the humble, You will strengthen their heart, You will incline Your ear" (vv. 14,17). This is an important point: the psalmist does not place his faith in what he sees (v. 1), because he sees very little relief from trouble, he puts his faith in what he knows that *God* sees. Righteous people do not live according to experience alone; they learn to build their hope on the promises of God.

We will deal with this subject at length in chapter 16, but the silence and hiddenness of God is part of His plan. We cry out for revelation sometimes—we want to make the right decision, to take the right path, to glorify the Lord—but still He is silent, distant. In this, God is giving us the opportunity to choose Him, and His silence is sometimes the very thing that can lead to our maturity in trusting Him.

The Contradiction of Biblical Writings to "Settled" Science. In Christian philosopher Alvin Plantinga's article "Darwin Mind and Meaning," he uses similar quotes from two prominent atheists that show what we are up against in the area of science. Daniel Dennett wrote in his book *Darwin's Dangerous Idea,* "To put it bluntly but fairly, anyone today who doubts that the variety of life on this planet was produced by a process of evolution is simply ignorant—inexcusably ignorant." In a *New York Times* book review

Richard Dawkins wrote, "It is absolutely safe to say that if you meet someone who claims not to believe in evolution, that person is ignorant, stupid, or insane (or wicked, but I'd rather not consider that)."[4] Here is the hurtling train that the Devil has used to undermine our faith. The belief that life on earth has evolved, without the need of creation, is a virulent doubt producer today. This hypothesis has become the sword used to eviscerate belief. It is not a desultory battle but an organized all-out war.

I do not think that we can be too strong on alerting people to the fallacy of the teaching of godless evolution. However, we need to be careful to define our terms.

We do believe that change takes place, and that survival-of-the-fittest (natural selection) goes on, even in observable ways. Predators pick off weaker animals, which cull the herd; bacteria develop resistance against some antibiotics and vaccines; some animal species have become stronger, larger, and more resistant to disease; humans have developed a more advanced cognitive function in light of natural challenges. We also purposely use selective breeding to produce, for example, better horse or dog breeds designed for a particular purpose. We affirm this kind of change, often called microevolution, or variation *within* kinds. However, this is not what the term evolution has come to mean today.

Evolutionary science teaches that new genetic material was passed on as the result of adaptive changes, mutations, or even as proposed by the late Stephen J. Gould, *punctiliar equilibrium* (bursts of change), causing the earliest life forms to evolve and eventually result in humans, as well as all the other creatures on earth. Where the creationist allows for a rearranging or separating of *existing* genetic information, this evolutionary model accepts the addition of a large amount of *new* genetic information. This evolutionary explanation of human origins leaves little room for the God of creation.

Some Christians incorporate the evolutionary model into biblical teaching (theistic evolution), but I have yet to find a convincing example where this works. The Bible's clear statements that God created Adam and Eve separately and subsequently from the rest of creation, brought this about with His breath of life, and established them to be in dominion over creation, seems to preclude human evolution from lower forms (Genesis 1:26-31, 2:7).

Putting aside strictly scientific or theological discussions, we should point out that both sides make assumptions.[5] I believe biblical assumptions are more reasonable.

The evolutionists assume that life began spontaneously, mutations occurred favorably, the earth is old enough for these enormous changes to happen, and we are simply advanced and evolved animals.

Those who teach creation or intelligent design assume: life must have been designed, because it is far too complicated to have happened by chance; the sheer variety and beauty of the created order points to a Creator; there is no observable evidence that supports mutations resulting in new genetic material; and man is a special and separate creation.

We have to ask some obvious questions to test the assumptions of evolution:

1. Why are humans so advanced in adaptation over all the other creatures?

Did the others not get the survival-of-the-fittest memo? (I raise this question, while sitting in a home, in an ultra-modern city, fully clothed, fortified against the rest of creation, which still fights "red in tooth and claw.") I am aware that the evolutionary model does not exclude the possibility of apes existing at the same time as humans, since they teach that we have a common ancestor rather than being direct descendents; however, why is there such an enormous gap between humankind and the rest of creation? Why am I discussing the origin of life while the most intelligent animals still just go about surviving without giving a thought to *meaning*?

The evolutionist often presents evidence that they assume shows the advanced thinking and wonderful nature of the various animals, probably in hopes of bridging this gap. I recently watched a documentary about bears where an evolutionary woman extolled their *gentleness*, just before she said that they were *as* intelligent as we are. She paused at that point, and I was hoping she would not say that they are *more intelligent* than we are. She did not...but I think she wanted to.

The difference between the animal and human is extensive—surpassingly so. Is it reasonable to believe that we are advanced adaptations, in light of the fact that we are *so* advanced?

2. How likely is the evolutionary model?

We have to remember that the theory of evolution requires an enormous expanse of time to work. The likelihood of life arising, first from nonlife, and then developing through mutations and biological accidents—by means of natural selection—to result in the many varied creatures that we see today seems a stretch, and a very long one. Logic has always been a hallmark of scientific study and we should not reject it as a means of testing this theory, so, I am asking this question: is it logical to accept this model for life origins?

Evolutionist theory goes further back than to the first single-celled "self-replicating" organism; it would go back even to the beginning of the earth as a very large, lifeless rock. The question would be, then, not whether we descended from other animals, but whether we can agree that we evolved from a rock. Eventually, evolution teaches, on the rock a "primordial ooze" came about after millions of years, and in this ooze there was a chemical reaction. This chemical reaction, possibly catalyzed by lightening, resulted in life! Life resulting from nonliving matter may seem unimaginable, but we have to take this first step in order to follow evolutionary theory.

If this living cell were to "happen," it would have to reproduce, or the process would start again—nonlife to life. Assuming the cell did reproduce, it must go through incredible successive stages to complete the evolutionary chain. It would need to swim, by developing the mechanisms to do that; it would need to develop mouthparts, eyes. Some would eventually crawl out on land; others develop lightweight bones, feathers, and then fly. Keep in mind that all of this would happen through favorable mutations or biological accidents.

There is no intelligence in the evolutionary model, so all the successive changes could only be preserved by chance. There was no guidance. Adaptations like muscles, connective tissue, bones and sockets, skin, hair, follicles would all happen accidentally and be preserved by a nonintellectual force. Even incredibly complex processes like respiration, blood circulation, reproduction, and the intricate coded information found in DNA would have just happened! All of these changes through "adapted" creatures would have to be passed on to the next one before death, and it would logically take millions or billions of years of mistakes to preserve these changes, which would mean multiple millions or billions of creatures would have to be formed and die to pass them on.[6]

Skeptics of evolutionary theory believe there was not enough time for these changes to happen were we to accept the current estimates of the age of the earth. For the author, the likelihood that this process would happen by chance is unbelievable even if there was unlimited time.

3. How do we explain the intricacy of natural design without a Designer?

It is unbelievable to me that some can see the complexity of this world and not opt for design as the reason. I wish to present one creature in this section that can focus this question of intricate design, though there are *many* others just like it.

We cannot read far in creationist or intelligent design literature before encountering a discussion of the Bombardier Beetle. This remarkable beetle has a storage area in its body that keeps two different chemicals that it manufactures separately. When it is threatened, it mixes those chemicals and shoots a strong foul-smelling acid mixture at its opponent. It can aim in any direction; can shoot accurately into the eye of an enemy at the rate of 29 times in four minutes. Each "bomb" is made up of 500 pulses per second in the insect's body. The acid it shoots comes out of the beetle at the temperature of 212 degrees Fahrenheit and at the speed of 26 miles an hour. The beetle manufactures a special inhibitor chemical that keeps the acid from hurting itself. Seriously, how could this have evolved by mistake and mutation, even to the point of a manufacturing plant within the beetle's body to protect itself just at the time it sprayed its first shot?[7]

This beetle is just one example of what has been called *irreducible complexity*. Michael Behe coined this term, which suggests that a mechanism is a sum of its parts, all of which must operate cooperatively and simultaneously.[8] In my view, there is no way in regards to the Bombardier Beetle to accept that all these interdependent factors could have evolved by happenstance or accident. The creation of this creature (and many others like it) simply *had* to be guided by intelligence vastly superior to anything on earth.

Incidentally, I have read many attempts to show the steps that could have happened to evolve this beetle. I find the explanations unbelievable. As my mother-in-law likes to say, I do not have enough faith to believe that! A design solution is much easier to believe.

We can handle our doubts. We can face them directly, and we will find they are never as devastating as believed. Nevertheless, simply being in a defensive posture is not enough; we need to add our obvious reasons for faith.

Positive Views of the Faith That Sustains Us

Referring to a debate between J.P. Moreland (Christian philosopher) and Kai Nielson (Atheist philosopher) that he witnessed, Ravi Zacharias said, "The debate once again proved beyond any doubt that only ignorance or prejudice calls the theistic position uninformed or intellectually wanting."[9] It is unfair to claim that all believers are gullible or simply not inquisitive. This is not true. Yet, antitheists often hurl these kinds of scurrilous accusations.

In his book *Farewell to God,* the late Charles Templeton, who was previously a Christian evangelist, described his leaving belief to become an agnostic. At one point he said that he believed Christians had not read the entire Bible (His estimation of those who had: one in a hundred clergy and one in a thousand laypersons), and therefore did not know what it stated or claimed.[10] He inferred that if people would read it, they would not be able to stay faithful to its teachings. This, of course, *may* be true for those who have not read the Bible through. We cannot know. However, many sincere Christians have not only read the Bible through; they have done so many times. They have faced their own questions about everything they have encountered with their faith intact.

Templeton expanded on his conclusions in his chapter titled, "The Man in the Pulpit." He said that the preachers who *have* studied the Scripture and tenets of faith deeply, if intelligent, simply "set aside" their unbelief in the Bible to continue preaching because so much of the Christian tradition is good. On the other hand, he states, if the believer is unintelligent (fundamentalist, by his inference which includes, "zealous, unsophisticated men and women"), we can assume they will believe *anything.*[11] In other words, people who are smart enough to understand the Bible disbelieve it, and those who truly believe in it are not very bright.

Unfair or not, this will be the ongoing position of many who discount belief in God. In this section I wish to make the point that it is not the intellectually dull that choose faith. It seems ridiculous to have to say this, but many highly intelligent and inquiring people believe. I wish to list a few evidences for belief that assert themselves regardless of the opposition, or the name-calling.

The March of Civilization. When I speak of civilization, I am speaking not in a general sense of all that humankind has done and built, nor to the use of the word to define cultures or groups. Rather, I am referring to an awareness that has come to us that certain behaviors are acceptable and certain behaviors reprehensible in our dealings with each other. This must go beyond whether we have beautiful buildings or great art centers; we should reflect on whether the members of society know how to treat each other.

Videotaped beheadings happen today, but thankfully, they are roundly condemned and punished when possible. Such brutal behavior used to be standard fare. Increasingly, worldwide revolutions are happening because people are demanding democracy, or some other manifestation of self-rule. We even have rules that apply to war, through the Geneva Conventions and other enactments leading to international humanitarian law. It is no longer acceptable to believe "All's fair in love or war," if this were ever true. Most societies today abhor torture. In fact, today we spend a great deal of time trying to determine which of our interrogation techniques are torture and which are not.

Where did this good judgment come from?

Civilization marches, and those who have followed the teachings of Jesus Christ have become increasingly sane. The most "civilized" countries the world has ever known are built on the principles of justice found in the entire Bible. In fact, democracy itself received a boost through the American idea that *all men are created equal*, which was taught and demonstrated by Jesus and His faithful followers.

However, what civilization we have built will be destroyed when people began to think that we could undermine the foundation on which it was formed. Taking biblical morality out of society will not result in moral people free from the constraints of religion—it will result in decay and decadence.

Chuck Colson, in reference to G. K. Chesterton noted, "Liberalism does not lead to liberalizing the world, in fact, the opposite is true. The promise of liberation led to Marxist repression. Destructive higher criticism led to a church without beliefs and soon without followers, and then to the inevitable chaos of a society that believes nothing, lives for nothing. Liberalism, Chesterton argued, is actually illiberal, denying free thinking, denying miracles and unable to countenance anything not within one's own sphere of knowledge and understanding."[12]

Critics of Christianity will invariably throw the accusation of evil practiced in the name of Jesus. They will point to the Crusades, Galileo's treatment by the Catholic Church, the Salem witch trials, and other such events to show that Christians are just as uncivilized. All of these events, though in part unjust, have been strongly misinterpreted and taken out of context. Nevertheless, Zacharias reminds us that those who make these accusations need to remember that violence spawned by those who follow Jesus was never sanctioned by the scriptural Christ. On the other hand, the large-scale slaughters by Hitler, Stalin, Mussolini, Mao—antitheists all— "were the logical outworking of their god-denying philosophy." Zacharias went on to say, "Antitheism provides every reason to be immoral and is *bereft of any objective point of reference* with which to condemn any choice.

Any antitheist who lives a moral life merely lives *better* than his or her philosophy warrants."[13]

If we are to take away the foundation of a society built on the laws of the God of Judeo-Christian tradition (Yahweh), we have set up our own destruction. We can thank the teaching of the Bible for the foundation of the civilization we have today. The application of its teaching has always created the best people and the best society. There is fortifying power in this for those who believe.

The Phenomenon of the Bible. Those who say the Bible is manmade and not Holy Writ, should know as Ricky said to Lucy (from TV's "I Love Lucy") they "have some '*splainin* to do."

F.F. Bruce reminds us in his book, *The Book and the Parchments,* that over a period of 1400 years diverse writers, including "kings, herdsmen, soldiers, legislators, fishermen, statesmen, courtiers, priests and prophets, a tent-making Rabbi and a Gentile Physician"; wrote diverse writings, including "history, law...religious poetry, didactic treatises, lyric poetry, parable and allegory, biography, personal correspondence, and diaries."[14] These writers, without collaboration, put together this connected whole which shows the unfolding work of God to relate to and redeem His Creation. Bruce reminds us that this work is not an anthology (which is complied by an anthologist), but *grew together* under the direction of the Holy Spirit.[15] Men moved by the Holy Spirit wrote these words, the children of God recognized its authority, but God Himself brought it together.

The "Canon," which is a word meaning a "reed" or "ruler" is our term for the completed Old and New Testaments. The Canon is closed, nothing will be taken away from it, and nothing will be added until it is no longer needed when the final age has come. Some believe the Bible, especially the New Testament, is authoritative because church councils approved it, but this is simply not true. The church councils that agreed to the books of the Canon that we have today were simply agreeing to what was the prevailing view in the Christian community. Whether or not a book is in the Canon is dependent entirely on its special authority. Therefore, a book is not authoritative because it is in the Canon; the book is in the Canon because it is authoritative.[16]

All of the books that make up the Bible have remarkably the same purpose, were brought together without the premeditation of persons, and have changed millions of lives throughout the centuries. Although attacks against it have been vicious, and there have been many who have tried to declare its inadequacy, it has weathered this and has a stronger hold on the world psyche than it has ever had.

I love to read. I discovered the joy of reading at an early age, and I have never lost the fascination that the pictures in the imagination are so much more vivid and powerful than those projected on a screen. I read fiction and nonfiction of all genres. My tastes are eclectic.

One of the early books that moved me a great deal was *Ivanhoe*, by Sir Walter Scott. I do not even remember why its impact was so strong. I just remember as a boy when I closed the book on the last words I thought it was *wonderful*. I have not read *Ivanhoe* since. I have no desire to. In fact, I rarely read books twice knowing that there are so many others to discover. On the other hand, I have read the entire Bible over 25 times at this writing. This does not include all the hours I have studied it, read it devotionally, heard it taught, etc. Each time I read the Bible it has something new to say to me, on every page, through the very words I have read many times before. I cannot even conceive of this happening with any other book, no matter how good. The Bible is simply incomparable because it breathes God's revelation and presence.

On occasion—disoriented, anxious, depressed—I have sat down dutifully to do my daily Bible reading. Finding I had to go through the genealogies in 1 Chronicles, or some dry passage in Leviticus, I plodded forward and was surprised by feelings of peace; my worries fading to invisibility. Is this because, as some say, the Bible is a placebo? Is it simply the joy of what is familiar? Or is it as more strident critics say, the Bible a place to hide because we are afraid of the dark?

For many millions of us, there is only one reasonable explanation. The healing in the very words of this book is because it is God's Word, His spoken revelation.

Historical Interconnectedness of the Biblical Narrative. Ravi Zacharias argues that Christianity combines the past, present, and future unlike any other belief. All are important in the sweep of God's redemptive purpose.[17] The Bible is more than just a statement of belief, or a presentation of a religious philosophy; it is a recording of God's work in history—often miraculous in nature—where He reveals His redemptive purpose. There is no attempt of the biblical writers to keep the narrative separate from history; rather, they work hard to couch the events in verifiable historical settings. For example, in Genesis 14:1-12 we hear of the capture of Lot, Abraham's nephew, by a coalition of four kings under the leadership of Chedorlaomer king of Elam. These verses carefully set Lot's capture in eleven verses of historical background. The people of God were involved with other people outside of their nation, and they clearly recorded the events.

This is true in the New Testament as well. For example, in Luke's gospel we read these words:

Now in the fifteenth year of the reign of Tiberius Caesar, when Pontius Pilate was governor of Judea, and Herod was tetrarch of Galilee, and his brother Philip was tetrarch of the region of Ituraea and Trachonitis, and Lysanias was tetrarch of Abilene, in the high priesthood of Annas and Caiaphas, the word of God came to John, the son of Zacharias, in the wilderness. And he came into all the district around the Jordan, preaching a baptism of repentance for the forgiveness of sins; as it is written in the book of the words of Isaiah the prophet, "The voice of one crying in the wilderness, 'Make ready the way of the Lord, Make His paths straight. Every ravine will be filled, And every mountain and hill will be brought low; The crooked will become straight, And the rough roads smooth; And all flesh will see the salvation of God.'" (Luke 3:1-6)

Luke carefully outlines the historical setting, as well as verifies the family of John and the location of the events. Furthermore, he uses prophecy from Isaiah to verify the calling and career of John and connect it to God's eternal purpose. This is a clear attempt to set these events, not in isolation, but in connection to world events and persons.

The famous genealogies of the Bible are still another example. Found throughout narrative passages, these are attempts by the writers to connect the history of God's working with the generations of His people. This kind of listing can be easily traced (not quite so easy today as much is lost in the mist of history), so that a reported happening can be verified. Those who wanted to pass off a myth would not be so careful to use historical records, as their fiction could be easily researched and debunked. An accurate historical record is the calling card of a person telling true events, since the record offers proof.

Some today have tried to separate the two Testaments, Old from New. Most want to retain the New Covenant over the Old because it seems kinder, more understandable in today's setting. However, we cannot separate the Old and New Testaments without doing violence to the revelation of both. We will not understand the New Testament fully without understanding the Old, and vice versa. Bruce said that the "Old Testament is to the New as the root is to the fruit."[18]

Some years ago, W.A. Criswell, the pastor of the First Baptist Church of Dallas, Texas, preached a sermon titled, "The Scarlet Thread of Redemption." His basic theme was that this scarlet thread, likened to Rahab's scarlet thread thrown out her window before the destruction of Jericho (Joshua 2:1-21), runs from the beginning of Genesis to the end of Revelation. The Bible connects its testimony of God's saving grace throughout history. The books of the Bible are not separate opinion pieces, but a supernaturally inspired collection designed to communicate God's plan—and they hold together remarkably.

The interconnectedness of the Bible is also evident in the area of biblical prophecy. Though there are many examples, it will help to look closely at a few.

In the course of my teaching, I have prepared and taught on *The Feasts of Israel.*[19] The feasts I referred to are those that God told the Israelites to follow in Leviticus 23. They are harbingers of the Messiah, and as other biblical prophecies, their accuracy is remarkable. We will deal with these in brief, though I encourage the reader to research them deeply. These feasts happen in the order below in the Jewish calendar year. The parallel events concerning Jesus, the Messiah, are also chronological.

1. *Passover* (Leviticus 23:4-5), the feast designed by God to remind the Israelites of His provision of liberation from the bondage of Egypt is a foreshadowing of Christ's redemption, provided for us through His death on the cross. Therefore, the Lord's Supper resembles this feast in many particulars.

2. *The Feast of Unleavened Bread* (Leviticus 23:6-8), which follows closely to the Passover and has become almost synonymous in practice because of their closeness in meaning, points to the sanctification that Christ provides. The feast was to indicate the removal of *leaven* from the home and nation, which indicated the need for God's redemptive work. Jesus is referred to as the Lamb without spot (1 Peter 1:19, Hebrews 9:14), and three times Pilate was reported to have said in John's gospel, "I find no fault in Him" (John 18:38, 19:4, 19:6).

3. *Firstfruits* (Leviticus 23:9-14) testifies of the first of the barley harvest, that the first fruit to come from the ground promised more to come. Jesus, described as the first fruits in His resurrection (1 Corinthians 15:20) was the first resurrection, which leads to the resurrection of those who follow Him.

4. *Pentecost* (Leviticus 23:15-21) was to occur fifty days after the offering of first fruits. Firstfruits connected with Pentecost, especially through the waving of two loaves, called "first fruits" (vv. 17, 20). Recall that Jesus' resurrection is the firstfruit offering, and fifty days later came the day of Pentecost. We are told in Acts, that after Jesus' resurrection He was on the earth

for forty days before His ascension, and He told the disciples to "stay in the city (Jerusalem) until you are clothed with power from on high" (Luke 24:49). This event happened ten days after Jesus' ascension because we are told, "When the day of Pentecost had come," the out-pouring of the Spirit came on the believers gathered in the upper room (Acts 2). James tells us we are, "first fruits of His creatures" (James 1:18), which would refer to all believers when they are regenerated, but could be specifically applied to this coming of the Holy Spirit on God's people as He is the agent of regeneration (Romans 8:23).

There is a break of over five months between the feasts at this point. The next three feasts, in their New Covenant form, are yet to be fulfilled in the future. The first four feasts pointed to the work of Christ with accuracy, so do these; although we may be less certain in our interpretation.

5. *The Feast of Trumpets* (Leviticus 23:24-25) happens on the first day of the seventh month, or the beginning of the Jewish civil year *Tisri*. It is uncertain what the trumpets indicate in this feast, but a sign of redemption and calling to duty at the temple are their usual use. In 1 Thessalonians 4:16, Paul tells us, "For the Lord Himself will descend from heaven with a shout, with the voice of the archangel and with the trumpet of God, and the dead in Christ will rise first." For those of a premillenial mindset, this feast would point to the Rapture.

6. *The Day of Atonement* (Leviticus 23:26-32) is indicative of spiritual regeneration. It seems out of place, since atonement is the theme of the first four feasts. However, remember that there are more to be redeemed. During the Tribulation, many Jewish people will be killed in the terrible persecution (Zecharaih 13:7-9); however, we are also told that many will be remade into a kingdom (Jeremiah 31:31-33). Though God fulfilled this prophecy with the Gentiles, it is yet to be consummated with the Jews. The promise of Israel's salvation points to those who repent at the Second Coming of Christ, and so Romans 11:25-27 will be fulfilled. At the end of the Tribulation (The Second Coming), those who are repentant of Israel will be restored, which many believe includes the resurrection of the Old Testament saints who died in faith.

7. *The Feast of Tabernacles* (Leviticus 23:33-36, 39-44) shows completion. God instituted this feast as the Israelites journeyed through the wilderness. He instructed them to build booths and place provisions inside to remind them of their successful liberation from Egypt. The feast concluded with the added element of thanksgiving for the harvest. After the events of rapture and the Tribulation, the return of Jesus at the Second Coming will establish His 1,000-year reign (Millennium) on earth. This can also show the final consummation of God's redemptive plans when He puts down all opposition, remakes Heaven and earth, and literally "tabernacles" among us (Revelation 21:3). This may be the significance of the "eighth day," which is the day just following the seven days of this feast that is literally a "day of closing" or "restraint," where the Israelites were allowed to return to their homes in reflective Sabbath celebration (Leviticus 23:36).

Whether we interpret these feasts exactly as I have laid out does not matter. It should be obvious that Moses, when writing Leviticus through the inspiration of God's Spirit, set out feasts that would have significance in the flowering of events many years later in Jesus' work.

Add to this the hundreds of prophecies—called Messianic Prophecies—that clearly indicate Jesus' coming and His work on earth (e.g., Genesis 3:15; Psalm 22:18, 69:21; Isaiah 7:14, 9:6-7, 52:13-53:12; Micah 5:1-3; Zechariah 12:10). Many other prophecies of the Old Testament give accurate predictions of future events. For example, Daniel's prophecies show in detail the Medo-Persian, Grecian, and Roman kingdoms following the Babylonian rule under which he lived. The accuracy is so astounding, critics have tried to say there was a "Pseudo-Daniel" that wrote this *after* the events in the second century B.C. He was not a prophet, they say, but a historian. They have to gloss over the fact that Daniel also predicted the coming of Christ's kingdom while Rome was strong and prophesied of future events recorded in the New Testament that are not yet fulfilled, even today.

I believe that Daniel wrote the book bearing his name in the court of Nebuchadnezzar and in that of the kings immediately following, just as the narrative stated. Daniel explained the reason for the accuracy of these prophecies when he said to King Nebuchadnezzar, "There is a God in heaven who reveals mysteries" (Daniel 2:28), for it takes more than human wisdom to write the Word of God.

In the New Testament, in both Galatians 3 and Romans 2-4, Paul specifically tied God's work of grace from Abraham's time until the age of Jesus. He clearly showed the marvelous plan of God, which included

Abraham as a recipient of the promises, fulfilled in Jesus as *The Promise*. Paul showed that when God said that Abraham was to be blessed through his seed, the word *seed* was singular, and referred to Christ. Moses was the intermediate between the giving of the promise to Abraham and its fulfillment in Jesus. The Law, delivered by God with Moses as the mediator four hundred thirty years after the beginning of bondage (when Jacob and family entered Canaan for the last time), was given as a "side road," or as Paul said, "was added" (Galatians 3:19). The Law led us to understand that the original promise to Abraham, with Messianic fulfillment, was the only way anyone would ever meet God's conditions for righteousness.

How could the intricacy of these workings of God's redemption happen throughout history without Divine guidance? How could person or persons plan this, especially since it involved those who were not collaborating through a great expanse of time?

Man did not plan the Bible nor did he coordinate it. Yet, the phenomenal coordination of the books and the unveiling of the revelation of God can give those who believe great confidence in their faith, and should give those who disbelieve intellectual pause.

Steps That Encourage Our Faith in the Face of Doubt

In this section, I hope to suggest certain steps that will help us when we face doubt. Doubt itself is not necessarily a sin, but cultivating it would be. We should search out ways to make the culture of our lives such that doubt, like an unnourished plant, must eventually shrivel and die. In its place, the healthy growth of faith will be unhindered.

Step One: Realize that the Bible is trustworthy. We need to take our conclusions about the Bible from the theoretical to the practical. In other words, learning about the Bible is not enough; we should also learn to use it.

The Bible is God's Word. It is above reproach. In any discussion of doubt, we should keep this in mind. We should expect those who do not name God as Father to try to attack the Bible historically and factually. For us—those who follow Christ—the Bible is always trustworthy. We should approach all of our questions about its direct teaching and implications in a positive light, knowing that it will reveal itself as pure. The way to despair is to begin to judge the Bible and to look at it suspiciously. Though we are free to research the teachings of the Bible, we are not free to accuse it; and though we may cry out to God when we are in doubt, it would be unwise to shout at Him.

I was reading 1 Peter 2:6 once, and it struck me in a way that I have not forgotten. Peter quoted Isaiah 28:16 to make his point, "For this is contained in Scripture: 'Behold, I lay in Zion a choice stone, a precious corner stone,

And he who believes in Him *will not be disappointed*'" (1 Peter 2:6, emphasis added). Peter was telling his readers that Jesus is trustworthy. Others have reacted to the "word" (v.8) with offense; therefore, they oppose Jesus and those who follow Him. What struck me was the second phrase when Peter said those who believe "will not be disappointed." Literally, the phrase is translated "they will not be put to shame."

I like to say they will not be left *holding the bag*. This phrase originated in England years ago, and meant that if police officers were closely chasing a gang, the gang would leave a stolen bag of money with the gang member of the lowest rank and make their getaway. The one holding the bag was the diversion, and the dupe.

This will not happen to those who trust in Jesus. Though the ridicule hurled at Christendom grows in volume, we will stand assured because we have placed our hope in the Rock of Ages as revealed in the Scripture. One day, all those who mock us will see that we placed our faith in what is eternally true. Those who do not believe, in fact, will be left "holding the bag."

Step Two: Live confidently according to the Bible's teachings. We can overcome our doubt when we apply the Scripture, and live as if it is true! I am not suggesting that we "fake it," but that we "test it" by *doing* it. The teachings of the Bible when applied have the power to change our life and weaken our doubt.

We referred earlier in this chapter to James' words concerning looking in a mirror and forgetting what we look like. James is speaking of our need to apply what we read in the Scripture. He said, "But prove yourselves doers of the word, and not merely hearers who delude themselves" (James 1:22). Unlike that person who looks in the mirror and forgets what he looks like, "One who looks intently at the perfect law, the law of liberty, and abides by it, not having become a forgetful hearer but an effectual doer, this man will be blessed in what he does" (v. 25). One of the inward testimonies to the truth of God's Word is its regenerating power. When we truly live according to the principles the Bible presents, we find that we cannot imagine living any other way. Our doubts fly as the Holy Spirit completes and empowers us.

Step Three: Be assured that bias is an equal opportunity motivator. Belief is not always intellectual—sometimes it is intuitive and visceral. But unbelief is the same. We often believe or do not believe because of our predisposition.

Koenig said, "The 'bias' of the believer in finding something or Someone 'out there' is really the logical presupposition for faith. Some kind of personal commitment has to be made before we can see things truthfully." [20] Two people will look at the same facts and come up with entirely different conclusions. Even the most hardened unbeliever finds his heart softening before he believes. In a mysterious way, we both draw and are drawn closer to God: "Draw near to God and He will draw near to you. Cleanse your hands, you sinners; and purify your hearts, you double-minded" (James 4:8); "Therefore let us draw near with confidence to the throne of grace, so that we may receive mercy and find grace to help in time of need" (Hebrews 4:16); "No one can come to Me unless the Father who sent Me draws him; and I will raise him up on the last day" (John 6:44). To some extent, our bias toward faith grows *after* we have showed interest.

Almost one hundred years ago, Ella Wheeler Wilcox wrote her famous poem, which says in part:

But to every man there openeth,
A high way and a low,
And every mind decideth,
The way his soul shall go.

One ship sails East,
And another West,
By the self-same winds that blow,
'Tis the set of the sails
And not the gales,
That tells the way to go.

Those who mock us for our *desire* to believe, have an equally strong desire *not* to believe. We are no more credulous than they are.

Nicholas Wolterstorff, at this writing the Professor of Philosophical Theology at Yale University, lost his 25-year-old son Eric in a mountain climbing accident. In *Lament for a Son*, when asked why he could not give up his faith in response to this tragedy Wolterstorff said, "When I survey this gigantic intricate world, I cannot believe that it just came about…The experiment to abolish it does not work. When looking at the heavens, I cannot manage to believe that they do not declare the glory of God. When looking at the earth, I cannot bring off the attempt to believe that it does not display His handiwork." [21]

It may help to remember that it is okay to *want* to believe.

Step Four: Remember that others have handled accusations of unbelief before. Koenig noted, "Many objections to Christian belief, even in the age of science, turn out to be versions of older questions of the past. Opponents of Christianity do not realize how often their 'devastating' attacks are only variations on themes of more original heretics of the past."[22]

Solomon said years ago, "There is nothing new under the sun" (Ecclesiastes 1:9b). Though couched in different terms, or arising because of new discoveries, the attacks on faith are generally the same. To name a few: The Bible is unreliable in reference to modern knowledge; Believing in a God who does not show Himself is impossible in a world where we trust only our senses; Following one God is intolerant in today's pluralistic society; and God is unnecessary, because we can save ourselves. Others have handled these views in the past, and when we concentrate on them today, we find they are not difficult to refute. If doubt is a problem for us, then we might need to spend some time discovering the many resources available that combat disbelief. We do not need to keep looking for arguments that our forebears have already discovered.

Here is a chance to use the discipline of study mentioned in chapter 12. We should use what spare time we have to research what causes us to falter. Some of the books in the endnotes at the end of this chapter would be a good start, but there are so many. Study does not replace our daily devotional time but is its supplement. We should read books of faith, past and present. We can do the work necessary to meet our doubts head on. We cannot borrow our faith from someone else; we have to mine it ourselves.

If our faith has matured, it is also good to study the authors who directly *assail* the faith. I have found that many of their points are unjust, and they show in their writings that they do not know what we believe. One atheistic author that I read kept referring to the close Christian friends he had, and that being the case I wondered how he could not know Christians better! Were his Christian friends silent? When we see the weakness of the arguments against our faith, the clear prejudice, and the inability to handle our perspective fairly, our confidence increases. Handling these arguments head-on sometimes reveals the monster in the closet is just an old coat.

At other times when the skeptic's questions resonate with ours, we can look more deeply into that particular area. We can go with confidence, because our faith is true. It has been tested. Ever since the Bible was written some have tried to discount it, and as long as there have been Christians their veracity has been questioned (not excepting Jesus!). However, we do not stand alone, for many have gone before and many stand with us today. These tests have hammered against God's people and this rock of faith, and though we may be confused for a while or fearful as the onslaught breaks, the rock, at least, is unshaken.

Step Five: Embrace what is best in you. What is best in you is from God. For those of us who believe, through all difficulties, we have seen the most beautiful characteristics grow within us. Only a supernatural explanation is adequate for the sometimes-overwhelming presence of the Lord. There is simple wisdom in Ruth Tucker's assertion that though she struggles with doubt, she will never abandon her faith because it is deeply part of her history and God *has a grip* on her.[23]

When I am near to God, when I share His holiness, I am at my very best. Allow me to take personal privilege to say that my wife and son follow the teachings of this book, imperfectly as I do, and are some of the godliest people I know. Those who describe my wife, say that she is one of the most precious people they know, engagingly helpful and positive. My son excels in everything he does, and his parents are always told how respectful and what a delight he is. My point is simple. My family is special because Jesus is! We find ourselves radically and continually changed. What is within us is stronger than any assaults from without. We are inconsistent sometimes, we are not always worthy of the Revelation, but when we *are* worthy it is because He has made us so. We choose to embrace these things and believe.

Some followers of other faiths may think they feel a clear sense of their god's nearness, yet they end up angry, divisive, and violent. Alternatively, in other lives their belief causes passivity and otherworldliness, a kind of self-centered spirituality. In stark contrast, the free presence of God in a Christian's life results in love, understanding, joy, and centered peace. It results in wisdom, fearlessness in confronting sin, and willingness to suffer for what is true. How the application of Christian faith changes us is a testimony to its truth, and we should see that what has happened and is happening to us is one of the strongest defenses for our faith.

Getting Help

We mentioned in chapter 13 that when the storm blew up on the Sea of Galilee, and the disciples were terrified, Jesus asked the disciples, "Why are you afraid, you men of little faith?" (Matthew 8:26). He then calmed the storm. Rees saw the importance of the word Jesus used, "little faith" (*Oligopistoi*), as showing a "polarity of faith and fear." He suggested, "Faith here means to trust completely in Jesus, and 'little faith' or doubt means to trust partially in Jesus, while also attending to someone or something else. In these instances that something else is one's own fear."[24]

Once I read a book, which I am sure the author considered a "devastating" critique of Christianity. I read it through in one morning, so engrossed was I in the negatives. Afterwards, it was time for my jog and as I began running, all the clouds lifted and I began singing praises to God. I had not thought of ways to combat the statements of the writer. I had not marshaled my intellectual forces to bolster myself. I had simply prayed a simple prayer, "Lord, see me through this, and help me to see things your way." The joy and complete release I felt made no earthly sense, but supernaturally it made all the sense in the world.

Jesus seemed to understand doubt. Once He was asked to heal a demon-possessed boy in Caesarea Philippi who was often thrown into convulsions. Jesus' disciples had not been able to heal him, and the father brought the boy to the Lord. Mark gives the fullest narrative, and we read that the father asked Jesus, "If you can do anything, take pity on us and help us!" Jesus responded that He is able to help those who believe. The father said, "I do believe, help thou my unbelief" (Mark 9:14-29).

The Bible teaches that God gives each person a measure of faith (Romans 12:3), and some seem to have more than others do (Matthew 13:23; 1 Corinthians 12:9, 13:2). I believe we are not to pray for more faith, but that our faith would not fail (Luke 22:32) or that we would use what faith we have. The exercise of faith is our part; grace and power is in the hand of God. Faith puts us in the way of His blessing.

When this man with the afflicted son said, "I do believe," he was telling Jesus the truth. However, he did not think his faith was strong enough to meet the challenge of his son's healing, so He asked Jesus not to give him more faith, but to help where his faith faltered. He said, "I do believe, help me where I do not." Jesus did not rebuke this response; in fact, He stepped in to help.

Faith counteracts doubt—in effect, it disables it. However, our faith is often too weak to handle our challenges because it collaborates with unbelief. We should ask for help with this. When we have "little faith," it is because through fear we have displaced our full measure of faith. It is in Jesus that we will find help.

The apostle Paul summarized this idea in these important words to the Galatians, "I have been crucified with Christ; and it is no longer I who live, but Christ lives in me; and the life which I now live in the flesh I live by faith in the Son of God, who loved me and gave Himself up for me" (Galatians 2:20). Paul is saying that once for all, our lives are hidden in God. We joined with Christ in His crucifixion and we have been raised complete. We should no longer live in our strength, but in His, and we can appeal at any time for the help we need.

Holiness must include loyalty to God. When we waver in our understanding of His revelation, or even the fact of His existence, we should remember that Jesus is the Vine—we remain the branches. All the healing that we need is very deep in the everlasting roots, and we connect through our faith. Our Father, the Master Gardener, will attend to our health.

In his book, *March Till They Die*, Catholic priest Philip Crosbie tells of a forced march during the Korean War. In November of 1950, the North

Koreans being pushed northward took with them the American and European POWs as well as mostly missionary civilians. Many of the civilians were aged, some in their seventies and eighties. All of those forced to march were near starvation from long captivity. It was a terrible march. The captors forced the prisoners sometimes to go twenty miles a day, for a total march in eight days of over one hundred miles. Over one hundred prisoners died (more than two hundred more in twenty days after the march). POWs who could not keep up would fall back, and shots would ring out—they were executed on the spot. "The Tiger," the leader of the Korean captors seemed to be making good on his words, for he had repeatedly told them they would "march till they die."

Crosbie, one of the prisoners, passed close to those who were having a hard time keeping up and would say slowly and quietly, "God is near us in this dark hour...Beyond this night of pain and hate. His love is real...His mercy is real...His forgiveness...His reward is waiting for us..."[25]

We can agree that this is a dark hour, but we need to remember that God is near.

---

1. Frank D. Rees, *Wrestling with Doubt; Theological Reflections on the Journey of Faith* (Collegeville, Minnesota: The Liturgical Press, 2001), 199-200.

2. Richard Edwin Koenig, *If God is God: Conversations on Faith, Doubt, Freedom, and Love* (Wheaton, Illinois: Tyndale House Publishers, 1969), 39-44.

3. Ibid., 36-37.

4. Alvin Plantinga, "Darwin, Mind and Meaning," *Books and Culture,* May/June 1996: 35, quoted in Ruth Tucker, *Walking Away from Faith: Unraveling the Mystery of Belief and Unbelief* (Downer's Grove, Illinois: InterVarsity Press, 2002), 107.

5. I recommend studying this subject with attention to biological, theological/philosophical, and historical proofs. See the following references if available: Michael Behe, *Darwin's Black Box: the Biochemical Challenge to Evolution* (New York: The Free Press, 1996); William Lane Craig, *Reasonable Faith: Christian Truth and Apologetics* (Wheaton, Illinois: Crossway, 2008); Norman L. Geisler and Peter Bocchino, *Unshakeable Foundations: Contemporary Answers to Crucial Questions about the Christian Faith* (Minneapolis: Bethany House Publishers, 2001); Norman L. Geisler and Frank Turek, *I Don't Have Enough Faith to be an Atheist* (Wheaton: Crossway, 2004); Lee Strobel, *The Case for a Creator* (Grand

Rapids: Zondervan, 2004); Yandall Woodfin, *With All Your Mind: A Christian Philosophy* (Nashville: Abingdon, 1980).

6. Although these are my conclusions, the idea for the entire heading #2 came from Dr. Gary Parker's lecture in:

Kenneth Ham and Gary Parker, *Understanding Genesis [videorecording]: A Complete Creation Seminar and Apologetic for the Historical and Scientific Accuracy of God's Word* (El Cajon, CA: CLP Video, 1986), volumes 4 and 5.

7. Charles Colson and Twila Dry, *Creation vs. Evolution: The Real Story* (Nashville: Lifeway Press, 2000).

8. Michael Behe, *Darwin's Black Box: the Biochemical Challenge to Evolution* (New York: The Free Press, 1996), 39-48.

9. Ravi Zacharias, *Can Man Live Without God?* (Nashville: W Publishing Group, 1994), 10.

10. Charles Templeton, *Farewell to God: My Reasons for Rejecting the Christian Faith,* (Toronto, Canada: McClelland & Stewart, 1996), 17, 103. Templeton insisted he was an agnostic and not an atheist (which he stated is as untenable as belief; both requiring faith). Rather than saying there is no God, he said the agnostic would say, "I *cannot* know." However, his book is evidence he *cannot believe* there is a God of the Bible. He indicated he believed in an "Impersonal Life Force" (232).

11. Templeton, *Farewell to God,* 161.

12. Chuck Colson, *The Faith: What Christians Believe, Why They Believe It, and Why It Matters* (Grand Rapids: Zondervan, 2008), 204.

13. Zacharias, *Can Man Live,* 22, 32.

14. F. F. Bruce, *The Books and the Parchments,* 3rd ed. (Old Tappan, New Jersey: Fleming H. Revell Company, 1963), 88.

15. Ibid.

16. Ibid., 96.

17. Zacharias, *Can Man Live,* 156.

18. Bruce, *The Books,* 82.

19. This study compiled over the years with information from these sources: Kevin Howard and Marvin Rosenthal, *The Feasts of the Lord: God's Prophetic Calendar from Calvary to the Kingdom,* 5th ed. (Nashville: Thomas Nelson, 1957); Victor Buksbazen, *The Gospel in the Feasts of Israel,* 11th ed. (Fort Washington, Pennsylvania: Christian Literature Crusade, 2004); Alfred Holiday, *The Feasts of the Lord* (London: Pickering and Inglis Ltd, n.d.).

20. Koenig, *If God is God,* 21.

21. Nicholas Wolterstorff, *Lament for a Son* (Grand Rapids: William B. Eerdmans, 1987), 76.

22. Koenig, *If God is God,* 39.

23. Ruth A. Tucker, *Walking Away from Faith: Unraveling the Mystery of Belief and Unbelief* (Downer's Grove, Illinois: InterVarsity Press, 2002), 25-26.

24. Rees, *Wrestling with Doubt,* 193.

25. Philip Crosbie, *March Till They Die* (Dublin: Browne and Nolan, Ltd., 1955), 158.

CHAPTER 15

Regulating Our Emotions

We are emotional creatures. God made us this way. Our emotions, though sometimes unreliable, keep us from being something like robots—relational only as much as the Maker was to push our buttons. A free relationship with the Almighty is part of the *reason* for creation. Since holiness is simply an uninhibited relationship with God, emotions will come into play.

At the very moment of the creation of human beings, God was expecting things out of them. He set them on earth to have dominion over creation, to name the animals, to tend the garden. Furthermore, they were held to a moral standard that the other creatures were not. This is obvious when Adam and Eve fell, and were driven from the garden because they were responsible for their behavior. God did not establish this kind of reciprocal relationship with any other creature.

Devotion deepens when our emotions are involved. The Bible often describes worship in emotional terms, like we "thrust our hands out," "shout to the Lord," or clap, sing, and dance. Emotion is part of the makeup that God created for us, and we should embrace it.

Emotion is also necessary and beneficial in human relationships. If someone in relationship with another person is not willing, or unable, to respond emotionally, the relationship is in peril.

Today, email has largely replaced the phone as a means of business communication. However, it appears cold, so some of us have to include "emoticons" (those little smiley faces or illustrations that show our emotion). In other electronic communication like blogging, we attach words like LOL (*laugh out loud*), or ROFL (*rolling on the floor laughing*) to add meaning. Some people add tags like *sniffs* to indicate sadness, or *smiles* to show happiness. We seem to be uncomfortable if we cannot express ourselves. ☹

However, we all know our emotions may also get the best of us, resulting in a state of ineffectiveness if not downright destructiveness. For example, many men ruin their lives with anger and impatience more than with other overt sins. They may be hardworking, moral, and honest, even righteous, and yet find anger their fly in the ointment.

In my years as a pastor, men have spoken to me of their sadness over their shortness with their wives and children, the dearest people in their world. These men generally start with good intentions—a desire to manage the home or to see their children maturing well—but end up being a destructive force in the family. They agonize over the disparity of, on the one hand, their love and desire to protect; and on the other, their fury towards the very ones they want to nurture.

Men are not the only ones affected, of course. All of us find that in the hands of the enemy, emotions may inhibit our spiritual lives.

Christianity or Stoicism?

Before we go forward, we need to point out that there is an enormous difference between *Christianity* and *Stoicism*. I am unaware of any formal teaching of Stoicism today, but some Christians get its tenets mixed up with ours.

Stoicism was widely taught in the Roman Empire when Christianity was making inroads in the First Century. A Greek philosophical thought, Stoicism taught that the physical and the spiritual were opposed to each other, which resulted in dualism of spirit and flesh. The Stoics wanted to arrive at a state where they were unmoved by emotions. The height of attainment would be to see the dearest thing to them lost (e.g., a beloved child to die), and to remain unmoved emotionally. The Stoic would see such death connected to the "cosmic good."

The Bible does not teach such emotional neutrality. Christians are moved by pity, compassion, anger, grief, loss, doubt, and fear. It is obvious in the Scripture that we are not to suppress emotion, rather to manage or regulate it. Charles Swindoll said, "Becoming a Christian is not synonymous with becoming superhuman. Expressing one's emotions is not a mark of immaturity or carnality."[1]

Paul said, "Rejoice with those who rejoice, and weep with those who weep" (Romans 12:15). He was telling the Romans to express appropriate emotions. In contrast, he also said, "Not that I speak from want, for I have learned to be content in whatever circumstances I am" (Philippians 4:11). Emotion can get out of hand, so it is our task to *learn* to be content. Contentment serves as a cap on emotions, resulting in our control of emotions rather than their control of us.

We will look at a few emotions that seem to be in the forefront of our experience. The ones in this chapter are those that have a negative side, as opposed to the emotions like love and joy, which are usually positive and discussed elsewhere in this book. Although the following list is not exhaustive, it includes what may be the most powerful set. We will look at a biblical perspective on each one, positive and negative, and conclude this chapter with solutions.

Anger

This powerful emotion can control us. The authors of *The Angry Man* wrote that "Cliff," a normally adjusted and mild-mannered man, frustrated with his lawn mower that would not start, took his prized deer rifle and shot it three times. Without a word, he then "retired to the den to clean his gun, closing the door behind him." His terrified wife wondered what hidden emotions were to come out at another time.[2]

Many of the violent crimes that seem so epidemic today are driven by this emotion out of control. Anger simmers in some people, resulting in its tyranny over their behavior at an emotional moment. But anger is not necessarily a sin. We remember when Jesus drove the moneychangers out of the temple, "He made a scourge of cords, and drove them all out of the temple, with the sheep and the oxen; and He poured out the coins of the moneychangers and overturned their tables" (John 2:15). Most of us know this story, and that Jesus was righteously indignant because they were "making My Father's house a place of business" (v. 16). It may shock us to see Jesus use a whip, but it is *impossible* to think of Him using it without anger.

Anger can be a supernaturally imposed emotion. I remember the many Old Testament prophets *thundering* their words to a stubborn people. Later, when Paul said, "Be angry, yet do not sin," (Ephesians 4:26), he was pointing to the righteous place for anger.

James D. Whitehead and Evelyn Eton Whitehead in their book *Shadows of the Heart: A Spirituality of the Negative Emotions* speak of "honoring" the emotion of anger. They suggest we recognize that anger is not taboo, but a normal and possibly helpful emotion. "Honoring helps us hold this formidable emotion as expectable, inevitable, allowable in our life—without rushing into actions we will later regret."[3] Anger does not necessarily harm our holy life. Nevertheless, before his conversion Paul *was* sinful when he, "breathed out threats and murder against the disciples of the Lord" (Acts 9:1). It will be our responsibility to find out where we have reason for anger, and where we do not. An even more subtle threat may be the times when our anger, even righteous anger, morphs into sin when we leave it unchained. The Book of Proverbs speaks of wrath being fierce and anger a flood (14:7). We will need to seek God's help to keep it from flood stage!

Anger may not always be visible. We sometimes feed on bitterness and disappointment to the extent that internalized anger begins to destroy us just as it destroys relationships. This hidden anger can be just as devastating to our spiritual selves, and may be more insidious.

Fear

Tim LaHaye indicated that extroverted and confident personalities tend to anger, but the more introverted to fear. On the other hand, though we may be predisposed by temperament to one of these emotions, we experience both emotions to some degree. LaHaye added that anger can lead to fear, and fear to anger![4] Anger and fear may be the same emotion, turned upside down. Anger is a natural reaction to frustration, disappointment, or threat. Fear is a natural reaction to the same stimuli. Anger reacts outwardly: "I'll fix it!" Fear reacts inwardly: "Oh no, what if it fixes me?"

Fear is a powerful emotion, but is usually more self-destructive than aggressive toward others. It is outward in the sense that it can steal a person's effectiveness, weaken relationships, even drive him from relationships altogether; but it causes the greatest damage to the self.

Unlike anger, notice that the Bible does not once suggest fear as a viable emotion, except in the fear of God Himself.[5] Fearing man does not seem to have a positive aspect, and fearing God may be the *solution* to fearing anything else.

In Proverbs 1:7, the wise man said, "The fear of the Lord is the beginning of knowledge." A person can have a great deal of knowledge without a thought of God, but this verse is pointing to true and lasting knowledge. This knowledge, that which will survive the test of fire in the end times, comes from *fear* of God. This fear, akin to great respect, leads a person to true knowledge. It is not unhealthy, as if we are waiting for Him to smash us flat! Rather, it indicates a total respect for His power and preeminence, which results in our desire not to contradict His will.

In his first letter, the apostle John said, "There is no fear in love; but perfect love casts out fear, because fear involves punishment, and the one who fears is not perfected in love. We love, because He first loved us" (1 John 4:18-19). It follows then that our knowledge, perfected through the fear of God, results in our embracing God's forgiveness. Our fear of punishment, or fear of anything else, disappears in light of His love and protection.

Sadness

The emotion of sadness could show itself in us as sorrow, grief, woe, or distress. Any of these expressions of sadness can lead to anxiety or depression. Excessive sadness can hinder a healthy relationship with God and with others.

This world seems immersed in sadness sometimes. Financial doldrums, natural disasters, wickedness, crime, war; they all contribute to a general gloom. Christians may sometimes feel there is more reason for sadness on earth than for happiness. Whether because of the behavior of our loved ones, the loss of something dear to us, the spiritual decay of the world around us, or even something as simple as a general, nonspecific bout of the blues; sadness is *sad*.

Isaiah described Jesus as, "A man of sorrows and acquainted with grief" (Isaiah 53:3). Matthew Henry said, "Of Him we never read that he laughed, but often that he wept." Jesus taught the disciples that we are *blessed* if we mourn (Matthew 5:4). This is the result of our sadness over personal sinfulness, and the broken and sinful nature of the entire world. Therefore, it seems that sadness may be an indication of holy living.

On the other hand, sadness can be a sinful state when it eclipses our victory in Christ. We are told to rejoice at all times and to leap for joy over persecutions (1 Thessalonians 5:16, Luke 6:22-23). Paul said that we "overwhelmingly conquer" (Romans 8:37). We must balance real world sadness, even the spiritual kind, with a refusal to mope. Someone said, "Strength of grace has never been measured by length of face." The Christian who goes around dejected and bemoaning the state of the world will have little impact on those that are lost without Christ. Our confession is that we do have hope!

Some years ago, when I was in my doctoral studies, I was conducting interviews in the town where I was pastor. The town had about 3600 residents, so it was easier to know the state of affairs than it would be in a bigger city. One of the pharmacists in town told me that over 90% of the medication they prescribed was for depression-related maladies. This indicates, at least in that town, that emotional sadness overtakes many people.

In speaking of sadness, which can result in depression, Robert Hastings said, "How can one master depression? Really, this is setting one's sights too high, because everyone gets depressed at one time or another, to varying degrees. One does not 'master' depression. He learns to live with it, to balance it against his other emotions. He learns to take a certain amount of depression for granted without letting it pull him completely under."[6] We should add that studies have indicated that people who "ruminate" over the causes and consequences of the *symptoms* of sadness, are more likely to develop dysfunctional depression.[7]

It is possible that we spend too much time being sad about sadness, when we need to look forward to the victory promised in Christ.

Ecstasy

It may come as a surprise that I would list this emotion. First, it is not as frequent as most emotions. Ecstasy is for those unusual times when everything comes together to bring us a tremendous amount of joy. Second, in our list of sometimes-negative emotions, it is such an overwhelmingly positive emotion. However, just as anger, fear, and sadness are reactions to unusual circumstances, so ecstasy is as well.

As positive as it is, ecstasy can prove disorienting. Our euphoria may sometimes be followed by depression. Subconsciously, we understand that life is not normally like this and the contrast might be too much.

In 2 Samuel 6:14,16, we find this event, "And David was dancing before the Lord with all his might, and David was wearing a linen ephod...Then it happened as the ark of the Lord came into the city of David that Michal the daughter of Saul looked out of the window and saw King David leaping and dancing before the Lord; and she despised him in her heart."

This is a wonderful example of unfettered worship for David, and a sad example of sharp judgment from his wife, Michal. David is completely taken with joy that the ark is returning to Israel, so he dances before the Lord, seemingly oblivious to what others might think. Michal, on the other hand, lowers the boom when he returns home. "But when David returned to bless his household, Michal the daughter of Saul came out to meet David and said, 'How the king of Israel distinguished himself today! He uncovered himself today in the eyes of his servants' maids as one of the foolish ones shamelessly uncovers himself!'" (2 Samuel 6:20).

I hope our spouses would not react this way to our great joy! However, it does represent what often happens: if there is not some external pressure to forgo our joy, our own alarming thoughts may tell us to feel guilty for having a bout of ecstasy.

As we stated before, we should regulate our emotions rather than fear them. We can fully embrace our moments of ecstasy. We should just not expect them to be normal fare. I believe God gives us times of great joy, whether from a spiritual or natural source, so that we might get a glimpse of heaven and hold on to our confession of hope.

Some Solutions

First, it is important that we understand that emotions, positive or negative, are friends. Anger, if it is righteous, can point to the need for corrective action. Fear can show that we are outside of God's protection, or that we need to be reacquainted with the fact of His love (1 John 4:18). Sadness actually helps us to face reality, and can lead to a solution when we counteract it with spiritual resources. Ecstasy reminds us of the beauty of our existence.

Second, we are not at the mercy of our emotions. James and Evelyn Whitehead note, "A person is *overcome* by guilt, *consumed* by anger, *paralyzed* by fear. Each verb is passive, suggesting our surrender in the face of forceful feelings. 'I can't help it?' we plead."[8] The authors explain this is the wrong perspective and that we are not without authority in our own lives.

My brother is a successful businessman and at the height of pressure at one point in his life he told me, "No one can make you feel anything; you do that yourself." Think about it. Can anyone *make* us angry or fearful? Can anything *steal* our joy? Is it *necessary* to succumb to our emotions? Obviously, sometimes a powerful emotion (e.g., grief at the loss of someone beloved, fear in the face of real danger) is so overwhelming that we are carried along. Initially, we seem unable to resist. With God's help, however, we find resources that keep us from being victimized by our own feelings.

What I call "low-grade anxiety" is another unpleasant and irreversible fact. For example, on occasion most of us experience the familiar gnawing in the stomach or disturbed sleep. The cause may just be the awareness of some threat, including a natural release of adrenaline in response, rather than poor mental or spiritual hygiene. We can do little about this occasional problem, other than to refuse to escalate it with our own worry and then turn our attention toward spiritual resources.

I would like to suggest two concrete spiritual "truths" that are effective against unregulated emotions, and these are *grace* and *peace*.

The well-known New Testament greeting of "Grace and Peace to you," or some variation, was common in the First Century. Paul uses this greeting twelve times in his letters, Peter and John two times each. This greeting joined two great virtues in the minds of Christians. *Grace* is the Greek side and *peace* is Jewish. Together they express the removal of the dividing wall, which Christ brought down with His sacrificial death.

When I see this greeting in the Bible, which often follows with "from God the Father and through Jesus Christ," I see something that helps to regulate emotional flights.

Grace is God's work directed toward us, and it is an outgrowth of His love. Christ is the agent of redemption, and He freed us from a life of spiritual bondage. The grace He offers is the linchpin of healthy living, because it tells us first that God has extended His aid to us by saving us, and then He followed by showing us that He will continue this support forever. We are each moment Children of the King.

Peace follows. First, we should view this peace as "Peace with God." There is no longer enmity between us and the Father, for Christ brought us into eternal peace. Second, this peace is that which gives us the ability to live in victory moment by moment. The Greek word that Paul uses (*eirēnē*) has roots in the Hebrew term *shalom*. Robert C. Roberts said, "Shalom is constituted, most centrally, by human beings living before God's face as he has ordained them to do and by God's looking on them with approving joy and blessing them with the fruits of righteousness."[9]

Our eternal peace is secure and unassailable and needs no activation. However, we must claim our *living* peace day to day. How are we to do this?

The healing for emotions out of control is the same for every other ill: the calm and prayerful center. We find this by simply seeking the strength of the Holy Spirit, and He gives us power over these detractors. Holiness results in effective living. Though "Christianity is not a therapy for those who wish never to be upset,"[10] it does provide a solution for being overwrought. When the stress piles up on the back of our neck, we begin shaking, our voice constricts, or our breathing elevates or slows, these early warning signs show the Spirit needs more control. Our cooperation with Him at such a crucial time will be the best way to prevent hurting ourselves...or someone else.

Monitoring our thinking is important as well. When we consider peace and grace as solutions, how clearly we view them will lead to our full possession of their promises. I have found that at times I was almost paralyzed with some nameless dread. Possibly, it involved work responsibilities and imagination of possible disaster, combined with nagging real time troubles. These thoughts, difficult to pinpoint in isolation, would work together to create a poisonous atmosphere which sapped my strength. I learned the way to combat this was to remind myself that God called me, gifted me, and promised not only to protect me but to bless me as well! I learned to concentrate on the positive outcomes that were possible. After that, I found that events almost never went a disastrous route, but showed the positive results I was expecting. Our negative imagination can be vivid, and it can distort the true positive state of spiritual reality.

We are emotional creatures. God has made us this way. Emotions are sometimes...*emotional*. However, we find that by monitoring and presenting these emotions to the moderating influence of the Holy Spirit, they will positively advance our wholeness and holiness.

1. Swindoll, Charles R., *Flying Closer to the Flame* (Dallas, Texas: Word Publishing, 1993), 156.

2. Stephen Arterburn and David Stoop, *The Angry Man* (Dallas, Texas: Word Publishing, 1991), 11-12.

3. James D. Whitehead and Evelyn Eton Whitehead, *Shadows of the Heart: A Spirituality of the Negative Emotions* (New York: The Crossroad Publishing Company, 1995), 76.

4. Tim LaHaye, *Spirit-Controlled Temperament,* rev. ed. (1966; repr., Wheaton, Illinois: Tyndale House Publishers, Inc., 1983), 70-71.

5. In Genesis 31, several times Jacob speaks of his "fear" of Isaac in a positive sense, though we should note that God did not encourage it, and it carries more the idea of respect than true fear. When man is to be feared (respected) in the Bible, he is always God's emissary (i.e., Proverbs 24:21, Romans 13:1-7, 1 Peter 2:17; and especially Deuteronomy 6.13 and Proverbs 29:25).

6. Robert Hastings, *How to Live with Yourself* (Nashville: Broadman Press, 1966), 40.

7. Michael Lewis, Jeannette M. Haviland-Jones, and Lisa Feldman Barrett, eds. *Handbook of Emotions,* 3rd ed. (New York: The Guilford Press, 2008), 800.

8. Whitehead and Whitehead, *Shadows of the Heart,* 8.

9. Robert C. Roberts, *Spiritual Emotions: a Psychology of Christian Emotions* (Grand Rapids: William B. Eerdmans Publishing Company, 2007), 172.

10. Ibid., 175.

CHAPTER 16

Accepting Spiritual Dryness and Pain

I am not a mystic. I believe the mysticism of the Christian faith, most closely exemplified by the "contemplatives" of the Middle Ages, can be a detriment to the action of our faith. Our calling has a clear undercurrent of *going* (Matthew 28:18-20; Acts 1:8), and it is possible to overdo inward contemplation which can weaken our outward focus.

Having said this, I also believe that the Christian faith must have an element of mysticism. In this context, we define *Christian mysticism* as spiritual understanding that transcends our intellect, a union with God that we achieve through contemplation. It is possible to be so "practical" in our belief that we miss the supernatural that clearly must be a part of relating to God. If we are to pursue holiness then we must understand there will be times when God is working deep within us in a way that may seem counterintuitive. God sometimes leads us through difficulty so that we might discover more of His Light.

There is in Christian literature an experience often referred to as "The Dark Night of the Soul." St. John of the Cross, a sixteenth century Spanish mystic, struggled with this concept. His poem "The Dark Night of the Soul" and his subsequent commentary has been translated and discussed many times since, and though it is not in the scope of this chapter to discuss the book *per se*, it is this topic that draws our attention. We will need to walk through the valley of the shadow of death in our pursuit of holiness, for walking in holiness will likely lead to periodic trips through spiritual dryness and pain.

The Dark Night

I think it would be best for us to look at the concept of the dark night of the soul before we discuss our response to days of spiritual dryness and pain. As I write, I struggle with the tension of writing deeply enough in a small space to touch on the subject, but not to be bogged down. The dark night is not the focus so much as a launching pad to discover more about spiritual darkness in a general sense.

I have read *Dark Night of the Soul* by St. John of the Cross several times, and I have found much of its meaning unclear. I feel that the observations were sometimes arcane or elusive. I also take exception to his belief that God specially chooses some Christians (called the "progressives" or "proficients" in his writings) for this experience. He said, "The Dark Night is God's gift to those souls whom he most desires to purify and draw to the light of His presence."[1] This idea seems spiritually elitist. God calls all people to depths of holiness (Leviticus 19:2, 1 Peter 1:15-16), and the only ones who do not attain to it are those who do not so choose. I believe that we should not specifically *seek* the experience of spiritual darkness, or desire to stay in it longer than necessary. In this sense, God initiates the experience and He *does* choose us. However, God desires to "purify and draw" all of us equally; the method He uses is different for each of us and we should submit to His sovereign choice.

St. John of the Cross presented the steps of the experience of the dark night as clear and structured. My experience with spiritual darkness, on the other hand, has shown that spiritual trial is very fluid. There do not seem to be *levels* or *stages* of contemplation—as St. John presents—as much as an increasing awareness of God's presence as He strips me of my own stubborn self-centeredness, often through alternating success and failure.

I do not intend to criticize the writing of St. John of the Cross, because I believe he has done us a great favor in pointing out the effects and meaning of spiritual darkness. His basic theme is biblical and should be heeded: that when a person desires to walk closely with God, God must purify them, and so gives them this experience, as a gift, to draw them closer to His presence.

Saint John writes of a person's "purgation" (or purging) in the Dark Night of the Soul being made up of two parts: the Dark Night of the Sense and the Dark Night of the Spirit.

The Dark Night of the Sense is that which through aridity of the senses we lose the ability to sense God's presence or to experience joy in the spiritual things that have given us joy before. Through this process, we lose all hope in ourselves, in our meditations and musings, even in our prayer and spiritual exercises, which results in realization of our spiritual poverty. We find there is nothing that we can do that is worthwhile in spiritual things, but our hope is only in God Himself.

The Dark Night of the Spirit is more "horrible" still, where a deeper work is done. Spiritual darkness is the vehicle whereby a person goes through the utter loss of themselves, and according to St. John of the Cross, to an ultimate union with the Divine. He says that when God takes away your capacities (affections, desires, and aptitudes) "God is freeing you from yourself and taking the matter from your hands."[2] He falls short of actually describing this resulting "union with the Divine." It seems to me it could be defined as a settled spiritual rest and satisfaction in Christ.

Georgia Harkness, in her own take on this experience in her book *The Dark Night of the Soul* names four historical characteristics of this experience.[3] The first is *the lost sense of God's nearness or the frustrated quest for the divine Presence.* The second characteristic is *a union of self-distrust with self-condemnation.* The third is *loneliness, which means the bitterness of isolation both from God and man.* The fourth is *spiritual impotence.*

Where St. John of the Cross believes this experience is highly valued and initiated by God as a work on special souls; Harkness believes the experience has value but ultimately "…is *both* a sin and a disease."[4] Harkness does not discount this experience (she believes it is very real), but she believes a person should find their way out of it by the application of spiritual principles. She believes that the dark night is a purgative process that is used by God to great ends, "but it becomes so only as, while one is passing through it, one does all that one can to let the light of God shine through the darkness."[5] She echoes the thoughts of St. John of the Cross when she says, "it is when one ceases to demand of God health, or happiness, or usefulness, or any of His gifts, but asks only for God himself, that the light breaks and the shadows flee away."[6]

Biblical Precedent

It is important to see an experience like the dark night in biblical light. If such an experience does not have biblical precedent and cannot be squared with biblical testimony, then it should be viewed with suspicion. For that reason, we will look at a few examples of people in the Bible who experienced dryness, pain, and separation from God and man. We will attempt to understand what they experienced, and then work out later in the chapter what is our solution and right response.

Jeremiah

Jeremiah, a good and faithful man, suffered greatly *because* he was faithful.[7] He knew what it was like to be completely alone, to be isolated from other men with the burden of righteousness and to feel isolated even from God himself. When he expressed his pain, he cried out to God, "Because of *Your* hand upon me I sat alone, for *You* filled me with indignation," and he asked, "Will *You* be to me like a deceptive stream?" (Jeremiah 15:17-18, emphasis added). Jeremiah was clear that he suffered because he loved the words of God and was called by His name (v. 16). He was clearly not suffering in this way because he was sinful but because he was consecrated. In verse fifteen, he says he is sure that God "knows him," and that it is for God's sake that he "endures reproach."

What Jeremiah was experiencing specifically we can only guess. We recall that Jeremiah was imprisoned in the court of the guard, was beaten and imprisoned in a dungeon, and later thrown in the cistern and left to stand in mud (Jeremiah 37 and 38). He brought a particularly unpopular message to bring to his beloved Israel, that they must surrender to the Chaldeans or face certain destruction. Therefore, he was considered a traitor to God's people, expendable to the Chaldeans, and an enemy to the Egyptians. Later, he was exiled with God's people to Egypt, but even there his prophecies thundered, and he continued to speak of the vicious Babylonian king, Nebuchadnezzar, as God's servant!

It seems that being faithful to God's call brings its own pain. Here the dryness is not that which is evident because the believer cannot find God; in this case, God is present, but His word brings isolation.

Job

Job also suffered greatly because he was a righteous man. Job's experience was special, in that it was part of a conversation between Satan and God Himself (Job 1:6-11; 2:1-6). For this reason, we should be careful in trying to get a doctrinal pattern to follow from such an unusual occurrence. Nevertheless, much of Job's experience in response to his tragedy is exactly what God does with the softened clay of a person shaped by the Potter.

After his manifold sufferings, Job came to the point of cursing the day of his birth (Job 3:1), because it did not "hide trouble from my eyes" (6:10). He is stating the obvious: had he not been born he could have avoided this suffering. He longed for release from his pain. During this trial, four friends visited him: Eliphaz, Bildad, Zophar and Elihu. A summary of the advice of these erring "comforters" was, "Trouble does not visit righteous people." But Job's story denies this claim. Job, like Jeremiah, believed the hand of God was instrumental in his calamity. He said, "The terrors of God are arrayed against me" (6:4), and God eventually rebuked these men for their false comfort and accusation.

What terrors were arrayed against Job? By reading from the beginning of the book, we can see a few.

Job's experience *left him alone*: "my brothers have acted deceitfully like a Wadi" (6:15). Though Job stays faithful, the pain is *unremitting*: "But it is still my consolation, and I rejoice in unsparing pain, that I have not denied the words of the Holy One" (6:10). This pain is *not of short duration*: "So am I allotted months of vanity, and nights of trouble are appointed me" (7:3). It is *intense*: "He will not allow me to get my breath, But saturates me with bitterness" (9:18). Job's experience *resists positive thinking*: "Though I say, 'I will forget my complaint, I will leave off my sad countenance and be cheerful,' I am afraid of all my pains, I know that You will not acquit me" (9:27-28). *Righteousness* seems to be no cure: "If I am wicked, woe to me! And if I am righteous, I dare not lift up my head. I am sated with disgrace and conscious of my misery" (10:15). It is *embarrassing*: "I am a joke to my friends...the just and blameless man is a joke" (12:4). The experience *cannot be thwarted*: "He imprisons a man, and there can be no release" (12:14). Job is surrounded by *misunderstanding*, as he says to his friends: "You are all worthless physicians...O that you would be completely silent!" (13:4-5). He notices a *contrast*: "Why do the wicked still live, continue on, and become very powerful?" (21:7).

As we said, though Job's experience may be unusual in its inception, it is not much different from ours in its result. This kind of pain is very personal, sometimes overwhelming, but can result in a fuller knowledge of God.

The Psalmists

The psalmists sometimes bring us heartfelt cries from suffering. These psalms, sometimes expressed by individuals and other times by a chorus of voices, we call psalms of lament. We will look at two of these psalms written by David.

Psalm 6 is a psalm of distress that expresses David's heartfelt anguish over what seems to be the Lord's deafness to his cries. David says that he is "pining away" and that his soul is dismayed, and he says "but You, O Lord—How long?" (vv. 2-3).

I did a quick search in the Psalms to see how often these words "how long" express the psalmists' chagrin over lengthy suffering. Thirteen times the psalmists ask how long will the Lord withhold His mercy, how long will they suffer, or how long will the wicked prosper. Length of time, or the appearance of the same, seems to figure strongly in spiritual suffering. David says, "I am weary with my sighing; every night I make my bed swim, I dissolve my couch with my tears" (v.6). His suffering is without reprieve. He says that his "eye has wasted away with grief" because of his enemies (v. 7). Whether it is through the direct assault of enemies, or simply deep spiritual dissatisfaction, we recognize the long, constant assault of grief.

Psalm 22 is a psalm that we often apply elsewhere, because it contains the famous words, "My God, my God, Why have You forsaken me?" This psalm, longer than the sixth, deals with similar themes. David says in the first two verses that his words do not bring deliverance, and though he cries day and night, God does not answer. He says he is physically at his end: his "bones are out of joint...heart like wax" and he is "poured out like water" (v. 14).

"Be not far from me," David cries in verse 11, because God does seem so very far away.

There are other psalms that express these same laments from the faithful. A few that St. John of the Cross mentions are Psalm 39, 77, and 88. We should recall that Psalm 23, a psalm of hope, has that distinctive line, "Even though I walk through the valley of the shadow of death..." In this wonderful and comforting psalm there is still an undercurrent of threat as the words in the original Hebrew literally say, "I walk through the valley of *deep darkness*."

Our Response

We should remember that pain in this case is both the result of righteousness, and has righteousness as its end. Jesus is the "refiner's fire," He wishes "to burn the dross" away so that we might be vessels "fit for honor." What is this dross, except everything, *anything*, but Jesus Himself? This dross can be our pleasure, our comfort, our desires, and our finances; and yes, it can be our prayer, our worship, our success, our usefulness. Everything that must be burned away in order that only the Savior will shine in our lives will be targeted.

I have suffered through a long "dark night" that happened to fall during the writing of this book. I have served the Lord with all my heart, and have tried to be faithful. He led me to the pastorate which I undertook with all of my labor, integrity, and hard work, always with an eye to His enabling strength and command. I have served six churches as a senior pastor, and four others in support ministry positions, and yet, I feel as unstable in ministry as I ever have. Ultimately, God has led me here. He always opens new doors, writing and lay work being central for now. Although I am being faithful, I sometimes feel isolated, inadequate, hidden.

I receive comfort from the words of Thomas à Kempis in describing those who are to be fitted for eternal life:

You must still be tried on earth, and exercised in many things. Consolation will sometimes be given you, but the complete fullness of it is not granted. Take courage, therefore, and be strong both to do and to suffer what is contrary to nature.

You must put on the new man. You must be changed into another man. You must often do the things you do not wish to do and forego those you do wish. What pleases others will succeed; what pleases you will not. The words of others will be heard; what you say will be accounted as nothing. Others will ask and receive; you will ask and not receive. Others will gain great fame among men; about you nothing will be said. To others the doing of this or that will be entrusted; you will be judged useless. At all this nature will sometimes be sad, and it will be a great thing if you bear this sadness in silence. For in these and many similar ways the faithful servant of the Lord is wont to be tried, to see how far he can deny himself and break himself in all things.[8]

These do not *sound* like comforting words, but they are when you are experiencing something like this and wondering why the world has turned upside down. My experience might serve as a help for you, for in it I have learned three important concepts to remember when we suffer in this way:

I May Feel Alone but I Am Not

When I experience spiritual dryness or pain, I am in the company of great and godly people, past and present, who have endured the same. In this chapter, we have already looked at the experiences of some Bible characters who suffered spiritual darkness. There are many more examples in the Bible as well as in the history of the church. The author of Hebrews touches on this communal suffering in the first three verses of chapter twelve, "Therefore, since we have so great a cloud of witnesses surrounding us, let us also lay aside every encumbrance and the sin which so easily entangles us, and let us run with endurance the race that is set before us, fixing our eyes on Jesus, the author and perfecter of faith, who for the joy set before Him endured the cross, despising the shame, and has sat down at the right hand of the throne of God. For consider Him who has endured such hostility by sinners against Himself, so that you will not grow weary and lose heart."

We should realize that many have gone before having walked through the valley of deep darkness. They can show us the way, through their writings and testimony. They are *witnesses*, the word having as its root the idea of a martyr, encouraging us on as we fight to the finish. They suffered, too. Today there are many who are suffering—and there are always those who suffer more deeply than us—who testify to us of the grace of God in trial.

As these verses show, Jesus is where our eyes are fixed. Unlike the rest of us, He never turned once from doing His father's will, and yet He said from the depths of pain, "My God, My God, why have you forsaken Me?" He experienced a suffering so deep that the prophecy says, "His appearance was marred more than any man and His form more than the sons of man" (Isaiah 52:14). Just as it might sadden you if you broke a dish in your kitchen, but it would *crush* you if you broke some of your heirloom fine china: Jesus' face and form were so perfect in righteousness that the ugliness of sinful attacks from wicked men (including our wickedness) left Him marred more than any man. I understand that He was physically marred but I believe the violence at the spiritual level was much greater. Yet this Scripture tells us that He "endured the cross" and even "despised" its shame. He gave it no credence because of His purpose in joy.

We keep company with a mysterious but wholly benevolent Lord, and His faithful people are with us to witness to His faithfulness.

I Am Charged to Grow Through this Experience

In the book of Jeremiah we find the prophet lamenting that while he enjoyed being given the Word of God and was glad to be "called by God's name (15:16)," it had cost him dearly. He said, "I did not sit in the circle of merrymakers, nor did I exult. Because of Your hand upon me I sat alone, for You filled me with indignation. Why has my pain been perpetual and my wound incurable, refusing to be healed? Will You indeed be to me like a deceptive stream with water that is unreliable?" (Jeremiah 15:17-18).

God's response to Jeremiah was not void of pity, but showed a perspective that must have surprised Jeremiah. God said to Jeremiah, "If you will return, then I will restore you—before Me you will stand; and if you extract the precious from the worthless, You will become My spokesman..." (v. 19). Though God sympathized with His prophet, the Scripture assures us He is compassionate and invested in our reimbursement (see Psalm 56:8 and 126:5-6)—He was *more* concerned with Jeremiah's return.

In what way would Jeremiah need to return? It would seem that he was, like Elijah at one point, bemoaning the fact that he was the only righteous person left. He was singing from the song, "Nobody knows the trouble I've seen...Nobody knows my sorrow...life is just one long, rainy day." Jeremiah's return, like ours, would be when we stop concentrating on our pain and begin focusing on what is "precious." What is precious? In the context of this chapter in Jeremiah it is clear in verse sixteen, a rose amidst the thorns: "Your words were found and I ate them, And Your words became for me a joy and the delight of my heart; For I have been called by Your name, O Lord God of hosts" (Jeremiah 15:16). God had made Jeremiah a depository of His purpose and will, a veritable living testimony of His word.

God promised Jeremiah that if he extracted the precious from what is worthless, He would make him a "fortified wall of bronze," and he would be a spokesman of note for the people. The end result for Jeremiah was that he listened, spoke clear words of warning in God's name, and never turned from his difficult task.[9]

Realize that difficulty, if you remain faithful, may be adding nothing to those who attack you but judgment, but for you God has prepared mercy through training. He desires to use you. You must see the larger picture, which is that when you suffer, the pain cannot compare to the glory of God's using you as a faithful spokesperson. Indeed, you may see little of that glory here, but faith tells you that it is as certain, more certain, than life itself. Your redemption in difficulty is based on the very promise of God.

Being God's spokesman is a high calling, but it seems to me there is a more foundational calling to God's deep work through spiritual loss. That is to be His faithful child. The children of Israel went through spiritual darkness when they wandered in the wilderness, but God said it was for a purpose:

> All the commandments that I am commanding you today you shall be careful to do, that you may live and multiply, and go in and possess the land which the Lord swore to give to your forefathers. You shall remember all the way which the Lord your God has led you in the wilderness these forty years, that He might humble you, testing you, to know what was in your heart, whether you would keep His commandments or not. He humbled you and let you be hungry, and fed you with manna which you did not know, nor did your fathers know, that He might make you understand that man does not live by bread alone, but man lives by everything that proceeds out of the mouth of the Lord. Your clothing did not wear out on you, nor did your foot swell these forty years. Thus you are to know in your heart that the Lord your God was disciplining you just as a man disciplines his son. Therefore, you shall keep the commandments of the Lord your God, to walk in His ways and to fear Him. (Deuteronomy 8:1-6)

This deep work of spiritual pain and loneliness can drive us deeper into a faithful relationship with our Heavenly Father. This is ultimately our first calling. The Westminster Catechism says it well, "Man's chief end is to glorify God, and to enjoy Him forever." It seems that Jesus had to remind the church in Ephesus of this: "I have this against you, that you have left your first love" (Revelation 2:4). God sometimes has to remind us what is first.

I Am Becoming Reconciled to My Beloved
It requires a loss of the comfort of earthly things to fit us for heaven. We cannot serve both God and mammon (Matthew 6:24).

Some of you reading this might want to say here that you do not aspire to be a saint and earthly comforts are just fine for you! But we should honestly ask ourselves, which of us did the Lord call to be only partly surrendered to Him?

We must go further than losing earthly comforts, for spiritual matters, too, must lose their attraction in light of a relationship with God. Possibly the very dryness we feel in worship, the dissatisfaction in our fellowship with other believers, or the frustration of ineffective prayer, are cures rather than symptoms of disease. Spiritual dryness can awaken us to our utter dependence on God's mercy, grace, and presence. In other words, this inner work can drive us to God Himself with nothing in-between.

Job, one of our examples, reacquainted himself with God through his spiritual pain. We speak of "the patience of Job," and yet, he lost his patience. Toward the end of his ordeal—and we may sympathize with him if we do not agree with him—he "cursed the day of his birth" (3:1ff). He wished he had never been born. Though he did not curse God (if he had, he would have proven Satan correct in this test, see 1:11 and 2:5), he cursed himself, God's good creation. When Job listed some of the horrible sins of that day in chapter 24, he wonders why God will not let the righteous see judgment on such things *instantly* (probably the best interpretation of v. 1; see also Ecclesiastes 8:11). This is probably in response to his unhelpful friends who suggest that God always sets things right while Job still wallows in pain.

Job never cursed God, but he lost hope in his own situation. There is a disconnection here that Job had to see, for there can be no hopelessness if you believe that God has called you His child.

God then speaks to Job "out of the whirlwind" beginning in Chapter 38. Following two recorded chapters of rebuke (38 and 39); He asks Job, "Will the faultfinder contend with the Almighty?" (40:1), and Job responds, "Behold I am insignificant...I lay my hand on my mouth" (v. 4). Job discovered that human significance is only in a relationship with God.

God is not finished. He questions Job through the next two chapters (40 and 41) concerning the great creatures of the earth. God asks, "Will you really annul My judgment...or do you have an arm like God, and can you thunder with a voice like His?" (40:8-9). As if in response to Job's disrespectful remarks concerning his own birth, God asks, "Behold now, Behemoth, *which I made as well as you...*" (40:15, emphasis added).

The greatness of God's creation overwhelms Job and he includes quotes from God in his response: "I know that You can do all things, And that no purpose of Yours can be thwarted. 'Who is this that hides counsel without knowledge?' Therefore I have declared that which I did not understand, Things too wonderful for me, which I did not know. 'Hear, now, and I will speak; I will ask You, and You instruct me.' I have heard of You by the hearing of the ear; But now my eye sees You; Therefore I retract, And I repent in dust and ashes" (Job 42:2-6).

Job had heard of God, but now he *sees* Him.

When we know the positive outcome of spiritual work on us, we are more able to submit completely. St. John of the Cross speaks of "becoming reconciled to the Beloved" through the dark night. I said this "union with the Divine" was never fully defined by him, possibly because he was not sure how to describe it.[10] However, by putting aside the mystic element of this I believe we can see clearly what God is doing. The more He allows all comforts to be removed, even spiritual comforts, the more we find *only in Him* what we are looking for. It would be simple for us to believe God since He already told us this—and the results would be so much less painful—but it seems that we sometimes must lose all things to understand that Jesus is everything.

I have thought, while buried in my own spiritual darkness, what joy life will be when the trial is over. If we think in this way, however, are we missing the message of the experience entirely? For if the result is truly to be fully reconciled with Jesus as our only satisfaction, hoping for the experience to end would indicate our hope is for something else. None of us wishes to embrace pain, but we should desire the presence of Jesus more than our comfort.

In Philippians 3:4-6, the Apostle Paul was telling his readers that he of all people had things to boast about, but he refused to boast. He reminded them that he had an impeccable background in the law. He said he had lost everything, but did not even consider reaching back:

> But whatever things were gain to me, those things I have counted as loss for the sake of Christ. More than that, I count all things to be loss in view of the surpassing value of knowing Christ Jesus my Lord, for whom I have suffered the loss of all things, and count them but rubbish so that I may gain Christ, and may be found in Him, not having a righteousness of my own derived from the Law, but that which is through faith in Christ, the righteousness which comes from God on the basis of faith, that I may know Him and the power of His resurrection and the fellowship of His sufferings, being conformed to His death; in order that I may attain to the resurrection from the dead. (Philippians 3:7-11)

We can see in these words that Paul felt this surpassing "knowledge" of Christ was a gift, as it must always be, and not based on righteousness of his own. He explained that this righteousness only comes through God "on the basis of faith," and this faith (which is our work) is sometimes dark work indeed.

When we try to get around in a dark room, we stumble, feel around, and guess at direction. Our faith is like that sometimes especially when we walk through spiritual crisis. The result, if we have arrived where we should, is what Paul experienced: he had *lost all things* and had *gained Christ*. While stumbling with diminished sight he had reached out his hand and taken hold of God's.

Just a few verses later Paul spoke of not having "laid hold" of everything that Jesus *held on to him for*, but that "one thing I do: *forgetting what lies behind* and reaching forward to what lies ahead, I press on toward the goal for the prize of the upward call of God in Christ Jesus" (Philippians 3:13b-14, emphasis added). He "pressed on," having lost all things and having lost desire for them, because he had fully gained Christ. Consequently, he no longer stumbled.

In his second letter to the Corinthians, Paul spoke of a personal agony: "For we do not want you to be unaware, brethren, of our affliction which came to us in Asia, that we were burdened excessively, beyond our strength, so that we despaired even of life; indeed, we had the sentence of death within ourselves so that we would not trust in ourselves, but in God who raises the dead; who delivered us from so great a peril of death, and will deliver us, He on whom we have set our hope" (2 Corinthians 1:8-10). We have no idea what specific trial Paul and his companions faced, but they saw it as *God's* effort to reduce them to nothing but simple trust. Everything else was gone; all they had left was hope in God.

When we are truly reduced to Christ alone through our sufferings how could we be turned from our goal again? What would cause us to fail our challenges? How could we be moved by anything else? In Paul's undaunted courage through persecution, singing praises in prison, strenuous labor without complaint, and deep-seated joy in facing imminent death in a Roman prison, we have testimony that his encounter with the living Savior was very real. This should encourage us as we can have exactly the same walk with Jesus that Paul did.

What to Do?

I want to give some practical helps to close the chapter. These will help us face spiritual darkness in the proper attitude. They are not guaranteed to stop the darkness, which is God's business. However, we can choose an obedient posture so that God can teach us what He desires.

1. We Can Pray Faithfully

Harkness wrote, "Unanswered prayer is one of the most common characteristics of the dark night, and one of the most poignant sources of misery," and "recognition of the limits as well as the possibilities of prayer leads to release from the bitterness of expectations unfulfilled, but also to clearer understanding and more potent faith..."[11]

Praying faithfully is not always easy, but all prayers of faith are productive. In a sense, prayer should not bring us anything other than God's will. Prayers of petition will be natural during periods of spiritual darkness, usually in various forms of "Oh Lord, HELP!", but we should also turn our attention to prayers of thanksgiving and affirmation.

The psalmists, particularly David, showed this ability. The formula in the psalms follows the same general format: the psalmist states his problem, often with a variation of "Where are you God and why have you forgotten me?" Then the tone of the psalm changes and the psalmist begins speaking positively, stating that God will indeed save him. For example, in David's sixth psalm mentioned earlier his cries are agonizing in the first seven verses, "...I am pining away...O Lord—How long?...I dissolve my couch with my tears." Then the shift comes in verse eight and following, "Depart from me, all you who do iniquity, for the Lord has heard the sound of my weeping...the Lord receives my prayers...my enemies will be ashamed." When this happens in the psalms, there is no indication that God spoke from heaven or showed a sign, but that the psalmist willfully turned his attention from appeal to confident assertion. Though all manner of prayer is acceptable when we suffer, we should remember to pray with confidence, acknowledging the Lord's provision and salvation.

2.   We Should Read the Bible Fruitfully

The Bible is God's Word, a revelation of His person and will to us. The Scripture should support and verify every decision that we make and action that we take, both sacred and secular.

Spiritual pain drives us to the Word of God. When God sends us through a famine of the spirit, we need nourishment to survive. He desires for us to find this primarily in Him. We noted that fasting tunes our spiritual receptivity to hear from God, so spiritual darkness—a type of fast—augments our spiritual senses.

As we stay faithful each day in our Bible activity, we should expect the Holy Spirit to illumine the words in order to plant them deeply into our lives. We should pray before and after our Bible study that God would show us His desires as we concentrate on His word. When the psalmist said, "Your word is a lamp unto my feet and a light unto my path" (Psalm 119:105) he was projecting this idea. God's Word can make permanent changes in us.

While in spiritual darkness, the Word of God may seem very unattractive to us. However, when we begin allowing its truth to penetrate we find it heals. We may be tearful, feeling distance between what we read and are experiencing, but God is actively doing His work. The Holy Spirit will remind us that our righteousness is not dependent on our good feelings, but upon the truth of the promises of God.

3.   We Should be Active and Occupied with Redemptive Activity

It is possible to turn inward when we are in pain. Like injured wild animals who seek a solitary place to heal, we may be tempted to withdraw. Difficult times may limit our activity but should not extinguish them.

We also may be tempted during our spiritual darkness to sever our relationship with the local church. Well-meaning church people may ask questions about our trials that we are trying to forget! The embarrassment we feel when it appears that God has withdrawn His blessings can cause us to want to hide from discerning believers. Nevertheless, God has designed us to grow best in the company of other believers; we need their compassion *and* accountability.

Furthermore, this could be the best time to help others with their trials. It seems that suffering heightens our sensitivity to other sufferers and fits us to be better healers. The most compassionate people are often those who have suffered the most. As we help other people bear their loads, it lightens our load as well. Paul said that bearing another's burdens "fulfills the law of Christ" (Galatians 6:2). To say we can *fulfill* the law of Christ is saying a great deal! The spiritual benefit of helping others is incalculable.

There might be many ways to be obedient to God in our activity and we cannot list them all here. Your list would be one that you and God have worked out together. Remember that your quiet submission to the Father's will during spiritual pain is not only how you learn and produce during the process, it is the *reason* for the process itself.

4.   We Are to Trust the Lord

When we suffer, it is also possible to forget the Lord Himself. Actually, we should see Him as the focus of this experience.

Job excelled in this area. After his many calamities, he spoke what have become famous words: "Though he slay me, I will hope in Him" (Job 13:15). We might wonder how someone could hope if they were "slain," but Job is telling us His trust is in God at *any* extremity. He asks the question of the ages, "If a man dies, will he live again?' (14:14). His knowledge of the afterlife is inexact, as he seems not to hold to that hope in this world; however, he states in the following verse that *God will call and he (Job) will answer*. Job trusts in God's sovereign grace enough to think that He will bring him back from the darkness of *Sheol*. He reminds himself that however difficult his life is, "the righteous will hold to his way, and he who has clean hands will grow stronger and stronger" (17:9). Job was able to say this at his weakest moment.

Job builds his statement of faith to a climax that Handel included in his *Messiah*: "I know that my Redeemer lives, and at the last He will take His stand on the earth" (19:25). Job can see God's coming judgment with its relief and exoneration for the righteous. Regardless of the horrific pain that he was experiencing, he *knew* that God lived and that He is indeed Job's redeemer.

It may seem a difficult thing to trust God when it seems that He bears the knife; however, John Calvin insists this is natural for the children of God because their hope in Christ is unassailable. He wrote, "The pious mind, how much soever it may be agitated and torn, at length rises superior to all difficulties, and allows not its confidence in the divine mercy to be destroyed. Nay, rather, the disputes which exercise and disturb it tend to establish this confidence. A proof of this is, that the saints, when the hand of God lies heaviest upon them, still lodge their complaints with him, and continue to invoke him, when to all appearance he is least disposed to hear. But of what use were it to lament before him if they had no hope of solace? They never would invoke him did they not believe that he is ready to assist them."[12]

We are children of God and we *do* trust the Father in Heaven. What we must learn is to hurry to this trust in our dark night rather than take a meandering course. The way to the resolution of our spiritual conflict is to go where there is no conflict, and that we find that in full fellowship with Jesus.

In Conclusion

The weakness of much of the teaching of the "Dark Night of the Soul" or like teaching is that it seems to limit the poverty only to the spiritual realm. The modern Christian is also plagued with uncertainties related to mortgages, careers, spouses and children, retirement, house and car repairs. Spiritual or non-spiritual catalysts can bring on spiritual darkness.

If we lose a child to accidental or violent death, our spiritual darkness will begin there. If our career ends after many years of effort and there is no hope in sight, we may immediately walk in this "valley of deep darkness." In this darkness, whether it is a deep spiritual work alone or has a physical cause, we should be aware that God desires to draw us closer. The duration of this period of trial may not be ours to determine, but the positive results can begin immediately when we seek the One who is always seeking us.

1. St. John of the Cross, *The Dark Night of the Soul* translated by E. Allison Peers, rev. ed. (n.d.; repr., Garden City, New York: Doubleday and Sons, Image Books, 1959), 30.

2. Ibid., 154.

3. Georgia Harkness, *The Dark Night of the Soul* (New York: Abignon-Cokesbury Press, 1945), 25-27.

4. Ibid., 71.

5. Ibid., 77.

6. Ibid., 114.

7. I must make this plain, that the spiritual work that we are looking at in this chapter is the result of a life fully dedicated to God and longing for His will. We are not dealing with the separation from God's presence that occurs when someone is recalcitrant, self-willed, or in a trap of their own sinful desires. The spiritual darkness that we are speaking of is that of a committed person.

8. Thomas à Kempis, *The Imitation of Christ*, rev. ed. (n.d.; repr., Milwaukee, Wisconsin: The Bruce Publishing Company, 1940), 179-180.

9. See also Jeremiah 20, where Jeremiah's suffering and lament is mixed with his assurance that God will be a "dread champion" on his behalf.

10. Harkness, *Dark Night*, 151.

11. Ibid., 77, 79.

12. John Calvin, *Institutes of the Christian Religion,* rev. ed. (Grand Rapids: William B. Eerdmans Publishing Company, 1972), 1:487.

Section 7: What We Should Not Forget

"To the Work! To the Work!"

CHAPTER 17

Personal Holiness and Fellowship

When I was a seminary student, I was given an assignment to do an in depth study of the mystics and monastics. It was an interesting study and I enjoyed reading about these people who were utterly devoted to God. We can learn from their consecration. I soon found that they often missed a major component in spiritual living, and that is its outward focus. They went to incredible lengths to "train the flesh," but sometimes had little interest in reaching lost people, or fellowshipping with spiritual siblings outside of their closed society. In this sense, they were unlike our Savior and His disciples. (Some, like St. Francis of Assisi and Mother Teresa, were *strongly* motivated toward others.)

There is a strong outward orientation to biblical spirituality. Christians cannot be truly holy unless their focus includes the outside world. The next two chapters, arranged in this section "What We Should Not Forget," are concerned with what we *might* forget. Our joy in seeking the face of our Savior may lead to a reclusiveness that has no part in God's calling.

There is a section in a famous poem from Sam Walter Foss from days gone by that goes:

> "There are hermit souls that live withdrawn,
>   In the place of their self-content;
> There are souls, like stars, that dwell apart
>   In a fellowless firmament.
>
> There are pioneer souls that blaze their paths
>   Where highways never ran;—
> But let me live by the side of the road,
>   And be a friend to man."

It is a great poem, and he intends to express his desire to be close to humankind. Walter J. Gresham responded with his own poem and took it a step farther:

> "It is only a half truth the poet has sung,
>   Of the "house by the side of the way";
> Our master had neither a house nor a home,
>   But he walked with the crowd day by day.

"And I think, when I read of the poet's desire,
   That a house by the road would be good;
But service is found in its tenderest form
   When we walk with the crowd in the road."

We Are Grounded in What Christ Has Done

Jesus had fellowship in mind when He prayed this prayer to the Father, "The glory which You have given Me I have given to them, that they may be one, just as We are one; I in them and You in Me, that they may be perfected in unity, so that the world may know that You sent Me, and loved them, even as You have loved Me" (John 17:22-23). Obviously, our fellowship is inseparable from the godhead. In our pursuit of holiness, we have often noticed that much of what we do is an imitation of what Christ did. Better yet, our lives should reflect His life. If we are to understand fellowship, we should learn it from Him.

Jesus did not just tolerate people—He genuinely liked them. He often seemed to be at some party or another attending banquets and the like. These were no casual social occasions with Him, however, as His presence brought depth and sometimes trouble. Nevertheless, He was comfortable in the company of others.

Jesus' teaching drew large crowds wherever He went. His miracles were certainly a factor in this, but it must also have been clear that He loved those He taught. Like hungry children clamoring for their mother's attention, the crowds drew acceptance from Him.

Even so, we find that He never completely gave Himself to them. John tells us when many believed on His name, "Jesus, on His part, was not entrusting Himself to them, for He knew all men…He Himself knew what is in man" (John 2:24-25). Oswald Chambers commented on these verses by saying, "Our Lord trusted no man, yet He was never suspicious, never bitter; His confidence in what God's grace could do for any man was so perfect that He never despaired of anyone. If our trust is placed in human beings, we will end in despairing of every one."[1]

Our fellowship with Christ and His redemptive work validates our relationship with others. We are fallible and sometimes uncomfortable company. When we know others in and through Christ, we will come to realize that the perfection of our union is dependent on Him; we are free to love our brothers and sisters completely and truly, because we do not expect perfection of them nor give them total trust that belongs only to Christ.

Dietrich Bonhoeffer said in *Life Together*, "Therefore, let him who until now has had the privilege of living a common Christian life with other Christians praise God's grace from the bottom of his heart. Let him thank

God on his knees and declare: It is grace, nothing but grace, that we are allowed to live in community with Christian brethren."[2]

A Richer Concept than At First Thought

Among the Baptists, we have a room in most of our churches we call the "Fellowship Hall." We eat in this room a lot and we generally have at least one serving of the *Baptist Bird* (fried chicken). The kitchen is attached to this room on purpose, and we have pass-through windows going into the kitchen where we push food, and later, used dishes.

In the Fellowship Hall, we gather for...you guessed it—*fellowships*. In our thinking, that usually includes food, fun, a relaxed atmosphere, and a light devotional if the preacher feels that he *must*.

However, this idea of fellowship may have limited our view. Eating and relaxing together is certainly fellowship and an important part too, but there is much more. According to Donald Whitney, "Fellowship is more than socializing; it is qualitatively different. Any two people can socialize. Only Christians can fellowship, at least in the biblical sense."[3]

The biblical term used for fellowship is *koinonia,* which literally means "fellow," "partner," or "one who shares." It could be one person sharing what they have with another person or even two persons sharing mutually. In the following verse, the word koinonia is used once (translated "fellowship"), but the concept permeates the entire verse:

"They were continually devoting themselves to the apostles' teaching and to fellowship, to the breaking of bread and to prayer. Everyone kept feeling a sense of awe; and many wonders and signs were taking place through the apostles. And all those who had believed were together and had all things in common; and they began selling their property and possessions and were sharing them with all, as anyone might have need. Day by day continuing with one mind in the temple, and breaking bread from house to house, they were taking their meals together with gladness and sincerity of heart, praising God and having favor with all the people. And the Lord was adding to their number day by day those who were being saved." (Acts 2:42-47)

It is obvious that relaxed fellowship is part of koinonia, but it also includes an active partnership in the spreading of the gospel and the building up of other believers.[4] Whenever we gather in His name and for His purposes we are expressing koinonia. It will change our perspective, for example, when we understand that fellowship includes hearing a biblical lesson, listening, and applying the message. According to this passage in

Acts, fellowship includes all aspects of our relations with other believers—teaching, prayer, sharing possessions, eating together—and results in a testimony to the lost. God will bless us when we take His command seriously to love one another, and His blessing energizes us to bring others into His kingdom.

We Have an Opportunity for Intercession

The preceding passage in Acts speaks of the community of faith "devoting themselves" to prayer. Undoubtedly, the author had all varieties of prayer in mind; however, we consider intercessory prayer a high water mark for Christian prayer as it is a pure extension of fellowship. Our intimate link with others in Christ's work naturally leads to concern for each other's welfare, which is expressed in prayers of intercession.

Bonhoeffer wrote, "Every Christian has his own circle who have requested him to make intercession for them or for whom he knows he has been called upon especially to pray. These will be, first of all, those with whom he must live day by day."[5] It is not helpful to pray generally for "believers" as it is to pray specifically for those whom we have compassion. God has given us this compassion, and it is a tremendous opportunity! We participate in God's ongoing work through fellow believers.

Intercessory prayer requires discipline, because either sometimes we feel dry in doing it or we simply forget. We need to push through these barriers to pray for others because this prayer is tremendously beneficial in the kingdom, and it adds to our spiritual vitality. The discipline is worth it, so, start a prayer list!

We Bear Burdens and We Share

As we continue to walk in the holiness of the Lord, we find that we share His concern for the burdens of fellow believers. We pray for each other but we must also be ready to act to lift heavy loads. In his book, *Everybody's Normal Till You Get to Know Them,* John Ortberg wrote, "You and I were made to be in the life-saving business. We don't always see it, because we can be blinded by our self-preoccupation, but people around us have little mini-shipwrecks every day."[6]

Paul's words to the Galatians in chapter 6 are intriguing. He said in verse 2 that they are to, "Bear one another's burdens," but then he said in verse 5, "Each one must bear his own load." At first reading, it sounds like a contradiction. However, the word for "burden" in verse 2 can be literally translated something like *overload*, whereas the word used in verse 5 is something akin to a *backpack.* Therefore, we do not encourage believers to cast their *daily* load on others ("each one should bear his own load"), but we should realize that sometimes members are overloaded ("bear one another's burdens"), and will need our help.

A burden too great to bear could come in any guise, at any time, to any person. Physically, it could arrive in the diagnosis of a serious disease. A person may be overloaded socially when people reject them. Financial obligations could immediately become a demon if a person is laid off. When doubts overwhelm faith, a spiritual overload is likely.

Paul said that when we bear the burdens of another person, "we *fulfill* the law of Christ" (v. 2, emphasis added). As discussed in the last chapter, this is strong language even for the apostle accustomed to strong language. Jesus spoke in the same manner when He said, "Love the Lord your God with all your heart...and love your neighbor as yourself. On these two commandments depend the whole Law and the Prophets" (Matthew 22:37-41). Helping each other out is indicative of our love for God.

One biblical meaning for koinonia is to share with others what we have, and this must include our willingness to help with material possessions.[7] In the passage cited above, Luke said that the first Christians sold their possessions and "shared with those who had need" (Acts 2:45). Our churches have always placed a high premium on the willingness to give of our substance in our Christian fellowship. Actually, our possessions are not our own but are a stewardship entrusted to us by God. We need to be careful in our giving, following the biblical admonitions to give wisely; however, this will not keep us from giving generously, especially since God is so generous with us.

There are many small services that cannot be neatly categorized and they often come in bunches. I have found as a pastor that there have been times where I was resentful of the demands on my time. For example, we like to say that there are no convenient funerals. Sometimes, when I officiate at a funeral during an especially difficult week, I am ashamed to admit I have to fight a bad attitude. (In times like these, we see how when unguarded we are unlike our Lord.) If we think about it, inconveniencing ourselves to relieve the inconvenience of others might be the *definition* of service. Bonhoeffer said, "It is part of the discipline of humility that we must not spare our hand where it can perform a service and that we do not assume that our schedule is our own to manage, but allow it to be arranged by God."[8] Nothing short of the grace of God will help us to be cheerful givers. We should pray for this grace when we are impatient with other people's needs.

We Must Be Honest

Sometimes fellowship is enhanced by negative reinforcement. There are times in our fellowship when brothers or sisters collide, for lack of a better word (or because that is the *best* word). At such times, we should keep two things in mind.

First, true love will help us to see that *we all have a tendency to be the problem* in such circumstances. We should first look to ourselves. Jesus taught this in the Sermon on the Mount when He told us to leave our offering at the altar and be reconciled to our brother (Matthew 5:21-24).

Ortberg said the give and take of relationships is not something to be avoided in fellowship, but what fellowship *is*. Knowing we all are weak is the first step toward healthy community. He mentioned a magazine article he saw titled, "Totally Normal Women Who Stalk Their Ex-Boyfriends."[9] Maybe we should redefine normal.

He shared an anecdote that I think captures the condition of the church:

A man is rescued from a desert island where he survived alone for fifteen years.

Before leaving, he gave his rescuers a little tour of the buildings he had constructed as a sort of one-man town over the years. "That was my house, that was my store, this building was a kind of cabana, and over here is I where I go to church."

"What's that building next to it?"

"Oh, that's where I *used* to go to church."[10]

G. K. Chesterton had the right perspective. When asked with other noted scholars to contribute to a London newspaper the reason for the problems of the world, Chesterton famously sent:

Dear Sirs,

I am.

Sincerely yours,

G.K. Chesterton.

The shortest route to solving interpersonal problems is often directly to our hearts.

Second, there are times when *another believer is clearly wrong and the situation must be addressed.* Community is disrupted. In such cases, we do not have the luxury of avoiding confrontation. Ortberg said, "Avoidance kills community. Avoidance causes resentment to fester inside you."[11] We might think we are choosing the better part to ignore an insult, or overlook disruptive behavior; but the underlying cause never goes away. In such cases, we may find that the end of the matter comes through an explosion of resentment—theirs, or ours—which is obviously something to avoid.

We need to take the risk of offending a person or even developing a more serious problem, by approaching the one who is offending others. It is not in our providence to determine whether it will end well, we just sometimes must do it.

Jesus did not avoid confrontation. In fact, He was sometimes downright assertive. When someone approached Jesus to settle an inheritance dispute He used the opportunity to confront greed (Luke 12:13-34). A good man approached Jesus and wanted to join His team. Jesus frankly showed the young man that he was not ready (Luke 18:18-25). Jesus broke societal norms by speaking to a Samaritan woman, and He also took the conversation beyond a surface discussion of water and invaded her life with the gospel (John 4:7-30). There are many such examples in Jesus' life as well as those of the prophets and apostles. In fact, it was this manner of speaking that sometimes hastened the end of faithful people (1 Kings 22:1-28, Mark 11:15-18, John 5:16-18, Acts 7:51-60).[12]

Though we should take care before we approach anyone with a rebuke or correction, we should be sure we are doing so from spiritual motivation and in the appropriate manner (Galatians 6:1-5, Matthew 18:15-18). The fellowship we enjoy in Christ sometimes must include forthrightness.

Fellowship Reflects Our Common Cause

Birds of a feather *do* flock together. If we are not careful, however, we forget that many of the birds of other Christian denominations are on the same team. Chuck Colson said, "While we may never achieve perfect doctrinal agreement on all points, shouldn't we at least make common cause in defense of our common orthodox faith in Christ and belief in absolute truth?"[13] Although there are obvious differences between our denominations and we should preserve our distinctive messages, we certainly agree on some key and essential elements that affect our society; like the Lordship of Jesus Christ, adherence to His teachings in church and state decisions, and the need to evangelize the world. John Calvin wrote during the contentious reformation era that he considered "even Rome" as his ally against the "Great Deep" of atheism.[14]

It is a holy act for us to join with those who are like-minded to counteract, for example, the great evils of abortion-on-demand or societal acceptance of the perversion of the sexual drive. Our work together can mark the difference in legislation—or we could hope—the changing of minds and hearts. We should be unified in defiance of the decay in societal mores and undaunted in the face of the outright virulence of the opposition.

Furthermore, this understanding of our common cause has led someone to say that in the Lord's Supper (Communion, Mass) we meet at the *longest table in the world.* In effect, we sit down with every other Christian. We *should* distinguish in meaning in doctrine when we partake of the Lord's Supper in our denominations and local churches. However, we also join universally with all other Christians in essentials: we are exalting the Lord Jesus as Savior and Lord; we are remembering Him as the answer for all questions; we are working so that the entire world would be changed by His revelation; and we are preparing for His return.

Bonhoeffer viewed the Lord's Supper as the highest form of fellowship in that "the life of Christians together under the Word has reached its perfection."[15] If so, this points to fellowship being at its pinnacle when we participate together with others in our common confession of the Lord's greatness.

---

1. Oswald Chambers, *The Moral Foundation of Life: A Series of Talks on the Ethical Principles of the Christian Life* (London: Simpkin Marshall, 1941), 89.

2. Dietrich Bonhoeffer, *Life Together* (New York: Harper & Brothers, Publishers, 1954), 20.

3. Donald S. Whitney, *Spiritual Disciplines Within the Church: Participating Fully in the Body of Christ* (Chicago: Moody Press, 1996), 19.

4. Jerry Bridges, *True Fellowship: The Biblical Practice of Koinonia* (Colorado Springs, Colorado: NavPress, 1985), 18.

5. Bonhoeffer, *Life Together,* 85.

6. John Ortberg, *Everybody's Normal Till You Get To Know Them* (Grand Rapids: Zondervan, 2003), 89.

7. Bridges, *True Fellowship,* 18.

8. Bonhoeffer, *Life Tther,* 99.

9. Ortberg, *Everybody's Normal,* 15.

10. Ibid., 139.

11. Ibid., 132.

12. In the interesting case of Michaiah in the 1 Kings passage, he was thrown into prison at the end of his ordeal, not actually killed. However, we never hear from him again. Ahab was killed as Michaiah prophesied, and two successive wicked sons of Ahab then ruled the kingdom. When years later Jehoshaphat again calls for a "prophet of the Lord" (2 Kings 3:11), no mention is made of Michaiah, only Elisha. Was Michaiah still languishing in prison, or dead?

13. Charles Colson, *The Body: Being Light in the Darkness* (Dallas, Texas: Word Publishing, 1992), 103.

14. Ibid.

15. Bonhoeffer, *Life Together,* 120-122.

CHAPTER 18

Our Witness: Holiness in Motion

Possibly, the most important example of our outward holiness is in our witness to others. I use the word *witness* rather than *evangelism* as the title of this chapter because it is broader. Evangelism is literally "sharing the good news of Jesus Christ," a very active concept. However, our witness includes evangelism, but also shows our faith before others in nonspecific ways. Sometimes what we share is not intentional at all.

The word *witness* also indicates its origin: holiness by its very nature witnesses to the grace of God. Our witness points to something active inside of us. We might say a clear and flowing fountain indicates a deep spring. Having the gift of God brings eternal life and frees us to abundant living; it follows that our witness should naturally result from our blessings.

I have divided this chapter into two sections that will help in reflecting on our personal witness. In the first section, we will discover that a witness is a clear commission for all of God's children. In the second section, we will consider how we can take practical steps to be effective witnesses.

Our Witness is Anticipated

When it was said of John the Baptist, "He came as a witness, to testify about the Light" (John 1:7), the words *witness* and *testify* are both the same Greek word (noun and verbal form) translated differently in English for clarity. The root word is *martus (μαρτυς)*. We recognize it as the word translated *Martyr*, which is simply a witness unto death.

The Lord God sent John to be a witness to testify of the coming Messiah, and we are to carry on this good work to remind people that He came. This first section of the chapter on the theology of witnessing and its biblical groundwork/foundation might be even more important than the practical considerations later. We should strive to be practical, but without an understanding of why we are trying to do what it is we are doing, we might be half-hearted or even guilty of making a show. When the Lord touches us with the need of evangelism, with compassion for the lost, which is born in a heart moved on by the Holy Spirit—then we are on our way to a practical witness.

There are clear themes in the Scripture that show us that the Lord anticipates our witness.

Jesus Witnessed

We view Jesus as our ultimate example in living. Our efforts to be like Him are obviously imperfect, but we look to His example to determine what is important to us. It will help to remember that Jesus is always the focus of our witness, just as He witnessed about Himself. We can see this clearly in John's Gospel, chapter 5:

1. Jesus Bore Witness to Himself.

In verses 24-29 He said, "Truly, truly, I say to you, he who hears My word, and believes Him who sent Me, has eternal life, and does not come into judgment, but has passed out of death into life. Truly, truly, I say to you, an hour is coming and now is, when the dead will hear the voice of the Son of God, and those who hear will live. For just as the Father has life in Himself, even so He gave to the Son also to have life in Himself; and He gave Him authority to execute judgment, because He is the Son of Man. Do not marvel at this; for an hour is coming, in which all who are in the tombs will hear His voice, and will come forth; those who did the good deeds to a resurrection of life, those who committed the evil deeds to a resurrection of judgment."

2. John the Baptist Bore Witness to Him.

Jesus reminded the disciples in verses 33-35, "You have sent to John, and he has testified to the truth. But the testimony which I receive is not from man, but I say these things so that you may be saved. He was the lamp that was burning and was shining and you were willing to rejoice for a while in his light."

Compared to Jesus, John may not be an overwhelming witness but he was sent to alert the people to "greater things." Jesus said that there was none greater than John the Baptist (Matthew 11:11, Luke 7:29). How could this be when we think of such luminaries as Moses, Elijah, and Jeremiah unless it is because John, "testified [directly and imminently] to the truth" (v. 33)?

3. Jesus Bore Witness through His Works.

In verse 36, Jesus said, "But the testimony which I have is greater than the testimony of John; for the works which the Father has given Me to accomplish—the very works that I do—testify about Me, that the Father has sent Me."

We might make too little of Jesus' works or miraculous acts, but Scripture does not. His works are a clear witness to the veracity of His claims. Although He refused to do these works *for* show, they were nonetheless *to* show His authority. Paul later referred to Jesus' crucifixion as a critical proof, "For if the dead are not raised, not even Christ has been raised; and if Christ has not been raised, your faith is worthless; you are still in your sins. Then those also who have fallen asleep in Christ have perished. If we have hoped in Christ in this life only, we are of all men most to be pitied" (1 Corinthians 15:16-19).

4.   The Father Bore Witness of Him.

Jesus continued in this passage in verses 37-38, "And the Father who sent Me, He has testified of Me. You have neither heard His voice at any time nor seen His form. You do not have His word abiding in you, for you do not believe Him whom He sent."

It seems obvious that the Father must verify the Son's authority; however, this connection takes it a step further in that Jesus shows His authority *in* the Father. Speaking of those who reject Him, Jesus said they have proven that they do not even know the Father!

5.   The Scriptures Bear Witness.

Finally, Jesus speaking to the unbelieving Jews in verses 39-47, showed the power of biblical testimony, "You search the Scriptures because you think that in them you have eternal life; it is these that testify about Me; and you are unwilling to come to Me so that you may have life. I do not receive glory from men; but I know you, that you do not have the love of God in yourselves. I have come in My Father's name, and you do not receive Me; if another comes in his own name, you will receive him. How can you believe, when you receive glory from one another and you do not seek the glory that is from the one and only God? Do not think that I will accuse you before the Father; the one who accuses you is Moses, in whom you have set your hope. For if you believed Moses, you would believe Me, for he wrote about Me. But if you do not believe his writings, how will you believe My words?"

Jesus said that Scripture is the testimony of Christ or His revelation. Though the Scriptures are not in themselves the Christ, they will judge the one who does not believe.

The Lord Jesus is not afraid to testify of Himself. If anyone merely human were to ask to be worshiped, it would amount to heresy or lunacy.

However, Jesus unabashedly asks for worship, and commands the witness of those who follow Him.

The Apostles and Early Church Witnessed

It seems obvious but we should state it anyway: the apostles witnessed constantly to the redemptive work of Jesus Christ, as did the members of the early church. This witness was extremely important to the first Christians, why should it be any less so for those of us who live today.

Jesus spoke to the disciples just before His ascension, "You will receive power when the Holy Spirit has come upon you; and you shall be My witnesses both in Jerusalem, and in all Judea and Samaria, and even to the remotest part of the earth" (Acts 1:8). The starting point for the fulfillment of this prophecy was at Pentecost. In the second chapter of Acts when the power of God through the Holy Spirit fell on the small group of believers in the Upper Room, they began testifying of Jesus and His mighty works…and they did not stop! On that day, Peter preached, and three thousand were added to the church through repentance and belief. Just a little later we read that "day by day continuing with one mind in the temple, and breaking bread from house to house, they were taking their meals together with gladness and sincerity of heart, praising God and having favor with all the people. And the Lord was adding to their number day by day those who were being saved" (Acts 2:46-47). Pentecost came as Jesus promised and the church turned the world upside down.

The apostle Paul emphatically followed Christ, and so took up His cause by witnessing. Delos Miles said, "Surely one thing which all of us might learn from Jesus Christ…is to witness as Paul did 'by word and deed' (Romans 15:18)."[1] Paul imitated Christ so that he might win others:

> For though I am free from all men, I have made myself a slave to all, so that I may win more. To the Jews I became as a Jew, so that I might win Jews; to those who are under the Law, as under the Law though not being myself under the Law, so that I might win those who are under the Law; to those who are without law, as without law, though not being without the law of God but under the law of Christ, so that I might win those who are without law. To the weak I became weak, that I might win the weak; I have become all things to all men, so that I may by all means save some. (1 Corinthians 9:20)

Jesus' leadership and gift of the Holy Spirit begat (a good Bible word!) the apostles whose leadership and sharing of the Spirit begat the fiery early church. We should not compare our desire to witness to the church down the street or to the neighbor in the pew; our example is the Lord, and His example fleshed out in the apostles and the church.

Practical Considerations in Our Witness

We desire to be practical. Our training in evangelism, careful sermons on the subject, and the tone of our prayers indicate we want our witnessing to be effective. Individually, we might wonder about our personal attempts to witness. Are we growing more effective in witnessing? Are we seeing people saved? Have we forgotten to try?

Some thoughts come to mind that will help:

We Must Have a Witness to Witness

We alluded to this earlier, but something happens deep inside that leads to our witness. Paul told the Ephesians "We were sealed in Christ with the Holy Spirit of promise, who is given as a pledge of our inheritance" (Ephesians 4:13b-14a). What happens to us deeply will have a bearing on who we are. Paul explained it this way: we are "sealed," so the Holy Spirit has done a supernatural work on us. He changed us! In addition, this "pledge" that Paul speaks of is the inward assurance that propels us toward our inheritance.

How can we ever hope to lead anyone where we have not gone or are not going? Though the work of internal change in a person is always the domain of the Holy Spirit, we cannot think we will be effective in witnessing if we had no radical change in our lives.

I mentioned that Jesus commanded, "You shall be My witnesses" (Acts 1:8). Chuck Colson said, "So many Christians interpret those words as *to* witness, rather than *be* a witness. And so they see it as an activity instead of what it really is: the state of our very being." He reminded us that St. Francis of Assisi told his followers, "Preach the gospel all the time; if necessary, use words."[2]

The witness of our changed lives gives power to our words of testimony. Our most effective witnessing moments are likely to begin when a curious acquaintance asks, "What makes you different?"

Holiness *is* Compassionate

Without holiness, without a deep work of the Holy Spirit, we will not witness as we should for want of compassion. David Brainerd said, "I care not where I go or how I live or what I endure so that I may save souls. When I sleep, I dream of them; when I awake they are first in my thoughts...No amount of scholastic attainment, of able and profound exposition, of brilliant and stirring eloquence can atone for the absence of a deep, impassioned, sympathetic love of human souls."[3] Such compassion is obviously a supernatural gift.

God gave His only Son because He "so loved the world" (John 3:16). It helps to see that everything God does, even His judgment, is an expression of His love. This love could not be clearer than when He sent His Son to die.

Jesus also manifested this love for the lost. For example, just after He witnessed to the woman of Sychar in John 4, the disciples urged Him to eat. He said, "I have food to eat that you do not know about" (v. 32). Sharing the bread of life was more important to Jesus than eating. He said, "My food is to do the will of Him who sent me and to accomplish His work…lift up your eyes and look on the fields, that they are white for harvest" (vv. 34-35). His compassion moved Him to ministry.

In the Gospel of Mark, as Jesus and the disciples were trying to rest, the crowds found them. Instead of responding with irritation at being disturbed, Jesus "felt compassion for them because they were like sheep without a shepherd; and He began to teach them many things" (Mark 6:34). If the love of the Lord moved Him to minister and witness, then it should affect His followers in the same way. Brainerd said we need the "deep, impassioned, sympathetic love for human souls," but he was not the first to express this for we see in the words and actions of Jesus a testimony to the power of God's love for others.

We Can Pray for Opportunities and Stay Alert

What keeps me from witnessing is usually a lack of opportunity. I have served as a pastor for many years and I am often with God's people. Even when I am not in a staff position and serve as a layperson, I *still* spend a great deal of time with the saved. If your situation is like mine, or lost people surround you, we find opportunities best when we are prayerful and alert. Delos Miles tells this story in *Introduction to Evangelism:*

> Pastor Herschel H. Hobbs tells how the Holy Spirit guided him one afternoon to a woman in need of salvation. He was out visiting when he received an impression that he should go to the church building. Ignoring it, he continued to visit. Soon the impression almost became an audible voice. Finally he went. Five minutes after arriving, a woman came to see him. She poured out her story of a life of sin. The night before she had heard the pastor's sermon on the radio. From that moment, she had been impressed to see him. That afternoon she was saved, and that night she joined the church. Later she was baptized and subsequently lived an exemplary Christian life."[4]

Jesus said, "Lift up your eyes...(the fields) are white for harvest." I am fond of saying, "If your eyes are open, your hands are likely to be full." There is no guarantee of opportunities if we are alert, but they are easy to miss if we are not.

If I have not had a witnessing moment in a while, I pray that I will remain Spirit-led and willing to share; then I ask for opportunities. Both elements are important: praying and staying alert to those opportunities.

On the other hand, being open to witness is not the same as forcing an opportunity. Some churches baptize many people with too few of those who continue to serve faithfully in the kingdom. This often points to rushed evangelism (and sometimes, poor follow up). Proper witnessing requires our sensitivity to the "right time."

I have met Christians that I believe would notch their Bibles with each newly lassoed saved person if they could! In a church where I was the new pastor, during worship I noticed one of the existing staff members approach a first-time visitor during the "greeting time" (A Baptist tradition in some churches, where we greet each other and welcome our guests by "wandering" around the sanctuary). This staff member had his Bible out and was attempting to "evangelize" the man. I approached to greet the visitor, and like a drowning man, he reached out to shake my hand. Later, after the service was over, this same staff member approached the man and started where he had left off, holding him in his sway until most people had left.

We never saw the visitor again.

It is sad to see such insensitivity. This young man probably thought that such aggression in witnessing is commendable. I longed for an opportunity to witness to this man, *first* by getting to know him and invite him to feel comfortable with us, but I never got the chance. (I did speak to the staff member about this.)

Oswald Chambers once was walking with a "deeply taught" Scottish minister. Chambers was young at the time, and they would have passed a shepherd they met on the way had Chambers not left his older friend and asked the stranger if all was well with his soul! It appeared a good example of a ready witness. When Chambers returned to the side of his elder friend, he was surprised when the man asked, "Tell me—did you get the permission of the Holy Ghost to speak to that man about his soul's welfare?"[5]

No man leads a person to Christ—the Holy Spirit does that. We are necessary to the witnessing moment but are to follow the leader. Knowing this will not only enhance our positive witness and lead to better results; it will prevent us from trying to force ourselves on others.

Our Witness Is Not Finished At the Point of Decision

We mentioned those who have made a decision for Christ, and then have not stayed in the church or His work. Sometimes, this is a matter of nonconversion, such people "made a decision," but did not embrace the Lord. On the other hand, there are many times when such attrition is due to a lack of follow up with the new believer. If we have not done all we can to connect the person we have led to Christ with the local church and her work, we have not finished our commission.

We often refer to the famous verses in Matthew as the Great Commission, "And Jesus came up and spoke to them, saying, 'All authority has been given to Me in heaven and on earth. Go therefore and make disciples of all the nations, baptizing them in the name of the Father and the Son and the Holy Spirit, teaching them to observe all that I commanded you; and lo, I am with you always, even to the end of the age'" (Matthew 28:18-20). As we look more deeply at this command, we notice that it emphasizes following even more than the act of evangelizing.

First, these verses are bracketed by "All is authority is given to me...Go" and "I am with you always." The word "Go" is important. Some have minimized its importance by pointing out in the original construction it literally reads, "As you are going." This does not lessen the impact of the word as Jesus is telling us that *we must be going*. While we are going, He said He would be with us in authority. From the start to the finish, He is committed to this work. He did not send us to a destination (ending at the conversion of someone), but rather to be on a road, or a way. The course of action that He started begins with our *going*, and never ends as we do everything necessary to fill the Kingdom with true believers.

Second, Jesus said that we are to "make disciples," which is the central verb in this command. Evangelization is important as we must start with a new believer but there is much more. The word in the original language literally reads, "Make learners (followers, students)." Our commission is to bring people to faith, and then help them live in faith.

Third, the Lord shows our follow up is important when He tells us to *baptize*. Baptism links a person with a local body of believers (in most cases). It always physically affiliates the new believer with the work of Christ. Like Hernando Cortez, "we burn the ships" so there is no way back, we are encouraged to commit to Christ's work publically and finally in baptism.[6]

Then, as if to enhance the theme of making disciples, Jesus clarifies by stating, "teaching them to observe all that I have commanded you." Though this command is generally included in His command of "making learners," He considers it important enough to emphasize specifically that we are to teach believers to observe each of His commands. How are we to teach them if we cannot get them to hang around?

Our best efforts sometimes fail: either new believers are not assimilated in the church because they will not let us, or there is simply no way to follow up because we never see them again. Nevertheless, we should do everything that is in our power or attempt to refer them to someone else. I make follow up a part of the witnessing moment. If someone I am speaking to does not come to Christ, I will add, "I hope you make this decision sometime, but please consider connecting with God's people in a Bible-believing church so they can help you." If I have been able to lead them to Christ and I know I will lose contact with them, I share with them the importance of gathering with God's people using Scripture passages like Hebrews 10:23-25 or Acts 2:44-47. Often the person will give me permission to contact a local pastor for them so that the church might follow up.

Most times, however, we *are* able to follow up as the person lives in our community or is attending our church. We should consider this an opportunity! It is more helpful to spend time with a new believer in helping them become an integral part of God's family than to rush off and find another person to evangelize. Our witnessing is ongoing with a new believer, and we do great good for the kingdom of God when we encourage a new believer in this tender stage of growth to become a steady follower.

Our Sword Needs Sharpening

I have always liked the phrase "Sharpening the Sword," which means to sharpen our skills. I am reminded that the author of Hebrews compared the word of God to a sharp two-edged sword, which is "living and active" (Hebrews 4:12). We cannot improve the word of God, but we can improve in our use of it so that our lives reflect its principles. Then in us, it becomes living and active.

This applies to our witnessing. We should always leave room for spontaneity and personality. I believe we sometimes over prepare for the witnessing moment. We could end up sharing our faith by rote or find ourselves under self-imposed pressure to "perform." Witnessing is often unnerving, but it can also be personal and simple.

I occasionally play golf, and years ago, wise friends taught me that I should work hard in practice, but lay off the myriad adjustments when I actually play (and in my game, the word *myriad* is accurate). When I practice, I try to correct my bad habits, but remember to enjoy myself as much as possible when it is time to use the skills on the course. This applies in most all endeavors, whether it is playing sports, performing music, speaking publicly—or when we witness. We can learn to "sharpen the sword" privately, not so that we will have a *razor wit* when we speak to a person in need of the Savior, and certainly not to beat them in an argument, but to be "fully convinced in our own minds" of the truth of Scripture and able to express its personal impact on us. In the actual witnessing moment, we should enjoy sharing the truth.

Some ways to sharpen the sword:

1. We can study examples of those who witnessed effectively in the Scripture, primarily those of Jesus and Paul. Jesus and Paul were consummate witnesses, and we can follow their encounters and learn from them.

2. We can study books by those who have experience in this area. There are many good books on this subject of witnessing or evangelism. We need to read these not just for methods, but also for inspiration. We are better witnesses when we are motivated.

3. We can practice on each other. When I teach rather simple classes on personal witnessing, I will sometimes do public examples of witnessing encounters with volunteers, and then ask the attendees to split into groups of two and practice on each other. It is impossible to capture the exact personality of a true witnessing encounter this way, but it helps and it is safe. We can also seek help from those who are capable witnesses by accompanying them when they witness and learn from their example.

4. We can start, haltingly or confidently, by actually *witnessing*. There really is no substitute for this. When we make an effort, we become more natural and grow in our ability to communicate the Good News.

Some years ago, I read (I do not remember where) a story that has stayed with me throughout the years. A leader (he is Caucasian) in my denomination told of waiting at a bus stop. He said it was raining and he and the only other person waiting for the bus, a black woman standing several feet away, were huddled under their umbrellas. This woman, obviously nervous about something, shuffled back and forth occasionally glancing sideways at him.

Gathering courage, she sidled up to him and asked in a tremulous voice, "Pardon me, Sir. Do you know my Lord?"

"How lovely on the mountains are the feet of him who brings good news, who announces peace and brings good news of happiness" (Isaiah

52:7a). It is beautiful to share our knowledge of the Lord with someone else. We need to start somewhere and keep going.

1. Delos Miles, "Witnessing—A Biblical Perspective," in *Witnessing-Giving Life,* William M. Pinson, Jr., ed. (Nashville: SBC Stewardship Commission, 1988), 35.

2. Charles Colson, *The Body: Being Light in the Darkness* (Dallas, Texas: Word Publishing, 1992), 329, 330.

3. David Augsburger, *Witnessing is Withness* (Chicago: Moody Press, 1971), 57.

4. Delos Miles, *Introduction to Evangelism* (Nashville, Tennessee: Broadman Press, 1983), 209.

5. Stephen F. Olford, *The Secret of Soul-Winning* (Chicago: Moody Press, 1972), 10.

6. Upon arriving at the Yucatan in 1519, Cortez called for his men to commit themselves to the work of taking the land for Spain by ordering the burning of all their ships. When the men protested, he said, "If we are going home, we are going home in their ships."

CHAPTER 19

Each Step Lighter

I have attempted in this book to make a primary point without sacrificing the secondary one. The primary point would be that God's strength is necessary for us to claim holiness, and the burden of our holy living is on His shoulders. This is where it is *light*. We cannot hope to produce His fruit.

The secondary point is just as true: our discipline is required to release the power of the Holy Spirit that is available. This is indeed a *burden*. You may have noticed that it is difficult maintaining both themes at once.

I am an amateur cellist, and the cello serves as one of the best parables I have to illustrate this relationship between God's work and ours in holiness.

My cello is made from fine wood taken from spruce and maple trees high in the Himalayas. Trees grown in this area (also the European Alps) are highly sought for the making of instruments like the cello, because the consistently cold weather causes them to grow slowly. This slow growth leads to tightly grained wood, which results in the best resonance. The wood is then carefully hand carved to certain exacting standards: just thin enough in some places, not too thick in others.

The front of the instrument (usually spruce) is glued to the sides and back (maple) so that they form a seamless whole. The artisan carefully adds the ebony pegs and fingerboard, the synthetic core metal strings, and a carefully designed and fitted bridge that supports the strings.

These parts work together in a remarkable way to send sound by the pulling of the bow. My bow is also a great achievement of workmanship combining Pernambuco wood from Brazilian rainforests and Mongolian horsehair with its many small natural hooks that "grab" the string.

In learning to play the cello, you realize very soon how passionate *and* relaxed is the relationship between the cellist and instrument. If you play too hard, too intensely, the sound becomes strained much like the new student with squeaks and scratches. If you relax too much, you lose tone, tuning, vibrancy, and power. As you advance in playing, you learn to find a balance between work and release. Although it may sound clichéd; soon the instrumentalist and the cello become one.

For the purposes of this illustration, *you* are the cello. God has made you, has perfectly designed you with spiritual gifts and personality to produce His music. Just as the cello is inherently designed to make beautiful sound, so we are designed and gifted to be effective and pleasing to Him.

God is the cellist.

As living instruments, it is our place to learn to let God work through us. Each of us must learn how much grace He gives and how much effort we apply. We must walk with Him. Ultimately, no one can tell us how to do this, we must "learn from Him" (Matthew 1:29). We cooperate with Him to make beautiful music.

This illustration is inadequate in that God *never* plays wrongly and we are not *passive* instruments. We work to liberate the Master's artistry in our lives.

The apostle Peter wrote, "To those who have received a faith of the same kind as ours, by the righteousness of our God and Savior, Jesus Christ: Grace and peace be multiplied to you in the knowledge of God and of Jesus our Lord; seeing that His divine power has granted to us everything pertaining to life and godliness, through the true knowledge of Him who called us by His own glory and excellence. For by these He has granted to us His precious and magnificent promises, so that by them you may become partakers of the divine nature, having escaped the corruption that is in the world by lust" (2 Peter 1:1–4).

Peter made the point that God's divine power gives us what we need to be like Him. He did not stop there, however, but followed these verses by focusing on our responsibility. He used phrases like "apply all diligence," and "in your faith supply moral excellence" (v. 5). Therefore, it is just as clear that we have an active part. This is our privilege! We can learn daily how to walk sensitively with our Lord.

Difficult, Yet Easy?

Some people fall on the path of holiness. They give up because they perceive it is too difficult, or they might fail to pick themselves up after a fall. I want to conclude this book by calling our attention to the reward of continuing in faithfulness.

One of the fine examples of holiness throughout the centuries is that of Brother Lawrence. He was a monk, actually a dishwasher in a monastery, who lived from 1614 to 1691. He kept a journal of his spiritual journey, which he never suspected would be published. It was published posthumously as *The Practice of the Presence of God*. Brother Lawrence is an interesting study because of his awareness of God's great power in juxtaposition to his frailty.

For example, on praying without ceasing, Brother Lawrence "examined himself how he had discharged his duty; if he found well, he returned thanks to God; if otherwise, he asked pardon, and without being discouraged, he set his mind right again, and continued his exercise of the presence of God as if he had never deviated from it."[1]

He understood that failing in any spiritual exercise is not the end. Like Brother Lawrence, we should learn to let ourselves grow rather than *drive* ourselves to it. Once, when Brother Lawrence was writing of an erring sister, he remarked, "She seems to me full of good will, but she would go faster than grace. One does not become holy all at once."[2] He also wrote, "If thou perceive thyself ofttimes troubled or grievously tempted. Thou art a man and not God, thou art flesh and no angel."[3] Even though the power given to us from Christ is perfect, it is often imperfect when carried in our vessels of clay. Therefore, our hatred of sin does not mean we should degenerate into hatred of ourselves, for the Scripture tells us how wonderfully God loves us, for even while we were sinners Christ died for us (Romans 5:8).

Nevertheless, knowing we are weak should not lessen our desire to be obedient. Brother Lawrence wrote, "We must hinder our spirits' wandering from Him upon any occasion. We must make our heart a spiritual temple, wherein to adore Him incessantly."[4] And in what sounds like excessive desire, "Pains and suffering would be a paradise to me, while I should suffer with my God; and the greatest pleasures would be hell to me, if I could relish them without Him…"[5]

This mix of intensity and relaxation is reminiscent of the great instrumentalists who have learned to concentrate their skills *and* enjoy themselves at the same time. As we learn to be the instruments that God made us, and daily allow Him to apply His consummate skill, we will learn how "easy" this difficult road is.

The Easy Yoke

You may have noticed that I have highlighted only part of what the Lord said in the verses in Matthew. He said, "My burden is light," but also said, "My yoke is easy." I have shied away from the second phrase because of how some might interpret it in this ready-made fast-food world. Some are already "taking their ease" in spiritual devotion! Nevertheless, to conclude this book, I would like to look briefly at the concept of the easy yoke.

As mentioned in chapter 1, Jesus shares this yoke with us. We are not pulling alone. An *easy* yoke is one that sits on our shoulders well.

In Jesus' day, most of the yokes were made of wood. After a while, the wood would wear and the shoulders of the animal would become calloused to where the yoke sat more easily. Today, since yokes are often made largely of leather, the yoke is even more likely to change shape and soften with use. The more the animal surrenders to the yoke, the more it adjusts.

As we begin to walk with the Lord in holiness, His yoke may chafe. We may find His demands exacting and constant. When we surrender, our spiritual muscles strengthen, our necks adjust, and we stop fighting so much. Soon, we find His yoke natural and easy. As we continue serving the Lord, and seek to give all of ourselves to His use, we find that He does not put us out to pasture (in keeping with the metaphor!); rather, He increases the size of the field we are to plow. We will not be satisfied where we were before, but now must see and do more.

By way of personal testimony to you, the reader, I want to tell you that my sensitivity to the Lord is increasing all the time. I find my walk with Him lightens as it deepens. Like the athlete, I do not stretch out harder because I must, but because I want to. My spiritual muscles are gaining strength and naturally, I enjoy testing them. Also like the athlete, there are times when I do not want to use my muscles, but I must, because the race is not finished.

Although it is a challenge, my service to Jesus may be as light as anything I do. I understand when King David said, "I love You, O LORD, my strength. The LORD is my rock and my fortress and my deliverer, my God, my rock, in whom I take refuge; my shield and the horn of my salvation, my stronghold" (Psalm 18:1–2). I take hold of this fortress and shield, even if I am not in trouble, because I run into this refuge simply because I delight in His presence.

Sometimes I feel that I might just float, take off without warning...

Until that day, however, I will continue to plow with an easy yoke. My sinfulness is ever before me, but so is my continued desire to walk closely with my Lord and "partake of His divine nature."

Truly, His yoke is easy and His burden is light.

---

1. Nicolas Herman (Brother Lawrence), *The Practice of the Presence of God and Selections From The Little Flowers of St. Francis,* (London: SCM Press LTD, 1956), 21.

2. Ibid., 38.

3. Ibid., 32.

4. Ibid., 45.

5. Ibid., 42.

Appendices

Appendix 1

Following is a simple chart that will help us remember what our responsibility is, and what God does. We should keep in mind that what God does will require our participation.

What We Do:

We obey and surrender, which includes devotion.

We learn to rest in His effectiveness.

We rejoice, pray, and give thanks.

We apply spiritual discipline.

We trust Him as we overcome.

We keep fellowship and witnessing in mind and action.

What He Does:

He sheds love abroad in our hearts.

He gives grace and empowers.

He changes hearts.

He fills with the Holy Spirit.

He produces fruit and gives gifts.

He creates holiness in us!

He makes the calculations and gives final rewards.

Appendix 2

Reminder Card

I have designed the following summary to remind a person what they should do to free the Holy Spirit in their lives. I have highlighted words that the devotee could memorize. The acrostic, easy to remember, is SSRKDRR. This is also small enough to copy and carry as a reference.

Stay obedient. Be devotional.

Surrender. Stay filled.

Release the burden; move in His will while resting.

Keep rejoicing, in instant prayer, and giving thanks.

Discipline yourself for the purpose of godliness.

Rely on spiritual resources to overcome.

Remember to fellowship and witness.

Study Guide/Discussion Topics

Chapter 1: His Burden Is Light and His Yoke Is Easy

1. In what way is holiness not complex?
2. In the analogy of the vine in John 15, who is the vinedresser? The vine? The branches?
3. What do you consider the primary message Jesus gives us in the analogy of the vine and branches?

Chapter 2: Simple Devotion

1. Why do we need to walk closely with Jesus?
2. In your own words, describe the *mind as a pilothouse*. Describe *life channels*.
3. Write down in what ways you plan to improve your quiet time.

Chapter 3: Obedience as Our Joy

1. Does Christ rob us of personal freedom?
2. When we follow Jesus, why is dying to self necessary?
3. When has Jesus ever subtracted from your life? Name some things He has added.
4. According to the author, the "helmet of salvation" refers to what?

Chapter 4: Absolute Surrender

1. What is absolute surrender? Why consider it a "first step"?
2. What can we learn from nature about absolute surrender?
3. How can I be sure my surrender is absolute?

Chapter 5: Being Filled with the Holy Spirit

1. When are Christians first filled with the Holy Spirit? Do they need to repeat this step?
2. Review the five steps that are included in being filled with the Holy Spirit.
3. Name two benefits in being filled with the Holy Spirit.

Chapter 6: Resting in Heavenly Places

1. How do we go forward while being seated?
2. Why is being crucified with Jesus, being buried with Him, a good thing?
3. Why must we stop fighting before God can help us?

Chapter 7: Walking in Christ

1. It seems that man's nature produces the works of the flesh, but who produces spiritual fruit?
2. What is the Apostle Paul's main point in Romans chapters 6, 7, and 8 (there are many words but he drives a simple point)?
3. Where do we find the cure for our unchristlike behavior?
4. Describe what steps you need to take to learn to walk in the Holy Spirit's power.

Chapter 8: Our Stance in Spiritual Warfare

1. Why do you think Paul repeats the phrase "stand firm" in his discussion of spiritual warfare?
2. How does the Bible teach we should view the strength of demonic forces?
3. What does it mean when we say that as Christ's army, we primarily fight a defensive warfare?
4. Consider, can God commit His name to you?

Chapter 9: Choosing to Rejoice

1. Why do you think Paul insists on constancy in Thessalonians 5:16-18? Do you think he is literally saying that we should follow these commands *all the time*?
2. Why would we describe rejoicing as an act of faith?
3. Review the *avenues of rejoicing* (p. 59) and determine to implement these, as well as other concrete ways to practice daily rejoicing.

Chapter 10: Praying Without Intermission

1. How would you answer this statement: "Praying without ceasing is impossible"?
2. Define praying without ceasing in your own words.
3. Name some things that should be the focus of our prayers throughout the day.

Chapter 11: Giving Thanks in Everything

1. Why would the Apostle Paul change the emphasis from the constant nature of rejoicing and prayer, to the emphasis on thanksgiving in all *circumstances*?
2. Review some of the scriptural support for being thankful.
3. How can wonder help produce thanksgiving?

Chapter 12: The Importance of the Spiritual Disciplines

1. In Ephesians 3:20, how much is the Holy Spirit promising us?
2. Consider the disciplines listed in the chapter that you neglect the most. Which ones are you practicing with regularity? Determine how you will improve where needed.
3. In this chapter, *spiritual discipline* is a phrase that centers on the activity of the Christian. Why is the author uncomfortable with this?

Chapter 13: Loosing Worry's Grip

1. How does a dog "worry" a sock? How does this help define our worry?
2. Consider the phrase "Jesus was never in a hurry." Do you think this is true? Can we relax while not neglecting our duties?
3. Name ways that worry dishonors God.
4. What two simple steps will help defeat worry?

Chapter 14: Disabling Our Doubt

1. Does the Bible view all doubt as sin?

2. Among the *Doubts that Disturb Us* (p. 97), is there an area that often challenges your faith? Commit to spending time to manage it with the help of strong biblical resources.
3. Where will we find our primary help in counteracting doubt?

Chapter 15: Regulating Our Emotions

1. Describe the difference between Christianity and Stoicism as they relate to emotions.
2. List the emotions that seem to control you. Which emotions do you handle well? What action can you take to bring the troublesome emotions under the power of the Holy Spirit?
3. How can a better grasp of *grace* and *peace* help you to manage emotions?

Chapter 16: Accepting Spiritual Dryness and Pain

1. In your own words, how would you describe the *Dark Night of the Soul* to someone?
2. Compare the sufferings of Job, Jeremiah, and the psalmists. Were their sufferings the result of personal sin? Where was God in their experience? What was the result of their experience?
3. How would you say you are to grow through similar experiences?
4. Review the suggestions under *What to Do* (p. 132). Make personal commitments concerning how you will face the next dry time or the next bout with spiritual pain.

Chapter 17: Personal Holiness and Fellowship

1. How would you define *koinonia*? Name various ways it could be expressed?
2. How is "bearing one another's burdens" a fulfillment of God's commands?
3. Can we be intimate in spiritual relationships and always avoid confrontation?

Chapter 18: Our Witness: Holiness in Motion

1. Why did the author say he chose the word *witness* over *evangelism?* How is this significant?
2. How strong is the biblical evidence that our witness is expected? Take time to name several factors that would motivate you to be a better witness.
3. Meditate on the headings in the section *Practical Considerations in Our Witness* (p. 147).

Chapter 19: Each Step Lighter

1. Why would Brother Lawrence say that a person should not try to go "faster than grace"?
2. How does the load lighten as it deepens?

Made in the USA
Columbia, SC
14 November 2017